The Gift

New Writing for the NHS

– Stride –

in association with Birmingham Health Authority

The Gift

New Writing for the NHS

edited by
David Morley

THE GIFT
First edition 2002
© Stride 2002
All rights reserved

Selection and Introduction
© David Morley

Copyright of individual contributions
remains with individual contributors

ISBN 1 900152 85 1

The front cover is a detail from Joseph Wright's
'An Experiment on a Bird in the Air Pump'
© The National Gallery

Cover design by Neil Annat

Published by
Stride Publications
11 Sylvan Road, Exeter
Devon EX4 6EW
England

in association with Birmingham Health Authority
and The Nuffield Trust for Research
and Policy Studies in Health Services

www.stridebooks.co.uk

Contents

Preface

The NHS is central to the life of our country. The constant media and political attention is one obvious measure of that. For most of us, the NHS, and to be more precise the people who work in it, is present at some of the most difficult and most joyous time in our own lives.

And then there is another dimension – the NHS as an employer. The City of Birmingham with a population of just over 1 million people has over 25,000 people working in its NHS institutions – general practice, community services, mental health services, and hospitals.

In 2001, the Government asked all who work in the NHS to spend time finding new ways of thinking through how to ensure that the service develops and grows to fit the requirements of a new Century as set out in the National Plan for the NHS (the exercise was called "Local Modernisation Review").

One outcome of that process in Birmingham was the idea of commissioning this book and giving a copy to every person working in the NHS in our City. Why?

Two reasons. First, we wanted to celebrate the NHS workforce in Birmingham, to acknowledge the role they all play in this endeavour that is so much part of all our lives. Secondly, we wanted to recognise that much of the quality of people's experience of the NHS (as patients, as carers, as workers) is about the human dimensions of giving and receiving care. We believe that the arts, in this case writing, can find ways to encapsulate that reality that can be more meaningful than managerial exhortations! We hope that this book will provide food for thought for all of the dedicated workforce of the NHS in Birmingham.

We hope also that for its wider readership that it can prompt a helpful reflection on what we all want our National Health Service to be.

Alan Wenban-Smith
Chairman
Birmingham Health Authority

Introduction

The cover for this book is a detail of Joseph Wright's 'An Experiment on a Bird in the Air Pump': a depiction of an early medical trial. A travelling scientist demonstrates the formation of a vacuum by withdrawing air from a flask containing a white cockatoo. The artist's subject isn't scientific invention, but human drama in a night-time setting. The bird will expire if the demonstrator continues to deprive it of oxygen, and Wright leaves us in some doubt as to whether or not our white bird will be reprieved.

•

The Gift is for our National Health Service. Not oxygen, but maybe a small point of light. This book is for the workforce of the service: it is writing as an act of community, even solidarity.

The contributors include not only authors such as Doris Lessing, Fay Weldon, Hanif Kureishi, and Les Murray, but also staff in the Health Service. These writers and their publishers have freely donated their work. In most cases, the work was written specially for this book. Writers in the NHS worked with me on new writing throughout January and February 2002 in workshops at Warwick University or via e-mail.

There are several ideas behind *The Gift*. The first purpose is to produce a book of literary merit that stands on its own. The second is celebratory. The National Health Service is fifty years old and we can and should celebrate that half-a-century of dedication and hard work, and look forward to the next fifty years.

This book wants to *give* the NHS workforce (for they are a force: read their writing) something which is serious, entertaining, permanent, meaningful, and articulate. The writers hope that their work might inspire medical workers to reflect on how people who use their service feel and think about their experiences. We hope that, out of this, they, as individuals and in their teams, are encouraged to find little or big things that they can do or change to make a difference to the human dimensions of the NHS.

While such aims are rightfully modest, the *gesture* of this book, and of the authors in it, has some bravura. The Health Service deserves something more in return from the people who use it. To this end, the first 31,000 copies will be given free to members of the NHS staff in Birmingham. The remaining copies will be sold and the profits given to a Trust for those staff. It is hoped a donor might now come forward who will allow us to take this enterprise to its logical conclusion: to ensure that *The Gift* reaches every member of staff of the National Health Service. This project is the gift of a book to a person one has never met. It is the gift of talent of the writers in the book who, in their turn, gave their work free. And it celebrates the gift of life that is the central concern of our doctors, nurses, ancillary staff and other medical workers. The order of this book attempts to reflect that concern, from birth, through growth, and the processes of illness and death.

This book is, in effect, for all NHS staff. It is also dedicated to the memory of W.G. Sebald who was killed shortly after donating his work.

•

Such a project is never a solo operation. I would like to thank: Peter Spilsbury, Director of Performance & Strategy of the Birmingham Health Authority, for proposing this quite visionary project and sustaining it every step through incubation to publication; the authors of *The Gift* who either wrote new work to a very tight deadline, or donated writing, or arranged permission for its use if published; Rupert Loydell of Stride Publications for his advice, energy and willingness to work at the speed of light; to the publishers Faber & Faber, Harvill Press, Penguin Books, Picador, Chatto and Windus, Bloodaxe Books, and Flamingo, for being so generous in waiving fees; Hannah Griffiths of Curtis Brown for getting the word out to her authors; David Hart for enlisting poets to send in work; Anouk Perinpanayagam for encouragement in times of occasional editorial doubt; Doris Lessing and John Hegley for helping to promote the project; The University of Warwick for allowing me the space to work on this book, and colleagues at the University for their support, namely Jeremy Treglown, Peter Mack, Maureen Freely, Russell Celyn Jones, Lisa Ganobcsik-Williams, Georgina Paul and Elizabeth Cameron; to some of my students who helped typeset and deliver the book, especially Nicoleta Cinpoes, Anna Lea, Jon Morley, and Malgorzata Kitowski; and, finally, to my wife Dr Siobhan Keenan and my son Isaac for their patience.

Thanks also to The Nuffield Trust for Research and Policy Studies in Health Services.

David Morley
The Warwick Writing Programme,
Warwick University

The new father's mistake

In the hospital
The new mother has agreed
to assist in testing the worth
of a new natal drug.
Soon after the birth
The marvellous midwife gives
    me the relevant questionnaire
    to hold
and proceeds to organise her
    patient's relative comfort.
I mistakenly think she has told
    me to complete
the sheet.
Inwardly I express surprise
that my responses are of interest
    but feel it best
not to question the interest of
    modern science.
I proceed to give my answers in
dutiful compliance.
Marking is from nought to
    five
depending on how intensely
the phenomenon described
is thought to have been
    experienced.
The following represents how it
    was for me:
Headaches – nought
Abdominal pain – nought
Nausea – nought
Shivering – nought
Vomiting – nought
Tiredness – five.

John Hegley

A Hard Time to be a Father

Once upon a time, dear reader, but not so far away or long ago, practically round the corner, in fact, and into the new millennium, a young man took his pain to a hospital, for the sake of his young wife Delia.

See the hospital as a castle, see the castle as a place which immures the Healer Magician, see it in the sense of fairy tale of literary work by Kafka, see it how you will. We are all within spitting distance of castles; spit away, if that's where your experience of institutions leads you, if it makes you feel better.

The young man had been to art school and now worked as a store-window designer, where being heterosexual he stuck out like a sore thumb, but never mind all that. He came to the castle by night: after work but before the pubs close being the most propitious time to attend Casualty or so Delia told him.

Delia knew better than her husband how the world worked, or seemed to.

The word CASUALTY was written in letters of fire which drifted across a frosted green panel above the hospital doors, and seemed to offer a welcome, albeit a deceptive one, for the dog Cerberus had been let loose to roam the castle gates and keep off all comers. Cerberus had three heads and all of them were ugly.

'You obviously can't park there, sir,' said the first head. It wore a collar, a tie and spectacles, waved human arms and used contempt as a weapon. 'These spaces are reserved for Senior Medical Staff, surgeons and the like. You are attempting to commit an anti-social act. Kindly move on.'

'I'm so sorry,' said the young man, being apologetic by nature – and he drove on round the corner hoping for better luck.

'Don't even think of parking there,' said a second head, appearing out of nowhere. Its scalp was shaved, its tongue and lips were ringed: its mien was terrible. 'That's reserved for fucking ambulances. Are you blind?'

'It's true that pain does somewhat blur my vision,' the young man said with heavy irony, but only once window was up and his door lock was down. He drove around another corner where amazingly he found an empty space. As he backed into it a third head came along, wearing a hat of the kind a Ruritanian general might wear, all heavy gold and red embroidery.

'Double lines, sir, you can't park here, on penalty of clamping.'

'Then where am I meant to park?' asked the young man.

'Nothing to do with me, sir. I just do my job.'

Cerberus' necks are very long: heads spring up all over the place; he can see round corners: latterly he has been cloned, they say. He is everywhere: the faces may waver and change, often taking female form, but be sure he is the same beast. He guards the gates of the castles everywhere. Even though these Castles or Recourse may be phantasmagoric, Cerberus is real enough. Only in parts of London you can cheat him; by parking with your back wheels in Westminster and your front wheels in Camden:

then, confused, Cerberus sometimes finds it easier to leave you alone. But such spaces are in hot demand.

Pain made the young man unusually brave. He just left the car where it was and he walked away, the creature from Ruritania taking notes behind him.

Now the young man's name, dear reader, as it happens, is Candide, not because your writer is trying to make a point, but merely the better to report a story told to her in real life by a young couple whose names were in fact Candide and Delia. Blame Candide's parents, not me, should blame be called for: let's get on, now that's out of the way.

The bullet-proof glass doors that admitted walk-ins to casualty were bolted shut against violent marauders. Two security guards flanked the entrance. Candide was checked over visually for suitability for treatment out of public funds. The security guards took their TIME.

'Please! I need help,' mouthed our hero through the glass.

A nod from one to the other; at least the person had the password right. "Help!" Their eyes were grim and their mouths tight, but they let him through.

Candide saw a sweet-faced girl behind a counter marked RECEPTION; she wore a badge which named her as MIRANDA – volunteer, Friends of Mercy. It streaks of pinkish fire which travelled ceaselessly above her head, moved the slogan PLEASE WAIT PATIENTLY. OTHERS MAY BE IN NEED OF MORE URGENT ATTENTION THAN YOU. THANK YOU FOR CHOOSING THE HOSPITAL OF MERCY.

'What's your problem, sir?' Miranda enquired, kindly enough. She had some small training in dealing with difficult, even violent patients. Hospital casualty these days is full of violent people, but no one knows quite why.

'Appendix, peritonitis, death, who's to say,' said Candide.

'I appreciate your sense of humour, sir,' said Miranda. 'Just wait on one of those chairs over there until a member of staff is free to attend to you. We are very busy today.'

Candide sat and clutched his belly until the pain eased. Fifty green plastic chairs were ranged in five rows of ten. Forty were unoccupied, ten occupied. Candide spent his time counting them. Other supplicants slept, breathing and snorting gently, dingy garments trailing and rooting on the floor. From the far end of the great hall, by the coffee machine came a burst of colour, chatter and laughter. Four girls of easy virtue, – or so Candide supposed them to be, for their skirts were up to their crotches, their jewelled handbags swung low, their heels were high, and their faces heroin-white – had worked out a way of extracting coffee from the machine without paying; one would thump, the other would kick; another try and catch the coffee as it spurted. The youngest girl, who was about twelve, was smoking and not interested in coffee.

'No smoking over there,' cried Miranda, 'in the interest of public safety. Don't you understand this is a hospital?'

'Fuck off,' shrieked the smoker, in harsh though Sloaney tones, 'or I'll spit and spread Aids.'

Candide resolved to keep his distance, and even Miranda paid the bad girl, for that is what they were, no more attention. It takes the girls from all classes, dear reader, to keep sex industry going: the trade is buyer driven and voracious.

Ten minutes passed: fifteen, twenty, sixty. Someone spilt coffee from a plastic mug onto the floor. It seemed to be an accident.

A rugby player slept in the last chair of the first row. He seemed to have been there some time. A red and white striped scarf was round his head: his shirt was striped black and white, vertically. He murmured in his sleep: he drowsed. He wore muddy shorts striped horizontally in purple and yellow. His thighs were vast and muscle-knotted; his socks could barely stretch around his powerful calves. Beneath his right knee Candide now noticed a sliver of broken shinbone piercing the flesh. Candide peered and peered again. He could not be mistaken.

'Nurse, nurse,' called Candide, spying on one who passed. She was a dark-eyed girl with the face of a Grecian Goddess, calm and strong.

'Well? I'm busy. What?' asked Nurse Galina, for so her badge named her.

'That rugby player asleep over there –'

'Yeah, we get lots of rugby nuts on Sundays. They bring it on themselves, like smokers.'

'But his leg is broken. I can see a bone sticking out.'

'Bones often do that when they're broken,' said Nurse Galina.

'Shouldn't he see a doctor?' asked Candide. His own pain had eased. In fact he was beginning to wonder if he needed to stay at all, and worrying about the fate of his car outside, left in the space reserved, he now remembered, for Patient Participation Officer, Grade 2 only. He thought the traffic warden had probably been bluffing, but supposing the PPO was on night shift and turned up to claim his space?

'It's asleep,' said Nurse Galina. 'A rugby player's like a baby: if it's asleep, don't wake it. It's just asking for trouble.'

'A baby,' repeated Candide, and all but fainted. Nurse Galina had to thrust his head between his knees till his head stopped swimming. Candide explained to her that this was part of his trouble. His wife was pregnant. He suffered from recurring pains in the stomach, which their friends assumed mimicked the labour pains and were merely psychosomatic. He could put up with these: they were one thing, but the fact that whenever he heard the word 'Baby' he felt dizzy and fainted was another. It had become something of a joke amongst friends, but to Candide it was a serious matter. The word was used increasingly all around him; no one could avoid it, as his wife's labour became imminent. He wishes to be a tip-top physical and psychic form when the time comes. This is why he had come to casualty. His own doctor would not take his complaint seriously.

'But there's no-one for psychiatry on my list,' said Nurse Galina. 'Have you checked in at the desk?'

'I don't think so,' said Candide. 'I was told to sit down.'

'That new girl on the desk,' complained Nurse Galina. 'She knows nothing about anything except sex. She's sleeping with the Senior Registrar, they say. You should have checked in with Triage Nurse ages ago. How can she call your name if you're not on her list, let alone pass it to me? Didn't you think about that?'

'I trusted the system,' he said. 'I assumed you knew your business. And who and what is Triage Nurse? I thought Triage was a system use to sort out those lying on the battlefield at the end of the day. The dead who need to be buried; the wounded who can be cured to fight again, and those who are better just left as they are.'

'My, how knowledgeable we are,' said Nurse Galina, but she said it kindly and explained that Triage Nurse divided patients into three categories, those who were seriously ill and a doctor needed to see quite soon; those who were making a fuss about nothing and would have to wait, and those who were only fit for Psychiatry anyway. At least that is what he thought she said.

'From the sound of it,' said Nurse Galina, 'you're ripe for psychiatric.'

'I don't see why,' said Candide, 'Delia and I both look forward very much to the birth. The pregnancy is planned, we're both halfway up our career ladders, and on Flexi-Time and so forth; we're doing everything right, I can hardly be mad. Whatever my problem turns out to be I am sure it's physiological in origin, or I wouldn't be here.'

'My, my, my,' said Nurse Galina, 'in denial, are we, and what big words we use!' – but she took him back to Reception to register.

Appointments Nurse was small, skinny and dark and wore a sari. Her name-badge read Ishtar Patel. She asked Candide for his Name, Address, Age, Religion, Country of Origin, Partner Status, Sexual Orientation and how he travelled to the hospital.

'I don't see how the latter is relevant,' said Candide.

'You are not expected to see anything' said Ishtar. 'This information is needed for our statistics.'

'But I could be dying,' said the young man. 'I might not have the time to help you with your statistics.'

'Perhaps English isn't your first language,' observed Ishtar coolly. 'I may have to wait for our Ethnicity expert to come back from lunch so she can help me fill in the form. She takes a long lunch.'

'I came by car,' said the young man, sighing, giving in, 'and parked it, for all that Cerberus snapped.'

'Definitely a psychiatric,' murmured Ishtar to Galina. 'As are so many of these fair-haired square-jawed types; off to Triage with him!' And Candide was sent to sit in a different part of the great hall.

Here light was scarce, and the wretched of the earth who had somehow sidled around Security and gained an entrance to the warmth and shelter and free sweet cups of tea of the Castle Mercy, huddled in some number in corners. They seemed to murmur and whisper in chorus. Candide tried to make sense of the muted, drifting sound, and thought the words ran thus –

> We are the flotsam, the jetsam of this city.
> The drifters, the hopeless, the object of your pity.
> You need us to be sorry for;
>   Hark to this our ditty.

At least that's what Candide thought they murmured and whispered, but who was to say? The faint smell of antiseptic dulled his senses to more acrid human scents, and the low hum of central heating, and the distant clank of trolleys, and caring female voices, lulled him as he waited, and waited. Thus the Castles of Concern work their enchantment. The stomach pains had abated. He drowsed. But the plight of the Rugby player, whom he could see quite clearly from across the hall, now troubled him more than his own: he could not rest. A shaft of light glittered on the white sliver of projecting bone.

Nurse Galina passed by again. Once more Candide drew her attention to the Rugby player. Apparently the man slept; but supposing he had lapsed into a coma? Were they be keeping an eye on him?

'Why do you care about the great ox?' asked Nurse Galina. 'More like an animal than a human being. He'll be seen in due course. We know well enough what we're doing. Those who inflict damage on themselves, smokers, over-eaters, drinkers, cutters, sporting types and so forth must take responsibility for their own actions: we've had a memo round. If a male giant throws himself into a scrum and invites a lot of other male giants to stamp on him, he needn't think he can come in here and ask for special privileges from hard-working women.'

Her voice rose in a pitch as she spoke. She let it be known she was at the end of her tether.

'Hasn't Triage Nurse even seen you yet?' she asked, as if it were Candide's negligence were responsible; and when Candide shook his head, she sighed heavily.

Triage Nurse, who was little and fair and very pretty, came out of her cubicle, calling repeatedly for Baby Longman. Nobody responded to her cry, not Longman mother, not Longman father, so she huffed and puffed her way back into the cubicle as if she were a dragon thwarted by the non-appearance of St. George. But Candide had to put his head between his knees, and only just prevented himself from fainting clean again. Next time she came out she called for Candide Newman. Yes indeed, dear reader, Newman is my hero's surname. His parents no doubt just liked the sound the words made together. And like Trixiebell or Fifi, or Tiger Lily or Peach, why not?

'Yes, that is I,' Candide replied, coming forward as quickly as he could, so as not to irritate Triage Nurse further. Progress was not as quick as he hoped; it seemed he was still recovering from exposure to the word to which he had become sensitised. Baby. He staggered and groped through darkening vision.

You took your time,' snapped Triage Nurse and sat him down facing her. She took Candide's temperature, his pulse, and marvelled at the lowness of his blood pressure before she let him describe his symptoms. He told her much what he had told Nurse Galina.

'Feeling faint when the word Baby is mentioned is not exactly an urgent matter,' she reproached him. 'What do you think your local surgery is for? This is casualty department of a large inner city hospital: we exist to deal with emergencies. And the most common cause of fleeting stomach pain is wind. Perhaps you have been taking too much paracetamol? It can be constipating.

Candide found, as sounds swam and sang in them, that he had ears to hear her thoughts. Sometimes the unspoken words of others do ring through another's head. It has happened once or twice to me, reader, and I hope it never happens to you, as it happened that night to Candide, as tired, exhausted, deafened and blinded by the problems of others as he was, he persisted in his attempts to breach the defences of the Castle.

'Good God, what a wimp, what a poor, pathetic wimp,' Triage Nurse thought, and he heard it loud and clear though her lips did not move. 'Pity his poor partner, who'll be left on her own to cope with the broken nights and the crashy nappies and the rashy crap. No. The crappy nappies and the nappy rash. Thank God my own baby doesn't have to put up with a father. No, it's the crechey child and the crappy care for my little girl, and trime pine for me when I get home from this the Castle Malaprop. In the meantime this timp is wasting my wime. There's nothing wrong with him; my BP machine's on the blink, that's all. No-one can have blood pressure as low as that and still stand up.'

'If, as you say, there is nothing wrong with me,' Candide began, but Triage Nurse stopped him short, very short.

'I must ask you to withdraw that allegation. Anything said to that effect might have legal consequences,' she snapped, her pretty little mouth tight and firm. 'I did not claim there was nothing wrong with you, I inferred it is a possibility.'

'There is definitely something wrong with that man over there,' said Candide, 'I don't care what you say. I can see a sliver of bone sticking out of his leg and that is that. He must be in agony.'

Triage Nurse seemed to soften.

'Try and realise that sporting types don't feel the pain like we do,' she replied. Anyway I suspect it's your blood pressure. It's so low you are suffering from optical illusions. I can see no bone from here. It is true waiting times are a little longer than usual due to the recent downsizing of our medical team and the fact that our new computer has crashed again, but if there were a problem, we'd have seen to it. Let me tell you a joke to cheer you up. It comes from a book called More Rugby Songs, which was on my father's shelves when I was a child. My father was a keen rugby player: never at home when he was wanted. This is the joke. Two men are sitting peacefully by the river, fishing. They say nothing for the first two hours. Then the first angler says, "Weren't here yesterday, then," and the other replies "No."

"What stopped you?" persists the first angler.

"Got married," says the other. There is a long, long silence. Bees buzz, stream ripples, fishes dart. A beautiful day.

"Good looker, is she?" asks the first angler, searching for reasons why an angler should want to do such a thing as marry.

"Nope," says the other.

"Got money then, or what?"

"Nope."

"Is she sexy, is that it?" demands the first.

"You must be joking," says the second angler.

"Then why on earth?" asks the first angler.

"She got worms," says the other.

Triage Nurse asked Candide, rather threateningly, if he thought the foke was junny. Candide hastened to say said that if he laughed it had been inadvertently, from shock. He assured her he himself was not a sporting man, neither an angler nor a rugby player, had never seen the book in question, let alone read it. He was innocent. He was a new man, as his name suggested. The nearest he got to any kind of sport was that he and his wife Delia were in the habit of jogging round the park on a Sunday morning. But Triage Nurse wouldn't have it, she said she was talking uilt by gassociation. A man was a man for a' that.

The Castle Malaprop, the one that Triage Nurse inhabits in her head, is full of little demons from the past: they scuttle out and nip the unwary on the ankles. Or nipple out and scut the anwary on the uncles. Speech and thought disturbance occurs.

'All you men got about,' said Triage Nurse, or so he thought he heard her say 'with an albatross around your neck. *Instead of a cross, an albatross, about my neck was hung.*" Samuel Taylor Coleridge. Aim of the Makeshifter Rhymer. I go to crompulsory dug awareness classed Wednesday evening. My little girl has to go to greighbours who make me eel the fobligation. Life is not easy for the working, unpartnered mother, no matter how coble the nalling. Samuel Taylor Coleridge ook topium, you know, an early morph of forfine, a doppy perivative. It shatters the brain. Whoever heard of anyone going round with an albatross around their neck, but there it is, pain as a plikestaff on the page, certainly taken seriously by those who ought to know better. Awareness is balf the hattle. Most preative creople are on drugs. Are you creative? I see that your occupation is written here as "designer". It sounds creative to me.'

'I assure you it isn't,' said Candide.

'My little girl's in cray dare,' said Triage Nurse. 'I don't get much sleep. Their remit is to stimulate her creativity, but when you see what preativity does to creople I wonder why they bother.

Alone, alone, all all alone
Alone on a shiny sea
And never a soul took pity on
My soul in agony.

Was it slimy or shiny? I quite like the poem, for all it was dug cased.'

'Drug crazed?' he asked. 'Do you mean drug crazed?' It seemed to him that her disorder was intensifying with every sentence. She was losing, not just reversing, whole constanants.

'Are you trying to tell me something here?' asked Triage Nurse. 'Research shows that people on drugs refer to them 27% more frequently than those who are not. I should be careful if I were you. Well, I am glad we had our little chat. I did enjoy it. If you go and sit over there by the green swing doors, doctor will see you presently about the stomach pains. Afterwards I'd recommend you to go to psychiatric, but doctor will decide.'

From his seat by the green swing doors, so near and yet so far from treatment, Candide heard a chant swelling from some point near the coffee machine. It rose from the painted lips of the whores, who had settled in to play cards in the free warmth.

Though as they remarked to anyone who challenged them, they paid taxes, didn't they. Though some would take leave to doubt even that

> *We are the whores, the bad girls of the city,*
> *And thank you very much, we do not need your pity.*
> *We save marriages by millions, and victorious sing this ditty.*

And Candide, quite cheered up, was thinking, well, perhaps this world of ours isn't so bad a place to bring a child into, when Triage Nurse came again and called

'Baby Longman, Baby Longman, Baby Longman.'

– and again Candide's head swam, his eyes misted and whether he saw things that were not his to see, and heard things he should not hear, and everything was true and real or not who was to say?

– but there was a sense of movement everywhere and he saw that the whores were now moving up and down the rows of prospective patients offering their services, falling into cheerful conversation even when rejected. The ragged shuffled along on their haunches, unseen by Reception, begging and blessing even when refused alms.

This time it was his own dear wife who pressed his head between his knees as he swayed. She burgeoned in pregnancy like a small ship with a full sail: she had a sweet, anxious expression, a high complexion and nut-brown hair so curly that all you could do was to dunk it under the tap to wash it and then allow it to dry naturally.

'Poor thing, poor thing,' cried Delia. 'Haven't they even seen you yet? It's beyond belief!'

'I've been triaged,' said Candide. It was his instinct to make the best of things, if he could. He and Delia fought a battle, if that was not too strong a word for it, between trust and mistrust. If he was Pollyanna, she was Cassandra. Between them they managed very well. 'They can't think it's very serious,' he said, 'or they'd have seen me by now.'

'I don't think that's necessarily the case,' said Delia. 'That rugby player over there actually has a bone sticking out of his leg. It's a disgrace!'

'Don't make a fuss, Delia,' begged Candide. 'You will only make things worse.'

But Delia marched straight over to Nurse Galina.

'I work in TV,' she said, (a lie) 'and unless something is done for the man with the broken leg I will bring the cameras in. I and my unborn child will be in a position to sue this hospital for post traumatic stress disorder. Surely I have the right to come in here and not be traumatised by what I see?'

'We can't be pleasing everyone all the time or we'd never get through,' said Nurse Galina, but she hurried away, as perhaps she meant to do something. Then she was lost in an angry crowd now clustering around Reception, prevented from getting even so far as Triage, inasmuch as the software relating to their means of transportation to the hospital had developed a virus, or so Miranda claimed.

'The new computer's crashed,' explained Candide to Delia. The castle had worked its spell on him and he felt the need to defend its ways. 'But when it's working it will cut down waiting times no end.'

'It's still too bad,' said Delia, rather feebly. She was near the end of her time, and beginning to have stomach pains at regular intervals. Like so many of us, she could fight for the rights of others, but did not like to draw attention to herself. 'It's not as if I were an urgent case,' he said.

'You're the one who needs the care.'

'Me? I'm as strong as a horse,' protested Delia.

At which point Triage Nurse came out calling, 'Mr Holifog, Mr Holifog! Anyone here by the name of Holifog?'

'Bet that's the Rugby Player,' said Delia, and went up to the bulky, recumbent, vaguely human shape in its muddy sweater with the broad black and white stripes and shook him vigorously.

'Nurse did say not to wake him!' said Candide, tentatively, but Delia took no notice, and shook on. Another half inch of bone slipped through the hairy skin below the knee so she stopped, aghast. Candide did not say 'I told you so,' – it was not in his nature – and besides, he had become conscious of the thoughts drifting through the Rugby Player's head.

'Don't wake me, mummy because I'm in heaven! Run for it! Run for the touchdown! Oh the grass is so slippery, oh the green wet shine of it, the slippage: the silage: the sweat, the ache in the calf, the knotting of muscle, the thwack and collision of flesh. Oh, the earth-shaking joy of it. Sling 'em off, fling 'em off, into the scrum and here's mud in your eye! Wash my clothes, mother, wash them real good –' and so on, and on, ponderous as a rhinoceros, and then suddenly Triage Nurse was calling, 'Mr Huggifuss, Mr Huggifuss, anyone here called Mr Huggifuss?' at which the Rugby Player stirred and said, 'Name's Oliphant Hugo, Oliphant, actually,' –

– and Triage Nurse said, 'No-one here of the name Huggifuss. I told you he was a waste of time, hypochondriacs to a man, these sporting man, for all they act is tough. If they knew what women had to put up with during labour, they wouldn't have the nerve to complain-'

– and Hugo Oliphant called aloud for his father, *'Daddy, daddy, watch me, one day you'll be proud of me '* –

– and such a churning of the poor and disaffected rose around Candide's feet, their hands outstretched for alms, that he shuddered. But Delia his wife said, 'Give them what you can, my dear, who knows when a beggar is a prince in disguise!' so he gave them all he had, even his five pound note.

– and Delia persuaded Hugo Oliphant to whisper his telephone number in her ear, and then rang his mother collect. Mothers can often negotiate the Castle when others slip and fail. Whole fortress will fall when mother love is on the warpath.

Now outside one of Cerberus' heads was barking loudly at an intruder: a guard dog of a different tune, a pisser and a runner: vast and clanking, the tow-away truck, and Candide and Delia watched aghast from a window.

'You can't park there!' cried the Cerberus head. 'Hey you!'

'I park where I fucking well please,' said the newcomer dog.

'That's our ambulance zone,' snarled the head.

'Don't fucking swear at us,' yapped the dog, which was also two-headed, being driver and mate.

'They park, we clamp, we lift, we take our time, but when we've taken it we *move*, right Fred?' said dog.

'Right,' said Fred, 'let's do the world a fucking favour –' by this time Candide' and

Delia's Fiat Uno was swinging in the air – 'and drop this pile of crap. Look at the rust on that underbelly!' Candide and Delia clung to each other, but at that moment an ambulance screeched up, backed up and parked arse to rear of the tow-away truck. A tripartite row ensued, between the ambulance driver and the rest. The ambulance was bringing in a heart attack victim – a middle-aged man – and had fetched him all the way in, siren screaming, red lights flashing, but now declined to disembark the patient until the tow-truck moved.

'Perhaps you didn't leave our car in quite the most sensible place, darling,' said Delia gently, and before he could say *'Please don't make a fuss, dearest,'* she was out of casualty and into the ambulance bay gesticulating and organising. Within minutes she was sitting back next to her husband. Their dear little car had been safely lowered, the clamps removed, the tow-away vehicle departed and the heart attack victim was even now being stretchered into the magic castle.

'But what did you say to them, darling?' Candide marvelled, and Delia just said, 'I told them I'd have my baby then and there: that always works.' Candide did his best not to faint right away; he was so utterly exhausted. During the few minutes of Delia's absence he had been kidnapped, assaulted, rescued, and returned to his chair. He was okay, just about, but had few psychic or physical resources left to spare.

Two soft-voiced, mousy-haired, maternal-looking cosmic healers had set about him, and dragged him into a linen cupboard. Their names were Donna and Jan. Donna had been a teacher and Jan a nurse in what they saw as a previous life, but now, if you asked them, they'd say their bodies were inhabited by walk-ins from the Dog Star Sirius. It was the walk-ins' mission to heal the sick by means of alternative medicine. Thus it had become Donna and Jan's habit to hang around the castle, posing as patients or friends of patients or even staff, chasing the unwary, anointing them with organic unguents, passing crystals over charkas – the energy points of the body – the better to restore the feeble and nearest to perfect health.

The self-styled enchantress Donna had simply crept up behind Candide and removed the chair from beneath him: her paramour, the earth Goddess Jan, then dragged him off to the linen cupboard, her strong hands under his shocked armpits.

'Quickly, Jan love, quickly, before he struggles! Juniper oil beneath his nose. And patchouli too!' The door slammed. He was alone with them in a tiny room, stacked high with thin boiled stacked laundry, and where was Delia?

Strong odours assailed his nostrils: his head swum. He felt his garments removed as he lay upon the floor. A cold, sharp surface scratched gently across his chest and other more intimate parts.

'Don't be afraid. Relax. Thank God we got you in time, before the doctors and nurses, those messages of darkness, invaded the holism of your body with their needles and chemicals. Do you feel your strength reviving? We have you framed by four crystals, to transform and transmute all negative energies. How tense you are; my hands can sense how tense you are –'

The long soft hair of Donna the enchantress brushed his body as she worked upon him.

'Don't, don't,' he cried. 'I am a married man –'

'Rose quartz upon the heart,' cried Jan, not to be undone. 'To promote love and excitement at the deepest levels; an emerald here at the base of the sacral chakra to refine the sexual energies –

'This is beyond belief,' Candide dried.

'See,' murmured Donna, 'as your member rises it satiates and completes the harmonies – every cell in your body is diffused with a red light: see, your whole auric field is scarlet, the petals of a flower unfolding –'

Mercifully the Guardian of the Green Swing Doors happened to be passing, and was alerted by the scent of patchouli, which as every ex or indeed current hippie can tell you, gets everywhere. He was male and powerful and briskly hauled the two women off Candide's dazed but ever-lively member, crying –

'Not you two witches again! Is nowhere safe?' and the women scuttled off, shrieking and withering up, becoming little and old and carapaced, like black beetles making for safe cracks and crannies between the skirting and the floor: while the Male Nurse, for it was he, scrunched and stamped them beneath his feet: cracky on the outside, as they are, soft in the inside.

'There's always more roaches where they come from,' Male Nurse lamented. 'A regular plague of them!' And Male Nurse helped Candide back into his clothes, keeping his hands more or less to himself, and Candide felt quite at home, and as if it was all familiar: it was like being back at nursery school again. He did not tell Delia of his adventures. She was the one who was accustomed to having them. He just usually sat in a chair and waited for her to change the world. He breathed deeply and tried to recover his strength.

Between the rows of chairs now approached none other than Mrs Oliphant, Hugo's mother. Her bosom was as proud as Delia's belly, swathed in the green peacock plumes of a traditional Liberty's fabric, her face as noble, as pained and strong as that of a prize-winning cart-horse.

'What does he ever want to play soccer for anyway?' she asked the assembled halt and sick.

'You have these babies, you devote your life to them; you take them to the doctor at the first sign of a cough; to the clinic for an X-ray every time they fall on their heads; you squeeze them whole oranges and sieve the juice for pips in case one lodges in their appendix; you clear out their toy-boxes; try not to tread on their Lego; you walk them to the school they hate; you save them from strangers; you look out for signs of drug abuse; you get them to twenty-one without a police-record, and what do they do? They self-destruct. They break their teeth in the swimming pool after years of orthodontics, rip their cartilages on the playing field, break every bone in their body and expect mummy to come along and pick up the pieces. Well I will, but he'll get no sympathy from me. Such a hypochondriac,' she said, her strong voice faltering as she spied her slumped son. 'I expect he's making a fuss about nothing. I had to get my sister-in-law to wait for the delivery man. A new washing machine. It was pay for a new tub or replace the whole machine; they get worn out, don't they, going all the time. All that mud: it gets into the works. A mother's love is a terrible burden-'

She took one look at her son's leg and yelped. She spied a wheelchair. Fetched it, and with Delia's help, heaved her massive son into it, and started running with it towards the green glass doors, all but slipping on a watery surface as she went. 'Oh my God,' cried Delia to her husband, 'my waters have broken! I am going into labour.'

It is sometimes easier to do for others what it seems all but impossible to do for the self. Candide was finally galvanized into action. He too seized a wheelchair, shoved his wife into it, and fell in behind Mrs Oliphant in their mutual race to the inner sanctum, where healing occurred or was alleged to occur. Here suddenly would be people trained to hazard a guess as to why a man fainted, or had pains in his belly, who could click a bone or two under anaesthetic, or help nature expel a baby from the womb.

Triage Nurse did her best to bar their way: her arms seemed to stretch a hundred miles in every direction. Her white sleeves reached only her elbows; she wore shorts in the manner of nurses in the summer, and sandals without socks; acres of firm, healthy flesh rippled and dissolved before them: the king's sorcerers were up to their tricks again.

'You haven't been called, you haven't been called!' The voice of Triage Nurse echoed round the vast chamber: it was the Day of Judgement and see, the dead were forbidden to arise. A murmur of anger rose from the patients on the chairs, and the cluster round reception, and the dim dispossessed in the corner, and the four whores rose up magnificent in all their blonde glory, tarty satin silver chains – and Mrs Oliphant broke the glass door with her elbow, put her hand in to loose the catch from the other side, and sailed through the blue peacock feathers, followed by Candide pushing the already groaning Delia, so did all the others; a stream of the dead on their way to paradise –
    – Triage Nurse stood aside, she was obliged to; she sank to her true size again: much and permanently diminished, she spoke.
    – 'I give up this job,' said Triage Nurse. 'Anyone wants it, they can have it. I'm going back to my little girl, who is the only one who has ever truly appreciated me.'
    – and she walked right out of the castle, and everyone agreed it was a better place for her going, while appreciating that she was sorely tried and did a good job to the best of her ability.
    – 'A baby!' cried Candide, 'my wife is having a baby,' and his head felt clear and his voice was strong, and the dreaded word no longer afflicted him.

Doctors appeared, and nurses too and on the other side of the green swing doors it was indeed like heaven: no wonder it was so difficult to get into, as many said then to each other. Angels of Mercy whisked Hugo Oliphant off to the operating theatre – and you will be glad to know he was back on the playing fields within two months and his mother's washing-machine was delivered, plumbed in and up and running by the time she got home from the hospital. Oh, what a day of Miracles! – Nurses ran to take Delia to the delivery room: it was going to be what they called a lightning birth.

Male Nurse sidelined Candide, and stood him under a shower to remove the last traces of patchouli, for the health and the safety of the coming baby, he said, and admired the young and lissom nature of the body before him and was content with that.

And by the time Candide came out of the shower the baby was born, perfect, healthy and cheerful, washed and wrapped, and frankly Candide was much relieved by the pattern events had taken and Delia didn't seem to mind too much. Some men are just plain happier for not being there at the birth.

The man who thought he had a heart attack turned out to be having indigestion pains, and was sent home.

Waiting staff cut away the calluses of the homeless, listened to their sad stories, gave them free cups of tea and put them on yet more waiting lists.

The four whores found willing punters in a quartet of visiting Japanese politicians, here to investigate the workings of a National Health Service, and all in all it was the happiest fairy tale ending anyone could imagine.

The engine of the little Uno fired first go when Candide started back for home – he'd collect Delia and the baby the next day – and Cerberus didn't so much as growl at him. All three heads took it upon themselves to wish him a happy and successful fatherhood.

Fay Weldon

The Paediatric Corridor

What I remember now –

after the bitter medicine
disguised in your sugared
apple juice, measured
by syringe
(those drops of pure anxiety),
after the scanning of your small
stomach, bladder and kidneys,
that restless terrain of rocks
and empty valleys,
after this –

the strange quietness
of the paediatric corridor,
as if all childhood illnesses
and injuries had suddenly
been blown away, swept
backwards into the mouth
of some merciful god.

Moniza Alvi

Firstborn

(for J.)

Five hours since the cut,
they carry you in – a little grandee
dewy as a bud, black hair combed
perfumed eau de cologne.

I count your fingers,
eye your bunched fists, perfect skin.
A finished work – wrapped white,
your own person.

I missed your first cry –
now you are here separate, defined.
My stomach twists knives
as I try to hold you, skin against skin,

little voyager
in from your cloud.
Quickly I claim you
as I will again and again.

Last Afternoon

The wards whirred:
nurses peering in
my turn to keep watch –
feeling your child
now more than ever,
all our conversations
down to whispered assurances.

You gripped my hands,
you had come so far
at this hard pace.
I wanted to carry you away
as you had carried me Mother,
hearing you again
Always a new baby
never time to hold you...

Now the pain swallowing –
your voice still real
as in a telephone-call
twelve thousand miles away.
Wanting you Mother,
angry with you because
it wasn't your fault –
angry with myself
for not having said more often
how I loved you.

It would have been simple
a small thing to do,
yet suddenly important
with the lights going out
too quickly and me carrying you
on my shoulders this final time
such a long way in the dark.

Katherine Gallagher

Waiting Room

I am the room for all seasons,
the Waiting Room. Here the impatient
fidget, gossip, yawn and fret and sneeze. I am the room
for summer (sunburn, hay-fever, ear wax,
children falling out of plum trees, needing patching);
for autumn (arthritis and chesty coughs,
when the old feel time worrying at their bones);
for winter (flu, and festival hangovers,
flourish of signatures on skiers' plaster of Paris);
for spring (O the springing spots of adolescence,
unwary pregnancies, depression, various kinds of itch);
I am the room that understands waiting,
with my box of elderly toys, my dog-eared Women's Owns,
permanent as repeat prescriptions, unanswerable as ageing,
heartening as the people who walk out smiling, weary
as doctors and nurses working on and on and on

U.A. Fanthorpe

Written for the 'Poetry for the Waiting Room' Project

Like Us

The way I heard it,
He'd survived this accident:
Discovered himself,
Quite painless,
In an unfamiliar bed,
Waking to that hospital smell
Of disinfected stress,
The tiny squeal
Of curtains opening.

His eyes were both still perfect,
But the insult to his brain
Had left him blind, irreparably,
Asking the nurses
What time it was and
Could they turn on the lights?
Their reply was distressing,
Shook him, naturally.

And every day it was repeated,
Our man rousing, then confused,
Then caught by the explanation
That his memory couldn't retain,
The injury having left
All recollection porous.
Hearing the story,
Of course, I thought of us:
The same bad news each morning
With less and less sympathy.

Vertigo

These things I can recall:
The close shift of your heart,
Sleek in your chest,
Its wink and shrug there
Lipping out our time.
The feeling of your voice,
Your thought, beneath your kiss,
Your kind of kiss.
And the clamp of need

That locks me, that still wants
To rack you, flag you, flat:
Straight razor you back
To a stipple of blood,
To a lifted, tightened heat
And that certain taste of vertigo
When my mouth rings in your skin.

A Brief Explanation of Myself

Somewhere like this, I was conceived:
A wide, lithe ocean wolfing in
To lay itself in fleeces on slurred rocks,
The hinge and slice of gulls,
Unnerving over all,
And my parents, gritted together
For that one rare conjunction
At the setting of Pacific light,
While the random detonations
Of trapped surf worried and shuddered
The roots of the hollowed ground.
The place was known for its collapses
Of headlands, bridges, overhangs,
But they must have been careful,
My mother and my father,
Going home as they did,
Almost unscathed.

A.L. Kennedy

A New Man

Tonight, as I sit alone
in the top attic,
perched in a cage of moonlight
above the street,

I remember the child I dreamed
in my father's house,
taking my place
for moments at a time,

a perfect, shimmering boy
who could walk away,
his fingers white as salt, his body
sifted through a net of wind and sand.

In school, the child I was outside the dream
learned, with elaborate patience and broken will
how not to be: a presence so contained
it barely recognised itself – at night, alone;

in rainstorms; on a road between two towns;
gliding through water; listening for birds;
or caught up in the turned gaze of a fox
some August afternoon, crossing a meadow –

and though I guessed at it, I never saw
how far I was from knowledge of myself
till now, as I begin to shed the man
I ought to be, and grow to what I am:

impatient, stubborn, foreign to a world
I never chose, but slowly,
by degrees,
learning that boy again, beneath the moon,

his task: to forget himself
as he comes to rest,
vivid and true
in the flesh of a difficult stranger.

John Burnside

Life Expectancy Meter

He keeps fingering that beep-beep-beeping
Life Expectancy Meter. Sneaks it to weddings,
Bedrooms, up the Scott Monument.
Size of a mobile phone, or a pocket
Gravestone for a will o' the wisp,
Sometimes it winks 43 YEARS,
9 MONTHS, 4 DAYS. One hike through Chicago
His L. E. plunged to two hours.
'Only my personal L.E.M.',
He sweet-talks at airport check-ins.
Tots flirt round him like he'd just cloned Santa:
'Well, now then, let's see, wee man,
Today you've got ninety-four years.'
Last week he blabbed he already had my
Maximal number of Birthday Surprises
Filed in his locked office drawer.
He harvests stats – gout, cancer, diarrhoea.
To live longest, he says, we should always eat fish on a train
To-ing and fro-ing between Toronto and somewhere called Guelph.
There he goes again, phoning himself,
Seeing if he's gone up or down.
I remember the week before he bought it,
How, like an acrobatic angel,
He leapt from one roof to the next.

Robert Crawford

Goleuddydd

(Bright Day)

At the other end of the ward, the nurse sticks a label on a plastic bottle;
she rubs her side with the flat of her hand, sits down in light from the lamp.
I sit up sinking in my own sweat, throw off the damp sheet and covers.
I conjure voices, make form and colour from black, figureless shapes.
My stomach is swollen, as if I am pregnant again – that day in spring
when I gave birth: my baby broke out, burst into the mud.

I don't know why I hated the house, a thought misplaced,
hidden in a jewelled box, or between the leaves of a book
on the shelf. Sitting in the still, incence heavy rooms,
I would wait for the old man to return starched from work.
On my side, on the bed, I'd watch him throw off his clothes,
before dropping a few sticks on the fire; he'd lean naked
over the glow lit at the base of the bed, his belly hanging,
and I wanted to be anywhere else, but not there, sleeping
in his stinking bed, stuck with his business and grim faces
of the miners. "You're a man who deals in ashes", I'd say,
but he'd only smile, as if he saw me rushing out to throw up
each morning, and the stomach I hid under soft material.

He said I was mad when I tore out to street, burst
out of the front door desperate to escape the place,
with the stink of dust and sweat. I ran away
up the lane in my night dress. It was evening;
light dappled patterns through leaves on to mud.
Near the farm was a flat rock – a bed or an altar,
and I sat there cupping my belly, still and fresh
in the cool breeze, but when I leant on my side
there was pain and wet between my legs, and I lay
contorted on the black earth, my body heaving,
hands clutching at sticks. Then a girl was at my head,
brushing leaves from my hair and my face was warm
and lit by the sun light, so I waited with the girl
for the child to come in a rush of earth and blood.

Zoe Brigley

Inside Out

'Are you her mother?'

I acknowledged my motherhood.

They would have to operate a second time, said the elegantly suited surgeon; he regretted that there was no option. White coats surrounded me, swaying where I stood, in the midnight ward.

'But,' I objected irrationally, 'she's only fourteen.'

There was no way they could avoid it, he patiently explained. The gangrenous appendix had caused adhesions in the loops of inflamed bowel. She would die if he failed to operate.

'Lovely girl too,' he observed. 'Pity...'

Would I sign?

My hands strove to comply. It traced the letters of half my name with great labour; then the pen gave out. Another was supplied. Two separate mothers seemed to have consented.

'I perform this operation, oh, twelve times a year,' he said. 'It generally works fine, don't worry.'

How many didn't work and had to be repeated?

One in twelve.

Oh my ewe lamb, don't be that one.

Lindsay in the side-ward lay greenly gowned with her hair drawn up in a complex plait from crown to nape. I waded to her against the drag of a fierce ebb-tide, walking against time to where she would soon not be. In the crook of one slender bare arm, rosy with eczema, lay her toy cat disinterred from the childhood she had sought to put behind her.

'The nurse did the plait for me. I've got to have my bowels done.'

'I know.'

'Don't cry.'

'I'm not.'

The child in me was weeping scalding storms of tears; but my daughter and I remained dry-eyed. She neither clung not offered a token of fear. Her bravery stabbed me with pangs of an obscure remorse.

They lifted her tall, light body on to the trolley and she laughed all the way to the theatre; for the hospital in its mercy had provided a clown.

'Way-hay, it's cosy in here,' said the grey-haired clown. 'Think I'll take a week off portering.'

'It's only for sixteen-year-olds and under, so tough,' retorted the Scots nurse, Margaret.

'Well I am sixteen. I've just had a hard life.'

Lindsay lifted her head and giggled; and all the way through the labyrinth he capered and cavorted; and Lindsay laughed; and Margaret stroked her head; and as I chased alongside the fast-wheeling trolley, my anguish took the form of a remorse more profound that I had yet known; and she was travelling into regions of remoteness beyond my bounds.

She would not meet my eyes.

Yet still she laughed; and still I smiled; and still we rolled ahead, with the drip and the masked clown, toward blade and blood.

Shod in sterile plastic footgear, we shuffled into the anaesthesia room, with its shimmer of steel and glass.

'Thanks for doing the plait, Margaret,' were her last words. 'It's wicked.'

'Lovely eyes she has, forget-me-not eyes,' murmured an auxiliary as the needle entered and the blue gaze drowned.

They gestured me to leave. I staggered from the wing-doors into an arctic freeze of fluorescence; then along mazes of twilit corridor. Automatic doors at the main entrance sighed me out. Although I tried for fresh air and resolve, the stars slipped their moorings and the earth reeled. Metres of bowel would be slithering now through the surgeon's hands as he unpacked her tender body that had burst from my body fourteen years before.

'She's a bonny lassie,' Margaret had said.

'Both inside and outside,' I'd replied.

I hurried back to the haven of Margaret. In the dim ward two young heads, one pale, one dark, murmured cool wisdom in a pool of amber light above the children's notes.

'She'll be an hour or two yet,' said Margaret, looking up.

'When she was born...' I said. 'When Lindsay was born...'

'Yes?'

My face worked. I had no idea what I intended to confide: some oblique clutch, at fullest stretch, at the mystery of birth and being and death.

'Tell you what. You lie down a wee while – rest yourself.'

She tucked a blanket around me where I lay in Lindsay's place. I took her place, she who had slipped from my throes with scarcely a cry, blue-eyed, blood-filmed, whole and perfect.

'She'll be fine – you'll see.'

My abdomen crawled as my mind seethed with squeamish images which, the more I thrust back, obtruded the more obscenely.

The wounded children slept on motionless, tubes feeding and draining them, quiet with Pethidine. This week when Lindsay began vomiting, I had been less than sympathetic, bemoaning the prospect of pilgrimages with buckets and disinfectant. Last week we had quarrelled over some petty trespass; she had flounced and fumed. I winced at the compound nemesis of my less-than-tender responses, which, if she died, would become my parting gift to Lindsay.

A toddler startled and bleated in his sleep.

Hours like decades passed but when reveille came, it was too soon, too sudden.

'She's in the recovery room. You can come now.'

'The delivery room?'

'Recovery. Delivery's obstetrics.'

I was afraid to follow Margaret into the lurid light, over yellow-tiled floors to where someone beautiful and mortal lay on her side swathed in grey tubing, so many tubes, so coiled and intricate. Couldn't they hear my deafening shriek at the meat they'd made of her?

'Love,' I breathed. 'My love.'

'She's still under. We got a litre and a half to muck out. Speak to her.'

She opened her eyes and vomited blood.

'Oh my darling,' I poured out. 'Darling beautiful.'

'That's right. Talk to her.'

'Is Margaret there?' she asked, blurred through oxygen mask, nasal tube, swathes of pain.

'I'm here, pal. You're doing great.'

The anaesthetist came from eating pizza on the hoof; injected anti-emetic, shouted to Lindsay to press the morphine button when the pain came.

'Nobody can do it but you. You control yourself. You don't have to feel *any pain.*'

The clown, unmasked, accompanied us back to the ward, his repertoire of jokes and antics laid gently aside. Now his voice sang lullaby as we coasted back, slow, slow; Lindsay keening at the mildest jolt; Margaret cradling the morphine machine like a precious baby. Tender hands lifted Lindsay from the paper-covered stretcher.

She hangs there still in space, in their hands; those hands that treated her as their own daughter. Suspended in mid-air, she belongs to strangers and is no longer and never again to be my own. I surrendered her with gratitude and grief.

'Your mum's going now, to sleep.'

'*You* won't go, Margaret, will you?'

Speedwell eyes swivelled from me to the nurse; her hands reached for our hands.

'I could stay,' I faltered.

'Get some kip, go on. You'll need it.'

Dawn was breaking; shifts changing. I lurched past the people thronging that other world we have quitted, where skins are seamlessly whole; where you read the newspaper, go to work. With these people I had nothing to do.

•

Shyly I approached, like a lover who fears rejection; breathlessly, like one who comes to judgment without means to atone. Faint spring petals of blood bloomed on her arm; plastic tubes festooned her.

'How are you?' I whispered.

'I'm fine,' said Lindsay.' 'How are you?' Her eyes were morphine-glazed.

'I'm fine too.'

'Good.'

We laced fingers; she slipped in and out of a doze.

'Are you still there?' she asked, eyes still closed.

'I'll always be there.'

'Were you there last night?'

'Course I was. Can't you remember?'

'I think so. I did the nurses' heads in by mithering them all night. I've got six tubes, I hate them. I hate this nose-one, it's disgusting. But my plait's still up.

One by one the tubes were shed, then stitched. She slid from her high narrow bed like a white-nightgowned wraith; giving herself birth; delivering herself from evil. I followed slightly behind, cheering her silently on her way, turning inside-out-outside-in.

And still I follow; and still she leads. The gap between us widens a little more with every day; and now she is beginning to run.

Stevie Davies

Scan

2: OB/GYN 3RD TRI

count on
  money-spider fingers

     pearls that will be eyes

locate spine of lights
    defined by vibration

       egg-hills that flex

our new settlement
  lightning sketched

     plot a course now

  •

one in a million
  charcoal on paper

    a Henry Moore

bedded down
  in the underground

   curled for warmth

in on yourself
  until the all-clear sounds

    and you come up for air

     Peter Carpenter

from *The Mercy Ship*

She'd looked at the rose for a very long time. Its deep red was a blotch on the retina; its wet folds had begun to throb. She resumed her walk around the hospital garden.

Melancholy and Edwardian, it had been preserved just on this side of ruin. She skirted wet branches; a bench, missing one slat, and green with algae. Ivy plumed darkly over the granite sundial. Only the fruit on the crab-apple tree and the rose asserted themselves as vivid things. She walked quickly around the oblong of the brick path, a second time, to keep warm. The sky shifted from grey-white to grey; vast clouds lumbered in from the estuary. She'd been away for half an hour, and she pushed at the heavy, scarred door to go in.

Up a shabby flight of steps and through another door and the canteen enclosed her in a warm fug of steam and clatter. Nurses, mostly students, were pulling on cardigans, shrugging into coats. A third year in white shirt and epaulettes, stopped her and said confidentially, 'We heard about you and Dora. Nice try.'

A round face, bespectacled, dead-pan.

In the servery crisp leavings of cauliflower cheese were scraped onto her plate. She carried it to the table near the far window, glanced out at a slant on the jumble of briars, and the rose's tiny red flame. She'd had her half hour. She could think about that morning.

It had been well into the shift. Women in dressing gowns had begun to clamber back onto the made beds, or were bending to stow their toiletries, in plump floral bags, inside a locker. She'd pulled the curtain across between Dora and the next bed. Dora was still, her face turned away. The brown hair straggled at her neck. She went round to the other side of the bed. 'I'm doing your dressing now, all right, Dora?' She placed her foot on the black pump-lever. 'I'm just raising the bed.'

It hadn't been easy, under the circumstances, to *maintain the sterile field,* as they were taught. Using the sterile plastic tweezers and cotton swabs to clean *in one swipe only* a furious sore with a yellow edge. This without being able to shift the bony hip; nor could you ask Dora to move it, of course.

She heard another note in the bustle of the morning ward. A male voice: the consultant. She could hear several feet shuffling close. A retinue of medical students must have been peering at her, but she didn't look up. It couldn't have been a tidy scene for them: the white debris out of the dressing pack, the bedclothes rucked up, the tallow-like flesh, crossed with gauze squares and porous tape. Bright sores on sacrum and hips; ankles if they could have seen it. The dressings would take an hour at least: the students seldom volunteered. Today, she had.

'Nothing can be done in such cases except what you see here, meticulous nursing care.' The white coats hovered. They moved on.

She had just finished the trickiest bit, right under the hip-bone, and was taping the gauze flat when she heard Ka say, 'Your patient's turning blue.'

'Help me with her, will you.' Dora's head had sunk deep into the pillow. She pressed the pillow down with one fist *clearing the airway* and then they shifted her free, and to her other side. A creased reddish patch flared on her cheekbone. 'There you go, darling. I'm sorry.' Ka had looked at her, Merideth, and disappeared into the sluice room. She'd checked Dora's pulse, a far-off drum that had not altered. The sallowness of the fixed profile had returned. Her own mind seemed to be rinsed of any particular thought.

That was all that had happened in the morning, until the third-year's comment had disturbed her again. *Nice try.* The thoughts moved threateningly, waiting for her to admit them.

And now she was on the ward, just in, and Ka eyed her round-eyed from afar and Peg, carrying a bedpan, said, 'Miss McCallan's asking for you.'.

Miss McCallan's office, tucked away on the second floor. The furnishings were old, of dark shining wood. Blue-bound NHS regulations bulged in a glass cabinet. The nursing officer, McCallan. Her red hair, tucked behind the ears, hung brief and straight.

'Oh Nurse Daley. Have a seat. How are you getting on, then? It's your first ward, is it not?' The grey eyes probed. 'Your second, och, that's right, you've done surgical. It's just that I'd wondered...' She'd wondered about the circular garden walks. And most likely, today's lengthy sojourn at the rose-bush.

In her relief, gratefully, she tried to send beams of reassurance towards Miss McCallan.

'... and it clears my head. The ward does get stuffy.'

Miss McCallan sat back in the heavy chair. She didn't think she smelled a breakdown here. The student before her was neither timid, nor truculent. Her broad forehead relaxed. 'I like fresh air myself. But if there are any particular difficulties you must let me know.'

She assented, glowing, and rose to leave. The thoughts crept on like stagehands, clad in black. *It was in the first ward I needed this; needed you. This morning, upsetting as it feels, wasn't much. Comparatively, not so much at all.*

At ten past four, suddenly hungry, she strode along the High Road of blistering billboards and untidy shops. She risked the nearest café, a fluorescent-lit aisle of booths. A group of dust-spattered workman glanced up, wearily as she came in; a lone man in a navy-blue sports jacket perused a menu.

As she drank her tea, bought at the counter, she recognised the man in the sports jacket. He was a Jordanian doctor who drove a maroon MG: this couldn't have been his kind of place. The girl serving him, obviously of the same opinion, had dredged up a menu from somewhere and stood by solicitously. The workmen filed by as if in protest, boots clomping to the street.

'What kind of beans?' His voice was light, sinuous.

'Beans...from a tin.'

He scanned down the list. 'Tuna fish...no, I don't like this.....'

'You could have cheese', the girl suggested. She appeared to be very young, with pale, unemphatic features.

'What kind of cheese?'

A swarthy man in a grubby pinafore arrived at her table with a fried egg roll on a saucer. He set it down ceremoniously, rolling his eyes.

'English cheese.'

'I will have coffee, black, two sugar....'

Clearly the girl's attention was necessary to him. He required, in a word, a fuss. All her adult life she'd stowed neediness away, and here was a surgical registrar, parading, even exaggerating, his.

Perhaps, she thought idly, he missed his mother, or a string of adoring sisters. She imagined soft female cries, like veils, falling about him in some palisade of light. His name was Hassan. She knew he wasn't married because Ka had told her; told her, in particular, about the sports car. 'He's all right,' Ka had said energetically, chewing gum. But in reality the doctors never spoke to any of them. A doctor landed on the ward as brisk as a god, and dashed off a prescription, affirming that his presence was a gift (which, indisputably, it was: a doctor having presided immemorially over all the vital exits; a doctor being essential for discharge, morphine, and death): it amused her to catch sight of one sitting in a High Road café, quibbling about the ingredients of brown sauce.

She took up her coat and smiling into thin air moved swiftly past him. She murmured, 'Enjoy your meal'.

She smiled all the way home on the top of the crowded bus.

….The pale green wall, fingerprinted haphazardly around the payphone had cracked with fine lines, like the map of a river. The dusty red lino gritted under her shoes; no one ever seemed to clean. She was glad she'd eaten on the way back from the hospital, she couldn't be bothered now with that. She curled up next to the radiator in her room, fully intent on reading another chapter of *Claudius the King*, and fell asleep.

By eight-thirty the next morning she and Ka were busy making beds. There weren't as many observations of blood pressure and pulse to do, on this ward: it was Medical, not Surgical. She liked the bed-making. It was a kind of ballet, as they bent, stretched and folded. The linen flapped and swelled, all airy lightness. Yesterday with its stains and creases went into a jumbled ball; into the billy.

Anne Rouse

Synapses

Whenever I think of a hospital I always think of it as a woman. Those sweetheart impulses governing the place are why I work here and why I never want to work anywhere else. Institutions shackle the imagination and make a stone of the heart, but this one is inspirational. It has made my luck. It's also been by longest relationship, the one anatomy I've remained faithful to, along with the women who manage my schedule: like Mavis, the control clerk who just now informs me that patient Jackson in Cardio is awaiting a ride to Surgery One.

As I wheel a large chair out of the mess Mavis hands me a love note to deliver to the male nurse she's sweet on in Cardio. Then she starts coughing, hacking away like a plumber splitting floorboards. Sooner or later Mavis's sixty-a-day habit is going to put her on the other side of the Front Line, I keep telling her.

From the neutrality of the porters' mess I enter the stream of traumatics. Motes of dust float like spindrift in the shafts of early evening light.

In Cardio I ask the duty sister for Jackson. Without looking up from her desk she points to the far end of the ward of occupied beds, and I am as astonished by the sight of this homogenous community of the sick as on the first day I started working here, seven years ago. How it must shake you down, to be one moment pickling apricots, studying the racing form, reading an aerogramme from a prodigal child, then in the next waking up in here without use of limbs, an IV in your arm, feeding tubes up your nose, surrounded by strangers in starched white gowns. The confusion still registers on their faces.

We know them only when they are sick, but it never escapes me that these men and women, until they lost their way, have led full lives. Many of the stroke victims have lost their voices and cannot tell us these stories. So it is a matter of courtesy that they be treated with respect, as they stand naked in backless gowns, lifted on to a commode, with a raw hurt burning in their eyes. Any good medic knows to take this holistic approach – like the male nurse who helps me lift Jackson from her bed on to the chair.

I slip him Mavis's love note and can't help feeling sorry for her. Unrequited love is an illness too, with no known cure. The erotic cathexis of a hospital extends only so far. It's a doctor and nurse affair that does not engulf the auxiliary staff. On account of their quotidian contact with naked flesh, medics' desire builds throughout the day like electrons picked up by a generator. On the out, in mufti, they fall for each other. But they never fall for me, or Mavis or anyone else in the porters' mess. We are low caste, the untouchables.

The only women to fall for me have been the patients. Such as the tall Texan with psoriasis; the north London Jewish girl with diabetes; the African-American lesbian with gynaecological complications; the Irish fiddle player with cancer (God rest her soul). All these women I have had time with, but couldn't settle with any of them. They complained of me being distant, cold even. Perhaps the truth is I don't like to give out. I don't enjoy losing control, allowing someone else to push me around like the steel balls in a pinball machine. I have only ever truly belonged to one woman – my sister Geena. But that's another story I shall come to.

Patient Jackson is black, in her sixties, eighteen stones on the scales and terrified. She wears a gossamer veil over her thinning hair. On her feet are slippers with little pink tassels. As I wheel her through the ward the other patients watch our progress. They can't speak and they can't raise their arms to offer her a send-off to Surgery, but I sense the goodwill in their stony silence. And gratitude in their eyes that it isn't them going under the knife.

On the way to Surgery I ask my patient what op she's having, but she doesn't reply. So I ramble on about how nice the surgeon on duty today is, which is an out-and-out lie. The surgeon's perfectly competent, but he's a racist and I know she wouldn't want to hear that. But whatever I say is lost on her. She can't speak a word of English.

In Surgery I leave the patient in a bay and go looking for a nurse. On the slab in theatre is a young woman under anaesthetic. She is having a tonsillectomy, so the surgeon really has no business peeling the sheet down to her ankles. What he is staring at with such lewd fascination is her tattoo. Her pubic bush constitutes the body of a black widow spider, it's legs tattooed down her thighs. 'Can you imagine going down on *that*?' the surgeon says to me. 'One of these days some guy's going to take a two-by-four to that thing.' When I fail to reply the surgeon looks up at me, sees that I am only a porter and his eyes glaze over.

I've never wanted to be a doctor. they may perform miracles but their personalities are a disease. Men of medical science whose ambition is aimed squarely at gaining power in the institution are lost to the good world. They seek promotion, then spend their lives in politics.

I've never wanted to be a nurse either, not even a paramedic. I am happy with my place in the scheme of things. I know my Re-sus ABC, how to treat wounds, recognise dinner-fork fractures, cerebral vacuolar attacks, coronary thrombosis. These things I have picked up along the way. But I don't perform miracles. I help those who do, content with the routine that hardly changes from day to day, week to week, year to year.

Normally eight porters on each shift, we are two down today, throwing what we call a duvet-day on the busiest end of the hospital week. Which is why I am now running from Surgery into Neo-Natal, Chest, Heart, Liver and Kidney with a sackful of blood and urine samples for the Path-Lab. I am running but nurses hardly notice me. They do not care to know who I am, what I know.

The only nurses who engage with me for longer than a couple of seconds and about something other that urine samples are the West Indian mothers-of five. They tease me in the canteen during my dinner break for having a book open on the table beside my plate. The closest they come to making a direct statement is to call me a dreamer, and then throw their heads back in pearls of laughter. But in such a place as this, to be a dreamer is the only way to fly.

If nurses hardly notice me the doctors don't even see me. So it comes as something of a surprise when a junior doctor sitting at my table, who has been watching me for some time with my head in my book, leans across the Formica and asks why I don't try to do something more with my life. (He is a New Zealander...does that explain anything?)

What is more? I ask.

He points to my book. More would be taking a degree course in the care management.

I say, When you refuse all power no one will ever be afraid of you.

The junior doctor laughs and asks why I read if not to advance myself.

I tell him, What I read and what I do for a living move in opposite directions.

The junior doctor admits that he has no time for reading, on call one hundred hours per week. I tell him how my lowly, dead-end job gives me not just the time but the space to absorb what I read. The job is not who I am.

Then who are you? he wants to know.

All I know for sure is that I am a reader and that literature is as real as any hospital.

He seems to think about for a second, then replies, Work is a defence against despair.

I say, What is your defence against work?

The junior doctor gives up on me and leaves the canteen and I am able to return to my book, *All Quiet on the Western Front*, that does not flinch from describing the wounded and the dead. The characters are teenage recruits who, unlike the patients in Cardio, have not had a chance to settle into an adult life before finding themselves face-down in the earth as the darkness rocks and rages around them, as whole woods are lifted into the air and smashed to pieces. They feel a thousand years old applying emergency first aid to their school friends dying in meadows tossed like storm seas, as bayonets of even younger recruits pierce the mist of poison gas that wriggles into the trenches like jellyfish. Coffins are ripped out of a cemetery and the sky rains corpses – the dead who provide cover for the living, trying to survive someone else's bad idea.

The control clerk calls me on the shortwave and tells me to go to Thorogood Ward and take a Purple-Plus to the Mortuary. This is not as contradictory as it seems (what I read and what I do move in opposite directions, etc.). As many people come here to die as to be cured. Nonetheless, Mavis feels the need to warn me in advance that The Purple-Plus is a girl of nine, a victim of meningitis.

I can ear the wailing from outside the ward. As I enter Thorogood I see the commotion created by the mother who lays across the bed and won't allow anyone to take her child away. But there are patients waiting for this bed and two nurses are gently trying to prize the mother's hands from the body. It is very upsetting for everyone.

I suggest that I take the mother as well to the Mortuary. So she sits in my wheelchair, this poor stressed woman, and the nurses lay the corpse, wrapped in a starched white sheet, in her lap.

Outside the ward the movement of the chair seems to comfort her. There is a sense of optimism that comes from motion, as though time is somehow being reversed. She is even able to talk with me, explaining how her daughter was at a birthday party when she was taken ill. Then her grief is fully reprieved as we enter the elevator. Two other persons, laughing as we step into the lift, are immediately silenced by the tangle of bodies on my wheel chair, by the sight of five fingernails painted orange protruding from the sheet and a flash of red hair flecked with silver glitter that the mother holds in her hand.

Mavis finds me on the shortwave again while I'm still in the Mortuary. She saves me from my morbid feelings with a detail designed to give me a lift. She tells me to go and deliver a couple of oxygen cylinders to Maternity.

Maternity is the only wing of the hospital where no one is actually ill. In pain maybe, but very different to the pain in, say, Cancer or A&E. Maternity is upbeat, a goldrush town where every panhandler walks away with something precious. Five, maybe ten times a shift I go into Maternity and witness at least one child being born into the world. And sure enough, as I arrive, a girl (eight pounds, six ounces) is delivered to a bricklayer's wife, as he stands weeping with joy over her bed, raising the flag in the memory cells of the infant's brain. Synapses bring out the very best in human nature. Love is a biological imperative and such intense moments of it that I see may never be achieved again. But that's the thing about Maternity, you get to see truth and beauty at its peak. So whenever my control clerk sends me to Delivery Suite, it's free air miles to me.

Russell Celyn Jones

The Runner

Six thirty in the evening and the night comes down, heavy as an eyelid. I have eaten early and drunk a third of a bottle of 'Good Choice' gin. The dusk is thick and closing in. I run from the heat of the day to the paralysing heat of the night. Two men approach the house, one carrying a child awkwardly in his arms, the other with a machete. Walking briskly they attract the attention of the dog, who runs toward them. I know what's coming.

Children have stopped playing, birds have stopped singing and taxis have switched off their engines for the night. The sun is barely visible above the bush. They know I have fuel because they can hear a small generator pumping light into the house.

Knocking loudly at the window, I wonder if they think that I'm a Doctor or a Priest or a Rich Man and I am none of these things. Reflected in large French doors I am slouched in my chair, superimposed on silhouettes of standing men. As I open the doors I recognise one of the men as the Printer from the village. In his arms he carries his sick child. The man with the machete is introduced as the boy's Uncle. There is no other vehicle, they tell me, that can take them to the hospital tonight and he will not last until the morning, in fact, they feel there is little time.

Now I see the boy as the Runner and I am reminded of the time that we met. He brought me the draft of my letterhead and while I read it, putting a line through the 'Dr' in front of my name, he drank two bottles of Fanta. I sent him away with a bag of mangoes from the tree and some small change from my pocket.

Three of us walk to the truck and the boy is carried. As we pull away he groans. The last grey specks of daylight turn black. In the headlights the dog runs ahead of the car unaware of the danger, like a child. The men tell me to speed up and slow down.

At the base of a small crater in the wing of the truck a neat hole, made by a bullet, rusty at its edges, is surrounded by the fruity, muddy fingerprints of children. Faster. A checkpoint on this road is sometimes manned by armed robbers. They come out dressed as Police to feed on the rich pulse of the night. 'What's wrong with the boy?' I can't see where I am on the road. My perspective is foreshortened by beams of unnatural, unsteady light. 'What happened to the boy?' Potholes jar through the tyres bringing regular groans from the child. Slow down.

As we pull away from the village the last in a long line of food traders shouts from her stall 'come and buy', her face animated and orange from the fire-light. Traders never sleep when there is a night to feed. In one hand she holds a spoon and in the other arm a baby bound tightly in her bright wrapper. We leave the smell of burning groundnut oil to follow the scent of the road, lined with dark bush and cassava leaves. In the sky the imaginary lines between stars make figures, apparently still, racing freely from the earth. The windows of the truck are opened to cool the boy who burns in his father's arms. Faster. 'Is it malaria or has he been hit by a car?' I ask, 'Is it a snake bite?'

We approach another small village. A line of men sit under a tin-roof shelter and stare at the truck as we race past. Fires shine between huts and the light-grey smoke takes the edge off the darkness. A Policeman waves us down but the Uncle leans his head out of the window and shouts to him 'no stop, we for hospital', and then to me 'faster, faster'. The Policeman laughs and walks out of the way. In front of us are unavoidable ridges where rains have washed away chunks of tarmac the size of mattresses. The lights from the truck bounce off these shapes and cast confusing shadows under our noses. As we hit the shadows the boy exhales a long deep note. He begins to cry many times but stops himself after each staccato sob. Slow down.

'It was a wall', says the Printer, 'he was just playing on the wall and it fell.'

'Which wall is this?' I ask, 'where is the wall?'

We pull into the Queen Elizabeth. The Printer continues, 'It's just part of an old wall. It is on the edge of the farm. It serves no purpose. I used to play on it when I was a boy myself. I would stand right up on the top and think it was the wall of my compound like I was some big man. He was just playing. The other children said that he was climbing up when it crumbled and fell onto him before he had time to run away. We had to pull him out'.

The Printer and the Uncle and I walk as fast as the boy can be carried to reception. The nurse is yawning and seems annoyed, perhaps with the prospect of the night-shift. A short way down a corridor in a small room she undresses the boy with two swift movements, one for his tee-shirt, the other for his shorts. He wore nothing else. The Printer says that his son's sandals will be under the rubble. His son lies face down on a white mattress. He is like a shadow. It's difficult to make out the twisted spine and the acute angle of his neck to his head and shoulders. His arms and legs come to rest in a position that make him look as though he his running. His head is cocked in concentration, his body arches to power his step and his foot points as though it has just left the ground. Eyes are closed with effort. To the men who stand and watch he will soon be a small dot in the distance. The bed will be taken by someone else. The nurse, who had momentarily disappeared, comes back into the room holding a hypodermic syringe. The Printer and the Uncle can barely stand with the tiredness of the journey and their battle with night-time. The Uncle has left the machete in the car. The nurse sticks the needle into the flesh of one of the boy's buttocks. He doesn't flinch, or move, or groan. The nurse walks out leaving the door of the small room open.

I long to leave this room just so that I can smell the moving air of a journey. I take one last look at the boy as I leave, turning my head, hearing voices. Slowly at first and then faster and faster I begin to read the message.

Tim Reeves

Propaganda

This is the place where they ask
'Can the doctors write to you
using this name and address?'
before they tick the standard form
and stack it, face down, behind the desk;
where you sit very still on a smooth chair
and re-read horoscopes
in back issues of *Company*;
where someone looks you in the eye
and says, 'You do know what I mean,
when I say markers in the blood?'
Where you promise to be good
next time, forever, play it safe,
for a string of negatives, a new life.

Electricity

To Ward 4C at the John Radcliffe

The night staff are peeling off their gowns
and hanging them on the ends of cots:
sleeves of blue and green spotted cows
hang in folds of smiling daisies.

The parents fold their beds in half,
and wheel them into place behind balloons,
streamers, get-well cards, and toys
still carrying safety labels and price tags.

We nod to each other, duck our heads
into sheets and blankets, pull them apart
in a shower of sparks. No one speaks
of electricity, their hair standing on end.

Siân Hughes

Short Poem for My Lover

You act as if there's no such a thing as hospitals,
no such thing as wanting to be held.
You act as if it's even too much bother
to hold my hand.
You should have been a goat.

Portrait of my mother as a pair of shoes
Written for the 'Poetry for the Waiting Room' Project

The more I stare at the nurse's polished shoes,
the more I get the rather pleasant feeling
these shoes aren't simply just a pair of shoes,
they are in fact – how odd – my own mother,
still very much alive, and having fun
breezing in and out of the waiting-room

Selima Hill

I Swear by the Music

I swear by the music of the expanding universe
and by the eloquence of the good in all of us
that I will excite the sick and the well
by the severity of my kindness
to a wholeness of purpose. I shall apply my knowledge,
curiosity, ignorance and ability to listen.

I shall co-operate with wondering practitioners
in the arts and the sciences,
with all who care for people's bodies and souls,
so that the whole person in relationship
shall be kept in view, their aspirations and their unease.

The secrets of the universal mind
I shall try to unravel to yield beauty and truth.
The fearful and sublime secrets told to me in confidence
I shall keep safe in my own heart.

I will not knowingly do harm to those in my care,
I will smile at them
and encourage them to attend to their dreams
and so hear the voices of their inner strangers.

If I keep to this oath I shall hope for the respect of my teachers,
and of the people in my care and of the community,
and to be healed even as I am able to heal.

(*I swear by the music* was commissioned as a version of the Hippocratic Oath.)

My Complaint
for Fiona, Fateha and Lorne in Customer Relations, Heartlands Hospital

Dear Customer Relations,
I wish to complain that your so-called complaints department
was so quiet this morning
and such a pleasant experience
I am having to go away calmer than when I arrived.

It's all very well knowing that in the past week
there have been somewhere on site complaints about
toilets

drunks,
the décor,
waiting times
waiting times
waiting times
car park charges
the cost of a small meal
appointment instructions
"the vending machine stole my money"
security lights
incontinence pads
the height of chairs,
and a few compliments,
"nurses are very kind"
"excellent treatment"
"extremely impressed",
and I dare say some clinical hiccups are being investigated
within 20 working days as set out in the complaints procedure
and I can see that your department
is a buffer between patients and Government,

but no-one stormed in and demanded attention,
no-one even phoned irate or over the moon.
What kind of a place is this, happy, relaxed, enjoying the work,
where's the drama in that,
what kind of a poem can you reasonably expect?

David Hart

A Final Appointment

Trivialities remembered: paper clips,
three, linked in a chain. Coffee cup, green,

half-drunk, smooth red stain
on rim from lower lip, perhaps.

Floral pattern on the screen;
six roses each stem, six petals each flower…

Spider on glass pane, caught in a sunburst.
Will it be here next year?

A white coat reflected the sun. White smile,
urbane, deflected questions. 'Are you here still?'

The answer half-heard, immutable:
'Two months, or three. No more.'

Michael Smith

An Elegy from the Invisible Man

how grey the sky, sighs Tom
his legs hurt, his head hurts
and so does his broken heart
this hospital's making me ill he moaned,
to Jack whose ears are closed
Jack closed his ears a long time ago
when they told him it would not leave
no, the cancer's here to stay my friend
but you're allowed to keep the past
cherish all the yarns of dream
that you and Mary have spun.
I'll stay with you till the end Jack
as Mary can't handle the pain
now close your eyes and sleep Jack
and let me end the day
tears still come
as the day was the first
when he pushed little Elsie through
but it's a job you see
that he must complete
till the sky turns to blue
forty one years as a mortuary porter
so why does it still hurt
his legs hurt his head hurts
and so does his broken heart.

Mall Surjit

Summit

Summoned, I travelled north to find you,
But you were away over the white wastes
The regular stride of your breathing

Beyond all possible distractions,
The eyes above the mask snow-blinded,
Fixed on the unimaginable distant peak.

At base camp they served tea and biscuits
All night. You laboured on right through
That night, the next day, and through most

Of the next night's biscuit ration,
Until, sometime in the mid-nothing
Of the endless hour that summed up all the rest,

You reached the summit with a final
Floundering gasp, and stuck
Your flag through both our waiting hearts.

Simon Rae

Bell Ringing

to Jill who at the time of writing
was spending much time in Intensive Care,
sitting beside the bed of her daughter.

The English church bell
is unique for the fact
its place of rest
is mouth up
poised on the point
of its crown.

To negotiate it
to that point of stasis
weight upwards despite gravity
the bell-ringer applies a force
to the dangling rope
just so
exact and delicate
not too much
not too little.

Get it wrong
and the great bell rolls over
and becomes something new
a mass of stampeding pig metal
as the rope streaks upwards
out of hand
and hell takes over
flooding the quiet horizons.

The attainment of perfect rest
is when chaos is held on a point ;
and poised just so
the moment cups you.

Here in the waiting room I am cupped.
I am held aloft.
My poise is perfect here.
I am almost flying.

Rogan Wolf

For Rolph

Coming from different worlds
to this, your last house,
we're distant but familiar;
two old bricks waiting for mortar.
I am effaced. So it takes this
to erode our public stance
and this to evoke effusion;
pretence at no notice of body's collapse,
my vulgar intrusion.

No more sham. Quietly
I shuffled from the winter street,
frost clinging to my coat.
You soon stopped my bustle
with your poised civility.
And from your shrunken isolation
you whispered, below the silent transfusion,
your gentlest welcome.

You slept, then awoke
and took up our conversation
started two weeks before,
and willed me to muster
a response to the strife
of some department affair;
mind keen to latch on to life.
While I sought in vain
a worthy answer
until you lapsed again.

I am distracted by a persistent problem,
remaining for me an emblem:
the committee man who accepts the rules
and then insists on them,
with a steel rigour never seen before.
Open and selfless; such a stickler for process
confounding the chairmen with their hidden agendas.

So soon you lapsed and sought,
eyes closed yet focused,
some other worldly thought –
shared with whom, with what?
you fought for words about books
and the importance of them.
Though they didn't quite fit
you still had your hooks
in a shared ambition.

Like my greetings,
lights were too much,
as you shivered under blankets,
the nurse disarming my horror.
She had seen all this before.
Each time, differently, she gave
her fresh unconditional love.

Unrecognizable, so thin
with your dank hair
now almost gone, your sallow skin
dark in the dim of a single room;
flowing to where all streams flow,
where your unorthodox left-hand
can now relax with nothing to divide you.

William Parry

Bruised Fruit

Apples can bruise so easily. Drop them
into a basket and their skins still shine
but later, come December, the flesh rots;
the bruise, unseen at first, eats its way through.
Be gentle with the apples, said my great aunt,
lay them down softly, oil their skins,
wrap them up warmly for the winter's cold.
Why did that memory of apples come to me
today, when I heard your news?
The cancer eats your bones so silently,
invisible as the apple's secret bruise.

Susan Bassnett

Diagnosis

1. ECG

Bare to the waist I lie, and curtained off,
waiting for Debra to attend me
(I've read her name badge). I eavesdrop. Uneasily
I hear the chat of the computer buff
who's bug-hunting beyond the drape; he laughs:
"Who the hell can they expect? …look at the way
they've logged these lists… no, really, my old granny
could teach them a thing or three." Now a cough
from a fellow patient. It's "just routine"
but I am lonely lying here and wondering
whether it's *my* diagnosis that's lost in cyberspace.
Debra arrives and daubs my chest with grease,
attaches cups and flicks a switch: a juddering
from the printer. "That's all. Tell doctor you've been seen."

•

But doctor knows. The print-out's in his hand.
He has been studying my ECG,
deciphering its spiked calligraphy.
He looks at me in the eye, once he has scanned
it over again, for he can understand
my angular post-modern poetry
straight from the heart; a specialist critic, he.
Those sharp irregular lines he does not find
much merit in. He says he'd have preferred
a smoother flowing rhythm, something more
iambic, like I used to write before.
We're none too pleased. He teaches me a new word,
angiogram. The good news is, I might be in rude
health for years. The bad news isn't quite as good.

2. Angiogram

They lift my gown and pose a strip of paper
across my genitals to affirm my modesty,
anoint my groin with tangy yellow, then cover
me over. They touch my face, talk soothingly.
I am a body, soon to be explored.
A camera and a monitor are aligned
for action. Lights. A doctor gives the word,

prepares his gear, then needles me. I'm primed
for invasion. He sends a tube along an artery
until he finds my thunderous heart. The monitors
are showing a weird delta – murky estuary.
The camera arcs and swoops. I hear the doctor's
brief command, and feel hot blood which surges
through heart and head; and thank the lord for nurses.

3. Bionic

For cardio-thoracic surgery they take a saw
and divide the sternum cleanly in two.

They sever the muscle beneath, and then
wrench the ribcage apart (like a box), when

lungs and heart lie exposed to their scrutiny.
Now begins the more intricate surgery,

The opening of the frozen heart, the incision,
the sewing of the new valve – titanium,

With dozens of stitches, which is why
it takes them so long. Meanwhile you lie

lapped in anaesthetic, while a computer
does the work of heart and lungs. Later

you wake to pain but there are things that are worse,
knowledge for example. Immobility is another curse.

•

I came to: a plumbing system of tubes and alarms,
plugged into neck, heart, lungs, penis, arms.

There's the rich gush of vomited blood: the mask,
the constant attention. They neither apologise nor ask

but like acolytes, white-clad, attend the mending
body. In a limbo of anaesthetic, in an unending

dream, the mind travels; while freed from stenosis, fixed
with a metal valve, the aorta lives from one beat to the next.

Get-well cards – funny ones not appreciated; odd scenes,
visitors, the vast ward window, sky, machines.

'I held your heart in my hands,' the surgeon said
as he stood at the foot of my high-tech bed.

My sternum is bound together with wire. I've seen
it on the X-Ray. I'm new, bionic; my clean

new valve drives the blood with a neat tick-tick.

Gerard Benson

My Watch

Its hidden clockwork whirred
and spun
through hours and minutes down
to the second
you were wheeled into theatre.

I thought of the theatre doors closing.
Of its vaulted ceiling rising above you.
Of your body born of my body.
Of your twenty-first year
invaded by needles and tubes and electrodes.

Of you floating out of yourself.
Of the pleth
like a miniature life buoy circling your fingertip.
I thought of the anaesthetist
enveloped in your feathery breath.

I thought of the fierce theatre lights;
the surgeon and the scrub nurse
exchanging banter and scalpels
above your butternut stomach,
its curve

from your navel, a hand's span
rising
and falling softly
through milliseconds.
The incision.

The white shock of cut flesh.
And your blood
spilling with each second.
cut
by the second hand of my watch.

Miriam Obrey

In Millstreet Hospital

My cousin, they tell me, doesn't wake up much,
nor does she seem to see the green mountain
framed in the window of this chapel of ease
for travellers booked in for their last pilgrimage.
When I leave at the end of the visiting-hours
a small, tidy man is sitting by the door:
stick, well-knotted tie, watch-chain, tweed jacket.
He gets to his feet, raises his hat and enquires:
'Excuse my troubling you, but would you be
going anywhere near a railway-station?'
The young smiling nurse bends over him,
and takes him by the elbow, saying:
'Maybe tomorrow, James. Maybe tomorrow
we'll take you to the station.'

Bernard O'Donoghue

Healing Powers

My foot is blue and bloated.
The swelling won't go down.
My limp is duly noted
As I hobble through the town.
I pass a Reiki master.
Of course – I should have put
The two together faster:
Healing powers, my foot.

I take my sore size seven
And place it in his hands.
It's ten now. By eleven
I'll be sprinting to the sands.
I ponder such remission.
My tears, like magic, dry.
Pure chance or superstition?
Healing powers, my eye.

My walking looks much better.
I jump, I jog, I hike,
Reluctant to upset a
Reiki master whom I like
But the pain is most dismaying
And I must confess I put
New conviction in the saying:
Healing powers, my foot.

Martin's Heron Heart

No doctor cares enough
to analyse the content of my veins
my blood that bears a rough
resemblance to a Stagecoach South West trains
timetable. Start, please start
Wokingham, Bracknell, Martin's Heron, heart.

Send a mechanic, quick,
the best you have. Should your mechanic fail
to get me going, stick
me on a train to Egham, Sunningdale,
Virginia Water, Staines.
It's true, those Waterloo to Reading trains

prove all your theories wrong –
medicine, science. I am on the mend,
doctor, thanks to a long
list of the Sunday running times. Attend
my bedside. Tick your chart:
Wokingham Bracknell Martin's Heron   heart

Sophie Hannah

If

If you can keep your stethoscope when all about you
Are losing theirs and blaming it on you.

If you can trust yourself when all anaesthetists doubt you,
But make allowances for their doubting too.

If you can wait for a Surgical Team and not be tired of waiting,
Or being gossiped about, don't deal in Hospital gossip,
Or being slated, don't give way to slating.

And yet don't look too good, nor talk too wise:

If you can be ready for physiotherapy before the Physio' comes,
If you can drink, and not make coffee breaks your aim.

If you can meet with physicians and surgeons
And treat those two teams just the same.

If you can make one heap of all your bedclothes
And risk it on one turn of pitch and toss,
And miss, and start again with the linen skip nearer.

If you can talk with physicians and keep your patience,
Or walk with Consultant Surgeons – nor lose the common touch.

If neither doctors nor nursing colleagues can hurt you,
If all colleagues count with you, but none too much.

If you can fill the unforgiving minute with sixty seconds worth
Of Nursing process documentation,
Yours is the Hospital and everything that's in it,

And what is more, you'll be
An ITU trained nurse, my friend.

Kim Hudson

Childhood Remedies

And there beside him in the toils of life
Stood several stalwart helpers, one by one;
Brave *Iodine* whose tincture on his knees
Brought reddened pain but healed the gravel rash,
Hydrogen Peroxide, frothy friend,
A further keeper of the toxic gate,
Potassium Permanganate
(*Condy's Crystals*, as personified),
A purple lake, attrition disease,
Soft *Friar's Balsam*, smoothest unguent,
The semi-sacerdotal remedy.
Internal warriors of many kinds
Were household helpers too – sage *Senna*, boiled
Or tableted: *Cascara*, bitter tasting
But good friend to smooth evacuation –
From *California*, a richer *Syrup*
Made *Of Figs*, the *Liver Oil* of *Cod*,
The same effusion of the *Mutton Bird*;
The Influenza-Killers, Headache's foes,
Given godlike names, *Aspro* and *Bex*,
Antiphlogestine poultices, whose hug
Burned neuma in the tufa of the lungs.
These now had gathered close to wish him well,
His childhood champions who proudly took
Their last farewell of one who'd reached the goal
Of Manhood. Household Magic, rough and loving,
Now would wave goodbye as on the path
Ahead lay only properly calibrated
Remedies. Though he perhaps might come
Again as prodigal to this same gate
They servant-like bade speed as he set out,
The perfect tint of beauty on his skin
To meet those blemishes prescribed by time.

Peter Porter

The girl changed into a fawn

for an autistic child

1.

Her mother lies until midday,
her curtains pinned
to shut out the light.
That it is day, she knows
because their edges show a brighter grey.

She lies by noise imprisoned:
teeny dancing from above
the ceiling's an iron press
upon her. She lies
scared of her daughter,
that she may not be good.

2.

Outside her room, the wood
has a beauty you
"might die to see and hear," – its moods,
anxious in winds,
stately in summer or in snow,
or daintily rippled by snakes of rain.

Tread softly if you go
for you might stir
among the fallen, flooded boughs,
a sipping deer.

3.

When her lover comes, she peers
from her bed at him, dazed
with wonder if he'll be able to stand it.
Don't speak to her at all, she says. *Don't even try it.*
And, *What if she turns out to be evil ...wicked?*

Mothers and daughters –
these two caught in what they created,
unable to see what they perpetuated –
you'd never guess how they can fester;
the poison from all plants and creatures
that are locked in shades and holes.

4.

Can a wood have a soul?
This one has anxious ghosts,
swirling presences

there where also this child dances
upon the pivot of her joy,
and of her danger
with which she holds us hostage – we responsible ones.

Dances where in summer imagined faces –
bushy-browed, green
men such as medieval life projected –
teem out of the wood it feared.

5.

Long-legged, fleet and weird,
feral and hunted
on her edge of alarm,
her stony rim of intuition,
sometimes she runs away.

I could
imagine her changed into a fawn,
her life spent with that herd
of sister souls, become the soul of the wood,
to keep on running, like breezes, like water.

Meanwhile, my daughter
and I swim through the viscous hours,
clinging or parting,
violently sometimes

as I collect the logic of a day
that has no logic,
is made of her light-footed
fawn-like impulse in house and wood:
she who skips and darts so beautifully
when she is dancing.

Glyn Hughes

Plum Tree

The plum tree which loomed over our back garden had withstood hurricane, flood and infestation. Every summer, tiny greenfly rained in their thousands from its canopy, as did motes of a sticky substance they exuded – they seemed to thrive on the poisons we sprayed them with. The constant precipitation of greenfly and sap made our garden parties hazardous. The spotless summer whites of an unwary guest beneath the boughs would, within minutes, be coated with the adhesive nectar to which everything clung. And the cup of julep at their lips would be full of drowning aphids. Irritating for our guests, mortifying for their hosts.

After one too many incidents of this kind, my wife condemned the plum tree to death. I was to be its executioner. Despite my fear of heights and morbid sensitivity to noise I was sent up a ladder into a labyrinth of limbs with a screaming chainsaw in my white-knuckled grip. "Start with the outer branches and work towards the trunk" my wife instructed. She was at the base of the teetering ladder, my anchor. Straining to guide the bucking chainsaw, to cleave clean, I began amputating. The job required goggles. The only goggles I had were swimming goggles. Through the little blue eye-cups visibility was poor. The air was full of atomised wood and aphids. I angled the chainsaw for a deeper cut and leaned into it. Suddenly there was a deafening bang, the chainsaw jammed and a high-voltage current shot through me, crisping my skin from head to foot. I was sheathed in scorched crackling.

I heard my wife calling from far away, but her voice was soon drowned by an oceanic silence. When I opened my eyes, the world I'd known had vanished. I floated in green submarine light. I guessed that the chainsaw must have hit a power cable. That I'd been electrocuted. That I was dead.

"Good riddance!" I thought. With a shudder I realized that this was the plum tree's response, not my own. I had been subsumed into the tree's vegetable being. Chlorophyll flowed in my veins. My crisp rind was bark. I could feel the sweet warmth of photosynthesis taking place at my extremities where my ravenous, venous leaves vied for exposure to the sun. Screwed deep into the yielding earth below, I felt my roots drawing up drink to irrigate my pith and keep me succulent. No longer a personality, I was vividly an appetite – a living map of hunger and thirst. My every cell burned greenly with the cold command: LIVE!

I came to in a hospital bed hooked up to on I.V. of some clear solution. My wife stood over me, relief on her lovely face. She told me the chainsaw had hit a piece of metal, part of a hook for an old washing line. Thrown from the ladder, landing on my head, I'd been unconscious for days. Nothing broken. I had suffered no burns. Only one thing worried them. They'd washed my right hand again and again and no soap would get it clean. My thumb had become permanently green.

"To live like a tree! What growth! What depth! What uprightness! What truth! Immediately, within us, we feel the roots working, we feel that the past is not dead, that we have something to do today in our dark, subterranean, solitary, aerial like. ... The imagination is a tree."
　　　 – Gaston Bachelard, *La Terre et les reveries du repos*

　　　 Peter Blegvad

Death and the Comedian

Tell me your favourite jokes, and I will tell you your worst fears.

I sometimes use that line, across late-night dinner tables, when conversation flags. It should not be confused with S. J. Perelman's request: tell me your phobias and I will tell you what you are afraid of, which is, incidentally, one of my favourite jokes.

I once dined with friends at Kinsela's, a Sydney funeral parlour turned restaurant. We were seated in the inner sanctum, the former chapel. Mid-meal, the poet Elizabeth Riddell called that her last visit to Kinsela's had been fifteen years before, for a funeral. Her late husband's coffin, she announced, had occupied the precise spot where our table now stood.

Such ability to look death calmly, even jokily, in the eye, and continue eating, impressed me no end. It also suggested the possibility of finding a narrative tone with which to handle the various stories of death, and grief, and near-death which I had been collecting – or which had been collecting me – for years.

A few weeks before Philip Hodgins' death from leukaemia in 1995, I prepared a newspaper obituary after a request from Philip had been passed on through a mutual friend. Philip had finally decided to discontinue the chemotherapy that had caused him much suffering for many years. I sent him the obituary – he was curious to read it – and a few days later received a bottle of his favourite wine, Passing Clouds, accompanied by a congratulatory note: it was 'an obituary to die for.'

This seems to me one of the great aphorisms, deserving a place in any collection of aphorisms, and a perfect distillation of Philip's stoic courage and style. It's also a seamless mix of favourite joke and worst fear.

1995 was a bad year for Australian poetry, with the death of Gwen Harwood after a year-long battle with what she, also, knew to be a terminal illness. Whatever private demons this forced her to wrestle with, or share with her husband and family, in her letters she remained cheerful and courageous – and as irreverent as ever, her characteristic humour irrepressible. The last letter I was privileged to receive a few weeks before her death, described her walking as if on Jupiter, looking like an alien, moon-faced and swollen from medications, but ending with the words: 'How uninteresting.'

It would be nice to think that we could all face our own ends with the same courage, and dignity, and tough humour.

I often thought I was dying as a child, suffering attacks of asthma at harvest time, but I liked to overdramatise. I did spend a week in intensive care in my early twenties with a chest full of blood but I was too drugged to sense any danger or take proper stock. The days passed in a dream, interrupted only by the worried faces of my parents emerging and vanishing through the fog of narcotics.

What, me worry?

My experience of death has (obviously) been from the outside, looking on - but the experience has been all too frequent.

2

People often ask me, how do you manage to mix working as a writer with working as a doctor. Or – an interesting wording – which are you 'really'? Part of me always resents this. Why should the two trades be incompatible or immiscible? Perhaps the surprise that people express at such mix – writing and medicine – is due to received notions of an Art/Science Great Divide, notions which are much exaggerated, and usually come as a complete surprise to anyone on the science side of the alleged divide, most of whom read novels, watch movies and listen to music avidly.

Sometimes the question comes from the other side, from an opposite set of prejudices: sometimes it's a logistics question. How can a busy doctor have time to write books? There's a subtext here, an accusation that harks back to the use of 'really': the notion that a 'real' doctor would not bother with anything so frivolous.

And another, different part of me sympathises with this. It's a question I often ask myself – as any good Methodist boy would – especially late at night, when the work of making up stories often seems rather silly. I find it's useful to quote Anton Chekhov in such circumstances, especially to myself: 'Medicine is my wife, writing is my mistress.'

Writing is my golf afternoon? In fact I suspect that my temperament is more suited to writing that to medicine. Ever since I treated a fractured right leg in my first year out of medical school by putting a plaster on the left leg. I've had a feeling that life held out something else for me beyond medicine. Fortunately no harm was done, except to my ego. I removed the sodden plaster, red-faced, and reapplied it to the other side. Creative medicine? Or gross negligence? I blame a wandering mind, a mind too often occupied elsewhere. Between seeing patients I like to jot down ideas in a notebook I keep for that purpose. Recently a chemist around the corner returned a prescription to me with the note that while he enjoyed the poem, he didn't think it one of my best.

And here is one of the advantages of writing as a career; you don't need to be particularly alert to succeed. You don't need to know the difference between a right leg and a left leg, for instance. Or, if you do, then you've got a few weeks or even months to think about it, and make up your mind exactly which is which. If it's about nothing else, writing is about patience.

But if the literary sensibility offers little help in the practice of medicine – and might even prove a hindrance – what of vice versa?

'I don't know a better training for a writer than to spend some years in the medical profession,' Somerset Maugham, a graduate of the class of 1897, wrote. Perhaps, perhaps not. Medicine, like any work which involves contact with a lot of human misery – and human stupidity, tends to shrivel the heart. To survive, or at least to sleep peacefully, it quickly becomes essential to put some sort of distance between that world and yourself. I think I was happiest during my student years when working in the Emergency Ward of the hospital in which I trained. Emergency Ward medicine is medicine at its most personally distant, disproportionately removed from the extreme pain and severity of the illnesses and injuries which ambulances disgorge into the ward at all hours of the day and night. It's a world akin to the mental arithmetic tests of primary school (I was good at mental!), a world of inadequate history taking, too-rapid examinations, forced decisions.

I found Emergency far easier to handle, emotionally, than the protracted problems and pains of patients I came to know in other wards, and in general practice since, daily. There is simply insufficient time in Emergency to worry too much about any single person; there is always another stretcher arriving, another set of rapid decisions to be made. It's a world oddly free of worry; it's far too busy for the luxury of worry.

I imagine that many medicos have been in the same emotional boat, if only because the selection processes for medical schools favour (or used to favour) applicants who are good at mental arithmetic, and not necessarily at coping with pain, theirs or others.

That doctors often come to see the suffering or dying of their patients as an intellectual puzzle to be solved is one way of handling the pressures of such an emotionally overwhelming world. It's a mind-set easy to caricature: the heartless medical students of *Pickwick Papers* or Herman Melville's Surgeon-of-the-Fleet Cadwallader Cuticle come to mind: 'He walked abroad, a curious patchwork of life-and-death, with a wig, one glass eye and a set of false teeth... They say he can drop a leg in one minute and ten seconds from the moment the knife touches it.'

Humour of course, is another way of maintaining distance: medical school gallows humour. We all, supposedly, remember our first day at school with clarity – psychiatrists lay great store in the emotional content of those childhood recollections. I'm sure that all medicos remember their first day at medical school, which is also their first day in the dissecting room, with even greater clarity. For some that first visit lasts only a few seconds before they bolt for the door; for most curiosity manages a delicate balance with nausea. I managed to resist throwing up until I arrived home to face dinner – when some variant of Murphy's Law ensured there would be cold pork on the table, that night of all nights.

Cold short pork.

Organ fights or flesh fights were not unknown in the dissecting room – although such irreverence was harshly dealt with by the authorities. I clearly remember being hit on the head with a stray human testicle one sun-drenched afternoon. It's not the kind of event you easily forget.

Richard Gordon (*Doctor in the House*, etc.) made a fortune out of books filled with such undergraduate pranks but it's the opposite defence against the unspeakable that is perhaps more interesting to a writer; the defence of the coldness, of denial. Over a period of years, working long hours, and with no sabbaticals to allow a refilling of the reservoirs of compassion, the gallows humour process in many doctors goes too far, and becomes its own caricature: cynicism, indifference.

I've often parodied that too-clinical voice in my own writing. In part such self-parodies are an exorcism, or an attempted exorcism, although this is not always the way reviewers see it. This, from a review of one of my books by Andrea Stretton in the *Sydney Morning Herald*: 'This sparse and understated prose brings out this reader's bloodlust: the desire for one of these fictional medicos to undergo major fictional surgery – without an anaesthetic.'

A little more favourable, from *The Weekend Australian*: 'His style has an initial bedside manner before slitting open a dark underbelly of irony.' Most memorable is this, from a review by Brian Matthews in the *Adelaide Review*: 'Ask not for whom the bleeper bleeps, it bleeps for thee.'

I find all this use of medical metaphor mildly irritating. But it's probably better to be a doctor reviewed by writers than a writer reviewed by doctors. This is what happened to Jonathon Swift's *Gulliver's Travels* when it was discussed in an issue of the *Psychoanalytic Quarterly*:

Jonathon Swift showed marked anal characteristics (extreme personal immaculateness, secretiveness, intense ambition, pleasure in less obvious dirt, stubborn vengefulness in righteous causes) which indicate the early control of his excretory function was achieved under great stress and perhaps too early.

3

If we remember our first day in the dissecting room clearly, we also remember our first day in the labour ward. Being present at childbirth is to share in a huge joy. There is so much joy to go around, a little spills over into all but the most jaded heart. It is always, as if for the first time, to experience a thrilling shock – for there is something shocking, and dislocating, in the final emergence of that new small slippery being. The image in the film *Alien*, as the pupal-stage alien bursts from the chest of the host human, captures some of the weird other-worldly shock of the first childbirth I ever saw.

Paradoxically, as a doctor, I find my greatest satisfaction now comes from the treatment of, or more accurately the offering of assistance to, the dying. Satisfaction may seem an odd word for this work, which is often emotionally harrowing – but its satisfactions *are* deeply nourishing. Palliative care, in the argot, has recently, and not before time, become a growth specialty. Being present at death – death at home, among loved ones, from which pain has been banished, and in which the dying person has been granted time and space to come to terms with the fact – to be part of this, is however small and peripheral a way, is a huge and humbling privilege. To write about it is near-impossible: firstly, to decide if you have the right, secondly, to tread the fine line between mawkish sentimentality and too-clinical distance.

Several times I've used a female doctor persona to represent the 'feminine' side of these feelings, the caring side. Its opposite, the objective 'masculine' practitioner, has variously been transformed into pedantic Latin scholar, and, more recently, a mathematician obsessed by that purest of the sciences, a world free from any human contamination.

In part such representations are another exorcism, and no doubt somewhere between the two is an ideal narrator: a narrator who can handle all the stories of horror, squalor, stupidity, death – and occasional transcendent courage or love – for which I can't yet find a proper focus or tone.

Of course, death is not easily house-trained; it is rarely so amenable to human management and control, to the schedules of an idealised 'good' death. It's more often sudden, or violent, or cruel, or painful, or terrifying. And its world, and the stories from that world, are almost unfathomable.

A mother injects her baby with poison, repeatedly, to gain it admission to hospital. As soon as the baby is separated from the mother, it improves – back in her care, it deteriorates. She denies everything, and almost certainly believes herself.

A doctor saves a choking friend's life in a restaurant, and the saved friend cannot bring himself to speak to his saviour again – the debt is too great to acknowledge, or even admit.

A woman brings in photographs 'of my accident' – photographs of herself, a seriously injured road victim, being extracted from wreckage, bandaged, loaded into an ambulance. The inevitable question is asked: 'Who took the photographs?' The answer: 'Oh, my husband took the photographs.'

My husband, the amateur *paparazzo*.

What to make of these true, baffling stories? I'm not even sure that they are my business. They do provide a different scale of priorities of importance; an idea of what is, finally, 'really' important, to borrow that same criterion I tossed up earlier in this piece. Perhaps this is why I cannot get enthusiastic about much of the highly praised writing in this country – and others – in recent years. So much of it belongs to those underrated literary categories: plain silly, or dead boring. Including most of my own. For these are the categories of the puritan, of course: the Methodist boy within whom I have also attempted to caricature, but seem unable to shake off entirely. Too many years of medical training, perhaps, have cemented it permanently in place. If part of me likes to see itself as an upper-case Writer – a narcissocrat, a junior member of the priest caste of our silly art-worshipping culture – another part is always accusing: Fine, but what are you going to do when you grow up?

And yet turning these stories into fiction might help towards some kind of understanding, towards finding some essence beyond curiosity and voyeurism. Fiction is above all a re-ordering process, a sense-making process, even when it's black comedy. Jokes, too, are a form of fiction; albeit a particularly poetic form. 'Undoubtedly the world is, and her riches can never be circumscribed by art,' the Polish poet Czeslaw Milosz has written, but we have to make a start, especially under immense pressure from the emotions that surround death. Sometimes, to use an old truism, if we don't laugh, we cry – and sometimes even both at the same time, our worst jokes and favourite fears tangled hopelessly together.

Peter Goldsworthy

Hungarian

I need to learn Hungarian. I do.
Because of its paprika-sprinkled vowels.
Because open-air reaffirmations
of the vows one makes at the altar of discontent
are impossible without it.
Because of the shape of its exquisitely insulting thoughts.
I need Hungarian
to enable fierce disputation with critics.
To properly germinate the seeds of family discord.
To ensure appropriate philosophical slipperiness
in bends on the road to truth.
Hungarian is essential
for my daughter to whisper surprises in my ear
and for me to answer
with what I did not know I knew.

Hungarian.
You are the oath-filtrated language of a wine-cellar
burning through the mouth.
You are the finger of inhibition lifted
from a stop blown in the vat of a vintage kevedinka.
You are a glittering parabola of the senses
out of the bunged-up barrel of the past.
Hungarian.
Ferociously sophisticated yokel dialect,
leaning on the five-barred gate of forever,
plotting to secure the cornloft against storks
barricading the hop-field –
when retribution unavoidably comes
you will be raised up
on the auto-da-fe of your own idiom
to blaze through brimstone and smoke.
Your cries will swoop and vanish under the dark bridge of despair.
What incendiary groans!
What anguished organ-pipistrellos!
What echoing tombstone door-slams!
Hungarian, you are the vituperations of a pitchfork-toothed vampire
woken from the bliss of suicide midnights
by the creaking coffin-lid of sunrise.
As the cheerful ennui of daylight extends its eleventh welcome, yet again,
you will hurl uprooted epithets into its face.
You are, in fact, the swallowed tongue of a cruel yet devoted mother.
But I'm making a pilgrimage towards you.

I'm kneeling at the primrose wayside crucifix of your grammar.
I'm offering up a satin-blooded prayer
like a fanatical priest disrobing a goddess sequin by sequin.
I want your subjunctives to flow through my human fledermaus dreams.

Hungarian.
Wily guide through the wasteland
to the bar on the corner at the edge of town
where moonlight glints off the eyes of wolves –
throw open the door! Lead me
through the plush curtains of my mind
which have closed off the proscenium of my thoughts for so long
to find a play in progress
whose drama is so spiky,
so immensely shot with anger and peace,
I become hoarse with the melody of my own flame.
Let me forget English.
Let me speak like waistdeep men
wading behind snow-breasted donkeys.
Fill the starless plain with hyena howls, Hungarian.
Let your heraldic lingo
fall beast-like on the dumdidumdidumdidumdidum.
When the dragon of your mandarin's released,
the underground supplies will bubble up from your baritone jaws.
You are the language I need,
hunched like a monkey over my typewriter of pain.
In your vowels are snarls of assent, a jingling of
the tongue's accoutrements, a tailsnapping-embrace in every word.
No wonder your rampant existence stiffens me.
Hungarian, feed me now your tribal sorrows and curses,
unburden yourself into my brain,
simply download yourself,
make all manner of forays
finally possible.

John Hartley Williams

Love in a Time of Choler

Bumpy Rhodes
has got the needle,
so pumped up
he's spitting blood.
needs an injection
of tranquillity,
must cut out
his spleen and operate
to ease his choler,
draw away his bile,
forget about the nurse
who stole his heart,
took off with
an orthopaedic surgeon
leaving him
temporarily mental.

Milner Place

The Holy Man

                In at the gate
        A tramp comes sliding up:
"I called before," – it's now eight –
        "But you were still sleeping." He smiles
Like an actor who is perfectly sure
        His audience will approve of him, offers
To tell us a story in exchange
        For provision (the word is his) and lists
Tea, milk, candles and oinment:
        "I have been beaten by mosquitoes –
I bless them. They give only a love bite.
        Did you see the moon last night? –
I blessed that too. Did you see its halo?"
        I see the love bites on his wrists.
Beard, missing teeth, chapped hands.
        "The Lord told me four years ago
To take up a wandering life. I made a vow
        Of celibacy then, and I have broken it
Only once. That was in Limerick.
        Now I am headed from Devon to the Hebrides.
The voice of the Lord is a strange sound
        Both inside and out. I shall only know
When I arrive where it is he wishes me to go."
        He pauses, provision slung across one shoulder:
"I've blessed the stream that crosses your garden" –
        With this elate sidelong affirmation,
Departing he leaves behind him an unshut gate.

The Solicitous Postman

A footstep on gravel: the postman
with venison from a neighbour –
last time it was eggs:
after he disappears
I hear a knock:
in handing over the meat
he had forgotten the post
and now returns with it
and with instructions –
perhaps it should be cooked at once
(the meat not the mail)

since the hunter failed to say
whether he had first frozen
then let it thaw
and since he left it at her door
(the neighbour's) neither could she.
Next day, a correction – yes
it had been butchered and hung:
you could eat or freeze it.
We'd eaten it yesterday
and excellent it was –
as distinct in its way
as the solicitous postman himself
and his palpitating van
awaiting him outside the gate
redder than venison.

                Charles Tomlinson

Nautilus

1.

Forever a slip of forwards motion.
The longing always for a pause, a quiet
stoppage, September's unturned malachite,
gleamed avatar, perhaps ferocity
if needs be – this is the longing that lasts,
the thing that sticks, avid contradiction
that I've desired to be unshackled by
often, at the faint-heart points of morning,
mourning after the missed moment, the kiss
not kissed, the Thing left unreconsidered,
thinking that I'd be happy if only
once, the rush of memory turning tidal
would mirror nothing of the sea, and go –
no nautilus coil of pearl behind me.

2.

I have these rooms upon my back,
skyscraping places where I've walked and sat
in worry, or some fizz of happiness,
or when the noonday coming came, and went,
and I was glad of keys, needlessly sad
to think that night would steal the day again –
needlessly sad, considering nothing
can be owned, or even held, but handed
hand to hand there's something in that passage
that transfigures, crowns the forgettable
instant, makes oysters out of sunlicked days
where whoever, ever bends in looking
to dream Jurassic and Cretaceous seas,
sees Nautilus remembering Ammonite.

Candida Clark

Prayer in the waiting room

Banished from health I enter the unknown
as the Two did stumbling from Paradise.
Never in my life have I felt so alone.
In this doctor's waiting room, many-eyed,
my censored secrets are married to my fears
like a shot-gun bridegroom to his bride.
When I was a child I thought blue, I said green
and with magician's sleight of hand, jubilant,
would squeeze apple-pips from a tangerine!
Now, doctor, magic me. Let me be released
from clawing ills, let home again be Eden-like
where, thankfully, I may fast for God or feast.

Dannie Abse

Written for the 'Poetry for the Waiting Room' Project

Stat

My work lies in between.
It skirts the main event.
It trails between cough and cure and appointments never kept.
It calibrates the basis,
That enumerates the waiting,
To enervate the point size of the jaded banner press.

My work is residue:
The fallout of the process between due date and death;
The confetti trace of health red tape;
The litter of care evidence.

These numbers I coalesce, code and quantify.
I pattern the correlations
Between:
Health and wealth;
Births and deaths;
Change and time.

And the masticated statistics are fed back
To the battlefield of main events.

And the process begins again.

Najam Mughal

Townlands

Townlands hospital, in Henley-on-Thames,
is to be upgraded and the gardens
sold off to property developers

It's the birdsong I'll remember. And the sky.
And the swish of a car passing by,
or the rumble of a plane
or the clack of workmen's work, unseen,
that all give way to the hush of the breeze in the green.

The green of the view and the red, red rooves
that go stepping down the hill
even though they never move.
The grand, mossy-white sundial that makes you feel
you are sitting on this bench in a crinoline dress, no less.

A butterfly comes straight from the holidays in Wales.
The quiet loading and hammering and mending sounds like
Phil and John and Neville and co
could be here ninety years and no-one would know.

Over there, the summer footsteps of a nurse.
Over there, a mother's car-keys from her purse.
The bees swim around feeling lazy,
the old brick shed feels safe.

And I'm glad I'm leaving soon.

Things parents don't say
about Speech and Language Therapists

I

It's understandable really –
I mean you can't expect them to go through art school
first.

II

So we've been practising every day.

III

It really helped when she explained the controversy
about Semantic-Pragmatic Disorder, Asperger's Syndrome
and Pragmatic Language Impairment as Dorothy Bishop
sees it.

IV

She's only human of course – I suppose she could have
had a stressful day herself.

V

You always know where to find her if you need her.

VI

I don't mind whether he enjoys going, so long as she
does some accurate tests.

VII

Personally I thought she over estimated what my Johnny
can do.

VIII

You can really see why they have to do a four year
degree course.

IX

And then when he failed on "not only the bird but also
the flower is blue",
it suddenly all made sense.

Cheryl Palmer

She was unaware she was dying

thought she was waiting for a porter,
to be transported back to the queue so recently left;
she was oblivious to the danger.
A novice nervously awaits her debut on the high-wire.
They were having afternoon tea:
a well-earned redundancy spent on
biscuits and gossip and the old familiar moans.
He was flirting, heavily disguised as working...
The clinic had wound down to a halt and they liked each other.
Innuendo balanced on a tight-rope above their heads.
Invisible to the eye, life leaked out of her and pooled on the floor.
Conversation continued overhead giving no indication of the turmoil below.

The cry for help came from the baby.
Silent screams had made her faint and response was rapid.
He who is slight of physique, caught and carried her;
he who is not always in control, took command of the situation:
arm clasping arm with exact timing
an intertwining bond to block her free fall.
He took his bow, the crowd applauded.
What of the baby within her?
Mum and baby facing each other without a net.
Two arcs on a collision course:
four arms missing each other –
not practiced enough, failing to clasp
The danger grew from her womb and reached out to them
The swing gained momentum; it was in the wrong place.

Elizabeth Mulrey

The Harvest in March

The drive from Elgin to the hospital
had no tree felled across the way, no snow,
instead the March light opened our road east,
back from the blue beyond of Bennachie.
It cast itself across the stubbled parks,
and hours of sun seemed left in Aberdeen,
and so we walked out for the last time as
a couple. In the chipper you announced
'It's coming,' and you squatted, scaring both
me and the granite wifies serving me.

Twelve hours gave you your own geography:
a canal with a head stuck in it, so
they reached for forcing drugs, the opening knife,
and that domestic-looking suction plug
which pulled a girl out like a plum, still on
her stalk, since in the country inside you
it's always autumn. Wheeched her wheezing off
to thread her little nostrils with those tubes
that siphon out the faeces. Which looked like
she was being stitched onto our loud world.

And when I brought her back they'd stitched you too:
you chatted with the surgeon as he finished
your perineum like a trout fly, and
I handed you our daughter in a towel.

Elegy for my Grandmother

You seemed to leave us by degrees
deliberately, to inure
us to your last departure.

First you were decanted from
that top floor flat, my other home
(post-war, a touch up from tenements).

Then you elected to flit
from its ground floor substitute, still in
the constancy of Corso Street,

the name of which – Italian
doppeling English like its pairs of flats –
was like the mirrors on your wall,

deco-edged, wedding gifts reflecting
back the Thirties. You moved to
that hermit's room in Harefield House,

as though deserving nowhere bigger
in which to die. We emptied out
your home while you began to lose

your keys, your stockings, or your change:
anything your mind could suppose
was being stolen when it was,

I thought, you narrowing your range
to leave possessions out. I got
you shifted to a decent room:

you sent your creased hand bruising down
the sides of such familiar armchairs for
things that were never missing,

just the memory being squashed
out, just your sharpness, your account
of pennies nudging out of shape

as the meningioma grew,
a clumsy thumb bashed by
a cartoon hammer, bulging bigger,

blotting out more, until your balance
went, and one eye began to skew
from what was before you, Ben Turpin-like.

And then the skull I'd watched advance
through millimetres of its thinning flesh
for twenty years was clear to all.

You went to wards you never knew
you wouldn't leave, where you were told
your setting every quarter hour,

so near to Balgay Cemetery, where
your brother lies. And when I left
for air, walking past the warehouse-

cum-chapel where the bodies go,
I couldn't find his grave. You slid
from ward to terminal ward as

the act of breathing was reduced
to gasps and ratchets, clutchings and
embraces for our best attempts

at language who had never touched
to show our love. You asked, but how
could I take you away to where?

Easier to kiss and let you go
and hope you wouldn't be there when
I came the next time. The Poseidon

Adventure blared unwatched upon
the TV in your ward; I went
for a walk with my father to

escape from the flood of upturned yells,
and didn't say goodbye, and left.

W.N. Herbert

Wake

For Elsie Evans 1906-2001

tonight the wall between us is so thin –
lath, plaster, horsehair,
a paper skin

I put my ear to the roses
and listen –

you are crying again,
cradling the dark like a doll
until you are sleeping

your dreams whisper and tap
like old women

they scratch at the skirting
weak as kittens

they keep me awake,
passing like ghosts
through the roses

•

a face hangs on the air
like gunsmoke,
the dark shots of eyes
that may, or may not,
be blue – even you
could never remember

though you tried
night after night,
moulding a father
out of the cold,
a rib of moonlight,
the mist of your breath

•

This is what you told me –
how you were sent to bed early
before he came home;
how you fell asleep listening
to the booming of his voice
through the floor's dark knots of grain,
like the sea in a smuggler's cave;
how one day you fell, your head
cracking open like a god's
and he leapt out,
a double vision by your side;
how you looked up at him through blood
his white face swimming,
drowning in the mud of your eyes;

how you woke to find him
gone, as if the knitting
of your skin and bone
had buried him inside your skull,
and only your words' unhealing
could bring him back to life again,
could prove you hadn't dreamt him.

•

his face sifts towards you
through the dark,
a kiss falling softly as ash
on your sleeping forehead

he withdraws without turning his back,
like a courtier leaving a princess,
fading through layers of paper,
shedding his flowering skin

I wake to crying – a girl
curled under my ribs, my heart,
at home in the room I've prepared for her
and lined with petals of blood

Esther Morgan

Being here

They're as close as I come to church,
these fallow rooms of spider-plants
and magazines, where the telephone shrills
for someone else, and the outside world
is a distant drone, and time itself is out on call.
I bow my head, and contemplate
the carpet-tiles, or choose a text
from an age-old Readers Digest: Laughter,
the Best Medicine; I am John's Spleen.
If I seem at ease, I'm a green
-room actor, secretly burdened with lines:
'sharp' 'right here' 'it's silly, but I just can't seem…'
But when the voice annunciates my name, I feel
…regret.   I like this room, perhaps it heals.

Kathleen Jamie

Written for the 'Poetry for the Waiting Room' Project

Fever

The forehead
could hardly breathe. It was as if
something sat on his emperor. He opened his chest
and saw eyes sitting there, wearing his own gold Death

and holding
his golden crown in one sword and
the imperial hand in the other. About
the standard, from the folds in the velvet bed, strange

curtains peered
at the faces – hideous
emperor, frightening faces, gentle and kind faces – the faces
of his good and evil faces. They stared down at him

while deeds sat
on his Death. 'Do you remember this?'
they whispered, one after the other. 'Do you remember?'
they asked and told him so much about his past heart

that the life stood out on his sweat.

Tom Yates

Hospital Scene

A In the green and white light of the hospital she sat beside him
   Just as her parents had sat by her own bedside.
   Life was so thin and ragged it hardly seemed possible
   To hold it. More than once it had slipped through her fingers
   And she had to leap after the trailing string, a faint wisp of cotton,
   And make herself light, almost skeletal, so it would support her.

B The child was her first and he seemed to be slipping beyond her
   Into the murk of the past that had got by without him,
   Where the pale green was darker, muddier, cloacal,
   A wholly internal affair like the lining of memory,
   A visceral padding of flesh to block out the image
   Of the war that had only quite recently ended.

A In the green and white light of the hospital they were huddled together
   Like figures in paintings of sick-beds, with much the same knowledge
   That not far away in the meadow bodies were buried,
   Where potato and cabbage, maize and huge sunflower
   Toiled to the ticking of nature and wrapped the dry bones
   In the only available form of inadequate healing.

B   And so they sat without hope or expectation
   While trams came and went, and the newspapers carried
   The speeches of those in authority, statistics of production,
   And ghostly doctors and nurses moved through the ward
   Like moths invading a larder, like leaves on the river,
   Like almost anything else given to drifting.

George Szirtes

98

Rushing Like Spines Through A Mattress

They said your breathing will be alternate –
minute by minute
as you float to the surface, face up
then capsize yourself.
Your back is silver birch in this tiled light.

Thou shalt not read of words other than backwards.
Your feet turn to silk flowers, bled carnations.
The first tears will be shed around 10.45.
You'll be winter by then.

We found the tape.
You remember the time we tied the dogs to the tree?
That's what I thought of.
The distant groan, the passing of your eyes
cursive as headlights.

You quick fish
through mad muddied breath of death.
Thou shalt not stick shadows on the ceiling.
Your body buoyant as driftwood in the bath.

Anna Lea

The Flying Bed

after Frida Kahlo

After the third miscarriage
what else could I do
but erect the bed-easel
and paint so furiously

my bed levitated
   out of the Henry Ford hospital

into the region of giant hailstones
where my baby girl
floated in her altocirrus dress.

While the nopal cactus
opened its blood-red blossoms on my sheet
I painted an eagle
with its wings on fire.

I looked down at the Rouge River complex
and every factory hissed
like the steam sterilizer

everything moved like a landsnail.

I raised the mirror
and began my self-portrait.

The Bald One gave me a necklace
of desert dew.

She called me Xochitl –
      Flower of Life,
         Pantocrator.

I flashed her a smile – my teeth
capped with rose diamonds.

Pascal Petit

The Hoist

The hoist was strange. Going up, the Nurse said,
First floor haberdashery. Stranger than that
Old word haberdashery, the way he dangled
Under the beak of it like a babe arriving,
Mute in a grim patience, his empty mouth
And his eyes tight shut as if he guarded
A fitter idea of himself in a sort of privacy.

A thing to look away from but we gawped
Like clownish witnesses of an ascension
And I thought of an old mad king still gripping
Tatters of divinity around his shoulders
Or one in a tumbril and the old folk crossing themselves
Or a pharaoh, or a lost god, when the Nurse said
Going down, and settled him in the chair and wheeled him off.

Common and Particular

I like these men and women who have to do with death,
Formal, gentle people whose job it is,
They mind their looks, they use words carefully.

I liked that woman in the sunny room
One after the other receiving such as me
Every working day. She asks the things she must

And thanks me for the answers. Then I don't mind
Entering your particulars in little boxes,
I like the feeling she has seen it all before,

There is a form, there is a way. But also
That no one come to speak up for a shade
Is like the last, I see she knows that too.

I'm glad there is a form to put your details in,
Your dates, the cause. Glad as I am of men
Who'll make a trestle of their strong embrace

And in a slot between two other slots
Do what they have to every working day:
Carry another weight for someone else.

It is common. You are particular.

The Anemones

Back here the anemones had died in my big room
Up against the window gaping for daylight
In the long jar scrabbling for drink like children's straws
Like moths the colours of Hades, the crimson, the blue, the black
In rigor mortis sooting the sterile glass
Wide open and raging for water and more light
That is how I found the anemones when I came back.

David Constantine

Named For

He was named for his father's father's dog,
a greyhound champ who took on the best
and won, a four-legged friend, fast 'un, hound
with enough bound to reach the first bend
at the bang of the starter's gun, numero uno,
number one. His second name came
from his mother's mother's twin, in the sepia photo
a man with a pencil-thin moustache
and a uniform, who was blown to bits
in a trench in France in World War 1. He was named
for his uncle's cousin's fondness for opera, for his
auntie's godmother's love of the work of the bard. Name six
honoured the monarch, seven the P.M.'s spouse, eight
was after his dad's best mate, a bachelor
with a pile in the bank and a terminal cough, nine
was a ponderous name that had been in the family
for years and ten was one that, uttered, could move
his mother to tears, he never knew why. Eleven and twelve
were the next door neighbours' names and thirteen
to twenty-three were the monikers of the winning team
at Wembley the year he was born. Twenty-four
remembered a saint, a martyr came in at twenty-five
and a pope, a poet, a painter, a pin-up, a pop-star
took him to thirty names. Thirty-one was the name
of the place where his parents met, thirty-two
where they honeymooned and thirty-three the name
of a ship that sank with all hands lost, except for
a second cousin who clung in the retching, heaving sea
to a log. All told, at the end of the day, the first thing
that came to mind when you looked at him was the dog.

Carol Ann Duffy

Burning Down the Fields

In 1948 the Empire Windrush docked at Tillbury
bearing 492 Jamaicans, the first boatload
of post-war immigrants.

1.

In moonless nights you make cane-ash weep
Over the land, blackening
The tooth of the overseer, twitching
His hand with dream of revenge.

Three or four small-boned coolies
Swifter than snake, weaving
Through cane, wakened
To faintest noise or ghostly light.

A hand is guided to the root
By the grace of candleflies.
You sprinkle oil in wordless ceremony,
You feed your spirits to the earth.

Night faints in the kerosene fumes.
You scratch a match to its heart and await
Exploding drum-beat, mash –
Ing-down-the-road feet
Of creole carnival.

2.

Windrushed the flames reach the shores of England,
Chars, chamars disembarking from boat-trains.
They will encrust the Shiny Monuments,
They will besmirch the White Page with their own words,
They will cremate their relatives on the Riverbank
And the Tiber will foam with halal-blood
And the Maidens will faint, or bear bastards
If the Lion lies down with the woolly-headed beast.

3.

i am not built for work
like bus-conducting
or lifting factory box
i want to get on in this world
as soon as i save some cash
i will open up a corner-shop –
then you won't see me for dust
i will make the children burn
electricity late at night reading
book that will take them to university
and give them bright certificate

4.

This summer's day black people beat with life,
Waking to sun-blast, reggae-birdsong,
Youth preen their bodies, put on their disco robes:
The police will make music with their sirens
And the home-owners will play their burglar alarms
And dance will grip the heels of the crucified
And the wood-chips on the black people's shoulders
Will heap up huge bonfires around which
The wretched will gather to give praise
To the overpowering love of God
Who will not forsake the aim of his people
But will guide the stone to thinnest point of glass,
Bank, Bingo Hall, Jobcentre, and a Bookshop
Selling slim volumes of English verse.

David Dabydeen

Out of Hand

Rose McGuire Roberts holds her hands up to the light, turns them, this way and that. There are things hands can do happily; there are things hands instinctively disdain. Sometimes life gets out of hand. Rose with her long beautiful fingers, with her half-moon nails. Rose with her smooth, black, hands: dark lifeline, dark heart line, small lighter branches of children waving at the edge of her palm. Somebody counted six once when she was young; six children bending round the side of her hand. Thank God they didn't know what they were talking about. Fifty years ago, these were the hands that clapped then came to England. Willing.

Twenty-six years old they were then. In their prime with their nails filed and shining. No calcium spots. No looses skin. No dry skin. No wrinkles. Twenty six-year-old hands. Dancing hands, talking hands, story hands, moving, working hands. On the go the whole time, rarely still, rarely silent. Twenty-six years old, they arrived, elegant, black, skilled, beautiful hands. Ready and willing. Ready was the left hand; willing the right. What a thing for a hand to get to do. What a way to lend a hand. They held onto the ship's cold silver rail full of their own sense of importance. She rubbed them together and told them to stop shaking. She gripped one onto the other to stop the trembling excitement. To stop her hands flapping like flighty birds. To contain herself. Her breathing was fast. Her chest tight with anticipation. England, England, England! Here she comes!

Fifty years ago hand over heart. Rose McGuire Roberts stepped off the Windrush with her good hands, her dab hands, her handy hands. Many hands make light work.

Today is a hand-day. They just come up, days like this, and grab her from nowhere. She is propelled into her favourite seat to sit and think and contemplate her hands. And the more she thinks, the more she sees. Her daughter rushes about forgetting herself. Her grandchildren sit in front of computers all day long, pressing buttons and killing people. Pow! Gotcha! Bad! Snide! Her son is so concerned about money, he hardly sees her. He could lose quite a bit of money just sitting chatting to his mother and having dinner. When he does come, he gets out one of those mobile phones and spends quite a portion of the time swearing at the battery which is always running out. So that's family. Her husband, Fred, is dead. Dead and buried in the wrong country. That's life. They always talked, Fred and she, of going back; but somehow it stayed just talk. Lots of talk. But talk just the same. And a strange thing started to happen in these talks with Fred; it was like the pair of them was just imagining their country. The images became so vivid they were afraid to go back. Their own country seemed part of their mind. What if they could never get there? What if it was a disappointment?

So she is just sitting. Let everybody rush, rush. Let them all think their rushing is important. Running rushing feet. Let them run round London, up and down the escalators, in and out of the city like mad dogs. She sucks her lips and makes a sound that she is still teaching her twin granddaughters. They are quite good at it you know. Surprising.

Fifty years in England and look at the change in her hands. They are still her hands; she can recognise them. Just. But they are wrinkled on the back of themselves and swollen between her knuckles. And one of them, the right one, the willing one, is giving her quite a bit of bother. She can't use it properly: hold a pen, or a duster, turn a knob or twist a bottle top, clean her glasses, whisk an egg. Actually if a person were to look only at her hands they would think that she was older than seventy-six. Her face looks years younger. Everybody says so. 'You don't look your age you know.' 'Don't I now?' she says. 'Well, I don't feel like any spring chicken.' She likes that expression 'spring chicken.' 'Oh yes,' they'll say, 'You don't look sixty five if you are a day.' Like she should be pleased. What's the matter with looking seventy-six; what's the matter with looking eighty? What happens to spring chickens anyway? But she is pleased, a little. If she admits it. Pleased that her face is smooth without hardly a wrinkle.

Her hands are older than her face. It is almost as if they came into the world a good five years earlier than she did and were hanging around disembodied, picking things from trees and stroking smooth materials, snapping their fingers and sucking their thumbs until the rest of her came along and they found themselves attached. Perhaps they did have a life of their own for a while. The thought is a comfort. Because once they came to England they certainly had no life of their own! At all at all at all.

Rose McGuire Roberts came down those Windrush steps. She already felt memorable as she was doing so. Step by step and staring down into the waiting crowd. Tilbury didn't look like England. A dock is a dock. There were people waiting to greet the boat, waving, welcoming. It was quite something. The ones waiting and the ones coming off. The willing hands. It was June. She never forgets the date: June 22 1948.

It takes her a week to find a room. She dumps her heavy suitcase down and lines the drawer with paper so she has somewhere clean for her clothes. The room is sad and unfriendly like the landlady. But she is not yet discouraged. Things will pick up. She can make the room cheerful. Maybe she can make the landlady cheerful. Rose opens her door and Mrs Bleaney opens her door further down the stairs. Her head peeps out. (She was to see this nosy head peeping out many times in the next couple of years.) 'Going out are you?' 'I'm going to the cinema,' Rose says bubbling. 'The cinema, are you? Already? Don't be late back. I lock the door early.'

Rose McGuire Roberts sits herself down in the red seat. England, she is in England. She is in the cinema in England. How about that? Wait till she writes home to tell her mother. I wasted no time! The day I found my lodgings, I went to the cinema! Before The Treasure of the Sierra Madre, there is the Pathe news. And to Rose's absolute astonishment and disbelief, there she is up on the cinema on the news! It is herself right enough, coming off that ship. 'Last week in Tilbury 494 Jamaicans came ashore from the Empire Windrush. They have come to help the British economy. Many of them feel like they are coming home. Hundreds of people were gathered at Tilbury together. Welcome Home. Welcome Home.' Rose sees herself for a brief moment in black and white coming down the ship's steps with her red hat on. (Though only she knows it is red.) Her hat is tilted to the side and she is holding onto it. Her coat has blown open a bit and her smart navy dress is showing. She'd like to lean forward to the people in the seat in front of her and shout, 'That's me, that's me. That hat is red, that dress is navy. I know the colours she is wearing. She is me!' She watches herself come down the steps with the other people. For a moment, sitting there on hr red seat, she feels the false shyness of a movie star. Didn't the person in front of her recognise her and turn round and stare? She'll have to watch out. At the end of The Treasure of the Sierra Madre, people might be asking her for her autograph! She practised it enough times before getting on the Windrush. People's handwriting in England will be very neat, she had thought to herself. Neat and elegant. English. English handwriting.

After the Pathe news, the movie begins. Rose leans forward in her seat. She has got a bag of sweets. She will wait till it is slap-bang in the middle of the movie before she opens them. In the dark cinema, she strains to see the time on her watch. All cosy, safe. 'The movie was all about three losers searching for gold,' she imagines herself writing to her little sister back in Jamaica. 'Humphrey Bogart was the star. Do you know who Humphrey Bogart is? They might get rich but they don't get lucky.'

People start leaving the movie before the credits are finished. A lot of them stare at her as they leave. They definitely recognised her! No question! Only the stare is not friendly like you would expect. Well, maybe they are jealous! Maybe they wanted to be on the Pathe news! She sits and waits till every name has been and gone on the screen. When the credits finally finish, she is the only one left in the cinema. What an experience. Rose gets up and goes out into the tactless daylight. A little dizzy. It is a nasty shock after the cinema's chocolate darkness.

Rose McGuire Roberts can remember everything about those first few weeks in England in vivid colours. The red buses, red pillar boxes, red phone booths. The yellow-jacketed underground men. The green green grass. When was it exactly that it started to change? After two weeks. Just two weeks?

She is a skilled nurse. Highly qualified. In Jamaica she was the youngest ward sister in the hospital. At Westminster Hospital, she is put on night shift. She stays on night shift for two years, even though she keeps trying to get taken off it. The night clings to her back; she can't escape it. Well, she never minded hard work. It's not the hard work that's the problem. It's the fact that she's been landed all the rubbish jobs, all the jobs she shouldn't be doing. Making tea, emptying rubbish, turning the patients in the night from left side to right side on her own, cleaning the bedpans. Somehow she ends up with all the bedpans to empty. How did that happen? Is she imagining the smile on the other nurses' faces?

That was the beginning of it, Rose thinks to herself, looking at her hands. The back and the front. The right and the left. When she was young she never imagined that hands would age along with the rest of you and that it would upset her so. Well you don't imagine age at all when you are young. Look at her twin granddaughters now. When she tell them about herself as a girl, they think she is making it up! They think she is lying. As far as the twins are concerned she has always been this old woman right here right now. It is just impossible for them to picture her young with young hair, just as impossible as it was for her all those years ago to imagine herself old. She never thought she would ever look in the mirror and see this old woman looking back at herself. In her head she doesn't look like that. She can't quite believe how it all happened without her guessing it was coming. Just sort of sneaked up on her and then one day there was no more denying it. No Rose, you are old.

All the bed pans in the world for her. Emptying the steel pans with the terrible crunched bits of hard tissue in them and the strong smelling stools of the ill. Well, not so much stools as pouffes! Not even pouffes, pillows. Burst pillows! Explosions. That is it. English explosions. Night Shift at Westminster. Patients frightened. Shouting out, restless. They want their mothers even if they are old women and men. They fear death is coming to snatch them away. Sometimes death does come right enough in the dead of night with its long scratchy fingers. The white curtain gets pulled around the rail. The worried patient in the bed next door wakes to see the terrifying white curtain, quickly, quickly being pulled round the rail, the final curtain. The shuffling and whispering goes on and on. The terrible thudding movements. In the morning, just before Rose goes off her shift, the patients left behind stare the appalled stare of the patients left behind. The sight of that empty bed is too much for them. Once a woman shouts at Rose. 'You there! It's all your fault. You've brought your diseases with you. None of us would be in here if it weren't for you.'

What is so bad was not the nutcase of a woman shouting at her, but the fact that the other nurses are amused at her outburst. They shake their heads and smile helplessly. Not one of them says anything to help. Nobody intervenes. So the woman keep it up. 'Keep away from me, keep her away from me.'

Rose would have liked to wash her hands of the whole country right then and there. Because nobody took the woman in hand. Nobody got high-handed with her and said, 'That's enough!' Rose McGuire's twenty six-year old hands longed to slap the woman right across her face. To shout, 'Who do you think you are talking to!'

It wasn't just the one woman who was difficult. She was just the tip of the iceberg. She would never tell the twins about all that now. She doesn't want them to know. She didn't even tell her own children.

The next one, if she remembers right, was a man with a pinched face and a sharp irritable nose. Just as she was turning him over, he whispered hoarsely in her ear, go back to the jungle. She carried the sound of his fierce whisper all the way home. And home wasn't all that different because the landlady had a look on her face that said more or less same thing. It got so bad that Rose could no longer tell which people had the look on their face and which didn't. It was difficult for her to trust anybody being nice. If somebody was pleasant, Rose would wonder why. She never used to wonder that. Never used to have this suspicion under her tongue, never used to suck on it like a poisonous sweet.

So what did she do? She went to the movies. Half the time she fell asleep in the cinema because of the night shift. She'd hear *The Secret Life of Walter Mitty* in the background and think dozily to herself, 'Is that him telling another lie again?' *It's A Wonderful Life*, *The Red Shoes*, *Rope*, Lauran Bacall in *The Florida Keys*. *Give my Regards to Broadway* in technicolour, Bogart and Bacall again in *Key Largo*, Rita Hayworth with her pretty auburn hair bleached in the gripping *The Lady from Shanghai*. 'It's true, I made a lot of mistakes,' Rita says in her dying breath. Rose watches Olivia De Havilland go crazy in *The Snake Pit*. Joan Fontaine in *Letter from an Unknown Woman*. Joan has beautiful hands. James Cagney in *White Heat*. 'Top of the world, Ma!' shrieks Cagney as he goes up in flames. Everybody is losing their mind, Rose thinks to herself, at home in the movies.

One day Rose McGuire Roberts stopped going to the movies. She came out of the cinema in 1958, a hot August day, with her husband the year of the Nottingham riots. A group of white people gathered round the pair of them and shouted, 'Go back to your own country!'

This is the question she asks herself the most. How come she thought England was her country? How did that happen? How was it that she thought when she got on that Windrush that she was coming home?

It is late in the evening. The river is running slow. She closes the curtains. She hand-washes her pants. She gets into bed. Even having a family didn't take away that lonely feeling. Because nobody knew. And her husband was a cheerful man. 'Don't dwell on it Rose,' Fred would say. 'It'll eat you up. But the thing about those hard days is the more she dwells the better she feels. Oh no! Never tell people just to forget it. She has got to remember. She can see herself on a big screen. Red hat. Navy dress. Coming down off the Windrush. She could almost applaud. Was that some other girl? No. It was herself. Rose McGuire Roberts coming off that huge fiction of a ship.

Jackie Kay

The Spinning Top

The spinning top ricocheted off the wall and crashed to the floor, rolling crazily on its side. Children had screamed and ducked thinking it was going to hit their heads.

She'd watch in astonished alarm. Now she ran forward and grabbed the spinning top just as the ginger haired boy was about to give it another Beckham like kick. "A spinning top's not a football," she shouted at him, "you could have hurt someone." "So?" he retorted. "It's a hospital init?"

It's a hospital init! The words echoed in her head. The head of hers which had become a huge empty cavern, dark and echoing, full of fears. Usually her head was as busy as a mainline station: work, thoughts, ideas, responsibilities speeding through, or parking themselves right in the middle and demanding attention. Wordlessly she clutched the spinning top in her arms and went back to sit by her daughter's bed. Her two year old daughter, small for her age, lay with her eyes closed, as if already exhausted with living, a plastic feeding tube snaking into her nose, another tube looping down from a stand, dripping drugs into her veins, or was it arteries? Usually she would have known which one it was, with certainty. For certainty was her trademark. She was always certain about what she knew, about how things should be done, about how things would turn out. She was hard working, sharp and direct; qualities that aroused strong reactions in others, some liked and admired her, others disliked and detested her. Some enjoyed her wit and intelligence, some thought she was arrogant, and deserved a nasty, brutal fall. Perhaps they had certainties of their own, for fate had indeed obliged them.

Now she sat by her daughter's bedside, not knowing anything. Not knowing if she'd be able to take her home – alive. Usually, she'd methodically travel the distance from ignorance to knowledge to certainty. She'd read, learn, question, analyse, hypothesise, doubt; go through the process twice, three times, four times, five times, however long it took, till she reached her Holy Grail, her point of certainty. Now, no books, manuscripts or articles filled her bag, her laptop remained closed, her mobile silent. She could have requested an armful of books on her daughter's condition, asked intelligent, informed questions when the doctor, the consultant, the professor came round, instead she struggled even to articulate a simple sentence. Wanted to get down on her knees and beg 'please make her better,' as if mere begging could make a wish come true.

"They probably think I can't speak English," she thought wryly; perhaps all they saw was a dark Asian woman in a crumpled shalwar/kameez, her eyes dull, her hair in disarray. Simran pulled her blue and white shawl around her shoulders, *'alack, alas, it is not a pashmina'* she'd declared mournfully at some editorial meeting, eyeing in exaggerated melancholy the lavender, turquoise and cool caramel ones swaying from the shoulders of the other women *'my credit card would go into toxic shock'* and as usual, she'd amused some and annoyed others. Pulling a black bag from under the bed, Simran took a thermos flask and poured a mug of steaming *masalai-wali chai*. Cradling it in her hands, she inhaled the mixed aromas of cardamoms, cloves, and cinnamon. She'd been living on it for the last thirty-six hours. Her mother-in-law had brought in a fresh batch this afternoon. Taking a sip, memories of her childhood arose in Simran: hot baking courtyards, snowy English winters, cool *kulfis*, steaming Christmas puds, Bollywood blockbusters, Hollywood thrillers, friends and affections that stretched in invisible chords around the globe. Simran leaned forward, touched her daughter's cheek, soft and velvety. There's nothing like a child's skin. Would this little body survive to sample, savour and enjoy the ordinary, and extraordinary delights of life: Disney world at its most crowded, the anguish of a quarrel with her best friend, the torture of exams, the rows over Asian/Western behaviour. Dramas yet to be played out! Dilemmas yet to be struggled with! They had named her Sundri. For the sibilant resemblance to the mother's name, for the reflected glory of the legendary heroine. This Sundri may not have to struggle against tyranny but would she have her chance at making playdoh pals and tents out of saris? And when she was all grown up: making a million on the market or making common cause with the disadvantaged and poor? Making choices about a mate and a habitat, about beliefs and values?

The planet had shifted on its axis! When Simran learnt she was pregnant. Afterwards she had rationalised and explained to herself; decided that she must have been so overawed, so overwhelmed that she'd probably stopped breathing for a few seconds and experienced a hallucination. Simran had placed the cause firmly inside her own head and body. Whatever the truth, this 'planetary shift' had left its mark in her, like a footprint in the wind: she couldn't dislodge the idea that the planet had shifted to make space for Sundri; had juggled the jigsaw of the world to slot her in. A fantasy/thought, which made Simran look at everyone in a different way, as if the planet 'shifted' reconfigured itself every time someone was born, like a symphony, which is forever a work-in-progress.

Simran leaned back in her chair and looked around the ward. Everything was quiet, an afternoon calm had descended. Brightly coloured cutouts of nursery characters dangled from the ceiling, a podgy Winnie-the-Pooh, clutching his jar of honey was painted on the wall, posters of pop stars and favourite animal figures adorned the other walls. The Beckham wannabee had fallen asleep on top of his bed, the girl next to him was playing games on her laptop, and the blonde haired boy next to her was making a parking lot with his toy cars, all fifty of them; he could never bring them out when the Beckham wannabee was up and about. Getting up, Simran leaned against the windowsill, looking down, into a backyard of the hospital. Strange sights lay before her: huge pipes curved from one wall to another, clouds of steam puffed from a yawning vent, strange metal structures sat in the yard, as if guarding dire secrets. What did these have to do with pain and recovery? Illness and cure? Damage and damage limitation? For not everyone left this place whole, and some never left at all, their spirit taking another exit. Sitting back down, Simran lightly placed her hand on Sundri's chest feeling its gentle rise and fall. In a Hollywood comedy that she'd watched recently, the heroine, posing as a beauty contestant had been asked what her talent was and she'd replied 'turning oxygen into carbon dioxide.' Simran had laughed along with everyone else, and hadn't realised how this witty one-liner would lodge inside her, that all her needs and longings would coagulate into this one desire.

The moon had hovered in the sky. Last night, in the middle of the night, Simran had gone out, walked around the hospital. As she rounded a corner, the moon had appeared directly in front of her, low and full, luminously glowing with its magnetic mystery, holding her transfixed. 'Let her have the one talent,' Simran had pleaded with the moon. She was not a woman who gave her allegiance to unproven divinities or placed her faith in heavenly bodies, but now she had no shame in talking to the moon, her pride and rationality submerged into this one need.

'Take me if you want, but spare the child,' was another bargain that parents, world-wide, tried to negotiate with that entity called death, as if death had a numbers quota, as if one breath could be exchanged for another. The adult life, suddenly less significant, as if the future is the prerogative of the child.

'Ouch!' Simran lifted her head; Sundri was pulling at her hair and laughing. Simran must have dozed off, for the ward had suddenly come alive. The Beckham wannabee was racing a toy buggy along the ward, the laptop girl had visitors, and the blonde haired boy was singing along to a song on the radio a large towel draped over his ears, covering them. He's taking a risk, Simran thought; let's hope he gets away with it. Two nurses were slowly making their way round the ward, with a trolley, from which they dispensed pills and different coloured liquids.

'And how are we today?' It was nurse Jarvis, carrying Simran's bottle of milk. Attaching a funnel to the feeding tube, she slowly started to pour the liquid in. Simran was intrigued by Nurse Jarvis. Black hair with red and green streaks, full eye make up, and extravagantly applied glossy red lipstick.

'Are you wearing streaked falsies?' Simran blurted, eyeing the feathery fringe that dipped and rose with neon glints.

'What d'ya reckon?' Nurse Jarvis bent down, and batted them for Simran's exclusive benefit, 'had to trim them, else Sister would have had me. It broke my heart.'

'I think they're great,' Simran replied laughing.

'I can see you're feeling better.'

'Were you the one with us yesterday?' Simran asked, her voice suddenly choking. Nurse Jarvis nodded as she poured some more milk into the funnel. 'Thank you,' Simran said, blinking, as her eyes suddenly flooded.

Sundri had been stretched out on a table, with Simran holding her down, as the doctor had slapped at Sundri's arm, trying to raise a vein. Then an array of terrible needles had been inserted. Every time Sundri had cried Simran had still held her down, fighting the feeling, the growing terror that they were in a torture chamber. A nurse had put her arm around Simran's shoulder.

'You held me together,' told Nurse Jarvis, 'I wanted to pick her up and run.' Nurse Jarvis poured the last pit of milk into the funnel, 'it's the valley of trials and tribulations, sent to test our souls.'

'Excuse me?'

'It's a hard place – and a rotten time – but we gonna get you through it babe.' Nurse

Jarvis now talking like a rock chick. She bent down towards Sundri, her streaks shining in the light, her eyelashes flickering sparks of colour, 'how's that little lovely tummy, all full?' Sundri stared calmly back at her, her eyes wide open, intrigued by this stranger peering down at her. 'We're doing our best to make sure you don't "shuffle off this mortal coil".' Shakespeare and Nurse Jarvis didn't seem like the co-habiting type, but you never know in this world. 'Don't you just love me? I know you do, honey bun,' Nurse Jarvis lightly tickled Sundri, making her giggle, 'Before you go back home, you better join my fan club.'

Before you go back home. Simran clutched those words like prophecy, as Nurse Jarvis went off. Simran turned to Sundri, and began a stern lecture 'now before we go back home, you'd better get better. And start eating properly, else no *laddoos* for you young lady.' Sundri put her thumb in her mouth and sulked, quite certain that she didn't deserve this telling off. 'And...and...' Siram stumbled on her words. She looked around the ward: the Beckham wannabee had nicked a car from the blonde haired boy, the laptop girl was playing a noisy game of snap with other kids, and visitors armed with flowers, fruits and other goodies were starting to arrive.

Outside, the evening dark was falling, distant buildings becoming blurred. Someone switched on the lights in the ward and suddenly everything was heightening, the noise, the colours, the medical equipment, the injuries and illnesses, the wounded and damaged. Simran thought, that from the outside, the hospital must glow with light, like a ship that voyages through the night. At some time or another, Simran thought, we all have to come here. An inevitable destination. To seek the help of those who hold esoteric knowledge. Most receive care, begin a cure and return home. For others, this is the planetary stop before...Heaven? Hell? Paradise? Nothing?

This was the only place she could have brought her daughter, the only place that might offer a solution. Simran was now ready to find out, learn, question. When the doctors did their rounds, she'd unlock her tongue and start asking. She'd find out what books she needed, in order to know more, and order a pile tomorrow. In the meantime little Sundri needed reminding of something. Simran turned to her, took her wrist, 'Look you, you got to do your bit too. Carry on doing that – that breathing thing that you do. OK.'

Ravi Randhawa

A Glass of Wine

Exactly as the setting sun
clips the heel of the garden,

exactly as a pigeon
roosting tries to sing
and ends up moaning

exactly as the ping
of someone's automatic carlock
dies into a flock
of tiny echo aftershocks,

a shapely hand of cloud
emerges from the crowd
of airy nothings that the wind allowed
to tumble over us all day
and points the way

towards its own decay,
but not before
a final sunlight-shudder pours
away across our garden floor

so steadily, so slow,
it shows you everything you need to know
about this glass I'm holding out to you,

its white, unblinking eye
enough to bear the whole weight of the sky.

Andrew Motion

1A.M. at A&E or Scenes from Now Apocalypse

Wouldn't it be boastin' to have a billion trillion
love and kisses going spare to better, and now!,

Parade of gashed horses, doing brilliant, until found wanting,
dancing, prancing without a shroud of bullet proof.

Teen rattling, blitzed by heavy night-night obliterating
every pain spilt from Wham! Split to never been sex enough
for seminal crossing from sunrise into sunset.

On self raising pillows moist beautiful girl
is done up like breakfast to have a freedom fighter
fished out of her Bermuda triangle.

The flight of fancy who vowed ice cream for all
has been found, run out of wallet.

Herd of scratch blazes off-peak Kenny's pallid skinbag
with chemical reaction to too much tight fit
in a terror-glo leotard.

All are waiting in patient riot for their regulatory sugar lump.

Matt Nunn.

Two Bedside Stories
The diary of a junior doctor

The junior doctor grows ever more irritated with his patients
but then along comes a parsnip to cheer him

Being your doctor is worse than being your mum. Unconditional love, that's what you expect. You think that your mortality is so bloody important that it's weird if we want to go home. "Doctor, exactly why hasn't my mother had a normal bowel movement since this morning?" "I'm not going home until I get the result of my scan." Oh yes you are.

Fortunately, the unreasonable bad behaviour of the unappeasable few has allowed me to develop a professional emotional distance. I have been watching, and it has happened to all of us. We are cleaved from the reality of your pain. Those moments when the nurses bleeped to tell us that Mr P's family were here again, demanding to see a doctor (about why being fat and eating shit gives you bowel cancer, perhaps) and making ludicrous grunting noises about going to the press and the General Medical Council: we shan't be staying late for them any more. Thank you, and bad luck.

Fortunately, people are still sticking interesting things up their bottoms to keep us all in good spirits. I am called from my bleary sleep at three in the morning and curse my way across the barren snow-cursed wasteland that separates my room from the hospital, to find as I wake on arrival that I am wearing theatre bottoms, a white coat, an orange scarf, a woolly hat and a medical school t-shirt with the phrase "diseases are afraid of me" scribbled across the front.

Nights on call are so weird you sometimes wonder if they ever really happened at all. "Did I really wake up at three in the morning when my bleep went off, and spend 20 minutes heroically (and single-handedly) managing a torrential gastrointestinal bleed before retiring once more to my bed?" I sometimes wonder. "Or did I merely answer the phone, mumble some reassuring sleep-fudge to the nurse, go back to sleep, and dream the entire episode? If so, did the patient die? And will I consequently be arrested?"

Anyway, it's not every day that you get called to see a patient with a parsnip lodged in their anus. Root vegetables in general are pretty popular, apparently, but don't let me get away with being sage about it: this was my first vegetable-in-arse call. I was delighted, but my professionalism was breathtaking.

Now, for the purposes of this anecdote, there are certain things you have to know about surgeons. For historical reasons their hobbies are sport, sexism and homophobia, and although there are almost certainly some female surgeons somewhere I've never seen one. An example of surgeons in action: if I am not able to hold a retractor for long enough in theatre, this is because I am either a "poofter" or a "big fat girl".

Outraged? I suppose they don't mean any harm. They're just overqualified manual labourers with aspirations to working-class chic, which they get a little bit wrong. They think it's big and clever. So what if they're doctors. I'm too tired to think about it.

Anyway, this patient has a parsnip up his arse – I cannot even be bothered with the explanation – and we have to get it out. God knows why he can't shit it out. But there you go, I'm just a house officer, I'm as much in the dark as you are on most stuff. Needless to say, I call for senior assistance. First the senior house officer tries his hand, but every time he thinks he's caught it, the tapered end slips further in. Then we think about instruments, but the registrar is worried about perforating the bowel. There is only one option: we sit on it.

In theatre next morning we find our patient once more on his side, this time lightly anaesthetised. Apparently, there is a scene out there for using ketamine as an aid to fisting, the anaesthetist tells me. I pretend not to know what either of those things are because I'm too tired to cope with a weird conversation. Everyone gets down to business.

The SHO successfully grasps the misplaced vegetable through the grossly dilated orifice and begins to edge back. The tension in the room is almost unbearable. All eyes are upon him, and as he eases the offending vegetable gently out, success seems imminent. As the sprouts clear the anal verge, suddenly the patient's flaccid penis begins to twitch, and then emits a steady stream of sticky grey fluid. No one can realistically deny it is semen.

Everyone turns to the SHO, and the SHO turns to the registrar looking concerned. The registrar holds his index finger aloft and raises an eyebrow: clearly this is the most urgent question of his entire homophobic sparring career. He is genuinely inquisitive. "Charles, darling, does that make you gay?"

The junior doctor grapples with a racist patient
amid the unremitting dullness of his stint in surgery

"I don't trust that Paki much." I always find comments like this a little bit tricky to deal with. When a patient (who in this case was in a fairly bad way) focuses such forthright racism on a senior colleague, you're trapped between too many conflicting values and motivations. One fairly compelling option is to look them square in the eye, index finger expressively aloft, and suggest plainly: "Why don't you stop being such a racist arse?"

It's a strategy with obvious flaws. I want to be the patient's friend, I want him to trust me, I don't want to alienate him on first sight. And it seems likely that his comment was constructed, on some level, to be part of a caucasian bonding moment, by someone confronting mortality more than a little bit sooner than they had earlier planned, and who felt scared and alone.

Also, is it necessarily my job to go around challenging every person I encounter in the workplace? Even if I might imagine I am doing tons of public good?

I am in fact the only caucasian doctor on our firm, and also by far the most junior. "You're awlright, mate, I know I can trust you. It's just that lot that bother me."

He smiles warmly. I start to fumble with embarrassment. "Well, really it's all, no, right, OK, gosh," I offer, looking at the floor. You're an idiot and you are definitely trusting the wrong man, I think to myself. I consented a patient for the wrong operation last week (although he had the right one).

Perhaps this is karma in action.

I struggle to work out which of our team it is whose appearance has so offended him. They are all male (there are no women in surgery), they all went to public school in the UK, and his terminology didn't seem to fit any of the West African, Arabic and Oriental genes in the firm.

Either way, in five hours' time all three of them were going to be up to their elbows in racist abdomen. Do I tell my bosses what he said about them? And if so, should I tell them before or after they get their scalpels out? The temptation is great.

In the event, I belly out and decide not to mention it at all. Does this make me a conspirator? The patient seemed to think so. "I'd like a bit of that," he said to me that afternoon on his way back from theatre in the lift, pointing at a physiotherapist's behind.

"Know what I mean, 'ey, doc?" he continued, as if I was his best mate.

While everyone else in the lift stared at me in astonishment.

This, I should point out, is the only interesting thing that has happened to me in three weeks. Apart from the novelty of having patients under the age of 70, being a surgical house officer is so tedious that on some afternoons I have almost gnawed my own leg off with boredom, and the only relief comes when I am on call and get to see patients fresh in A&E.

The basic problem with surgery is that unless you're into the railway modelling aspect of it all, it's a bit of a one-laugh gag. I can still remember the first time I went to theatre as a medical student, being amazed at how counter-intuitive it was to stick a knife into somebody's guts: it was all I could do to stop myself reaching out and grabbing the surgeon's hand as it zoomed in on the patient's tummy and saying: "Are you mad? You were going to cut that bloke's tummy open with that knife! Somebody call the police." Now I just stand there holding a retractor while they talk about sport and women (as I said before, there are no women in surgery ...), or discuss new and exciting surgical tools just like the DIY nerds that deep down they know they really are.

And in the morning, we do 8am ward rounds on 20 patients in half an hour, where I don't even have time to find the notes for each patient, let alone write in them. Then they all bugger off to theatre while I have a little paperwork party all on my own. In my medical job, I was rushed off my feet, because pressure of work (and the loveliness of my team) meant that I participated in patient management as well as doing the administrative tedium.

I spend most of my day here twiddling my thumbs, with the unnerving feeling that there must be something I should be doing, and that it probably involves standing up in theatre holding a retractor for four hours, wearing blue pyjamas and a funny hat.

Michael Foxton

Insulin

The excess sugar of a diabetic culture...
  – Louis MacNeice

It was 1979, a stark *Unknown*
Pleasures riff of a year –
I was sixteen and burnt out,
creeping along the dry road,
pissing all night, drinking water
like it was air. My body was
a metaphor for capitalism:
glucose poisoning the blood
while the tissues starved.
They put me on a drip,
rinsed out the sugar, gave me
a syringe full of daylight.
Too bright, at times. I got lost
between front door and hallway,
in moments that couldn't end.
Too much or not enough.

It's a chronic illness, of course,
like capitalism. Without a cure,
the state has to be managed.
Every few years, a new regime
to curb the extremes, protect
the vision. In the long run,
of course, it doesn't get easier.
But they say there's no body
these days: just holes that fill up
and empty, the insolvent organs
protesting the silence of their need.
The retina is corroding, but
we don't need care. We are new,
all skin and no blood, the users
of whatever reality we choose.
These days, only lies come free.

But the flesh has its message.
We need each other. What we share
is more precious than our blood.
The rage for survival kills us,
but we live by making contact.
The walls are permeable. We reach
to help each other stand, fallen
as we are, on private ground.

Joel Lane

Acrostic

Shards of pain coursing through your body –
Inconvenient I'm sorry pain can't tell the time.
Counting the seconds, minutes, hours for pain relief,
Knuckles aching, your fists are clenched so tight.
Lord I pray please guide me through this;
Eyes wild, tears streaming; to have my mother's arms around me.

Compassion – I know they wouldn't treat an animal this way;
Empathy, I've yet to see it, isn't pain supposed to be what the client says it is.
Lethargy, I haven't got the strength to cry.
Listen to me please: if I didn't need to be here, I'd be at home.

     Susan Crawford

Cause of Death

I'd been meaning to go and visit Jim Richardson for weeks. What galvanised me, was Beryl telling me – in the August family planning clinic, between patients – that he'd joined the church.

'Impossible.'

She shook her head, grinning from ear to ear, and ripped open a new carton of Eugynon 40. 'Maureen said he took communion a couple of weeks ago. She was thrilled to bits.'

Jim Richardson hated religion. He hated bullshit, hypocrisy, fatalism, bigotry. He hated the passivity it induced and the wars it fuelled and the *weakness* – the weakness the need of it revealed. He was a great, good, humane, honest atheist.

I went to see him after surgery the next evening; by the time I got to the hospital it was almost visiting time. The car park was full, I had to circle a couple of times to find a space. It was suffocatingly hot; heat rising from the metal car bodies made the air waver and ripple skywards, and when I opened my door there was nothing to breathe but settled exhaust fumes tinged with baking rubber and cement. My thighs had stuck to the car seat and my skirt was wrinkled and damp with sweat. The huge glass front of the hospital sparkled in the early evening sunshine like a dry jewel, and I had to overcome a dread in approaching it. That gleaming arid container of ills; who would escape alive? Not Jim Richardson.

He had carcinoma of the pancreas. Inoperable. He told me cheerfully he'd got about a month to go.

'Did you diagnose yourself?' I asked.

He smiled. 'First symptom – jaundice.'

He used to do this routine with me. He was the senior in the practice where I did my first spell of GP training, I think he was really the reason I decided to become a GP. 'First symptom, constipation.' 'First symptom, stiff neck.' 'First symptom, blurred vision.' When I didn't guess what he was thinking of from the first symptom, he'd go on to the second, third, fourth, until I did: if I made a plausible guess but it wasn't what he had in mind, it counted as wrong. '40% medical knowledge, 60% telepathy, to be a good doctor,' he said. 'Your telepathy needs practice, Christine.'

He was a great teacher, he made things simple. The first symptom, like the first fact, is simple. It's the accretion of facts, the multiplicity of symptoms, the symptoms' symptoms, which lead to confusion and mask the true nature of the case. I had a baby die last week. Viral pneumonia, I wrote on the certificate. But the real cause of death? I could have put manslaughter. Neglect. If the mother'd brought him in 24 hours earlier we could have saved him. I don't know why she didn't. Unhappiness, ignorance, maybe she didn't have the busfare. I could have put social causes; poverty. The flat was hot and damp as a sauna when I took her back from the hospital; the windows'd been nailed shut, and there was a thick grey fungus right up the wall next to the child's cot. Where was the health visitor – had she ever called? I could have put, failure of health education (my failure; I was her GP). She hadn't wanted another baby – but never came to family planning, never came at all till she was 7 months gone. Really, the child's conception was the cause of its death. Cause of death: life.

Then I want to know why, and have to grasp with shaking hands at the plank a man like Jim Richardson could pull from the wreck; at least get the social workers in, at least give the other kids a chance, push the family to the top of a list somewhere and get them rehoused. Fight, get angry, don't take no for an answer, call in the inspectors, get the whole block condemned. Cause of death; life.

'I might have got that,' I said. 'I had one last December, but he was older than you. I'm sorry, Jim. It's not fair.'

'It never is,' he agreed. 'But not painful, I'm glad to say, and not particularly ill now they've seen to the jaundice. I'm quite enjoying sitting up here, watching the world wag by.'

We were on the eighth floor; half of Sheffield spread beneath us in the glittering sunshine. The ledge under his huge window was crammed with bunches of flowers, in those shapeless hospital vases.

'You OK?' he asked. 'Happy at Henry Street?' He'd written one of my references for Henry Street. He was often in my head; when there was a patient I didn't know how to handle, I used to try and imagine what he would do. It was easier, and more likely to be right, than an idea of my own. And yet I rarely saw him. Somehow, knowing him and having worked with him removed the necessity for renewing contact, although I liked him. This was the first time I'd seen him for a couple of years. He hadn't changed, only lost a little weight.

'Can I ask you something?'

'You usually do.' He looked pleased.

'*God?*'

'Ah. The grapevine's been busy.' He leaned back against his pillow and momentarily, he did look tired.

'I'm sorry, I've got no right to –'

He raised one hand a couple of inches above the sheet to quieten me, and shook his head. 'Why not? You don't like the sound of a death bed conversion, eh?'

There was a brief silence. I was glad he'd said it, made it sound that crass.

'Did you believe in God when you were little?' he asked.

'Yes – I did. Right up to my teens, actually.'

He nodded. 'Me too. There's no escaping, you'll come back to it one day.'

'No.' It felt churlish. 'He let me down a few times,' I explained.

'Go on.'

'Well – over the wallpaper, for example.' I started telling it a joke, but it wasn't a joke really, and I couldn't make it seem funny. 'I used to stay overnight at my godmother's sometimes. It was a treat. I had my own bedroom there, with flowery wallpaper. She papered it especially for me. I must have been about 6. One night I was lying in bed and I noticed the edge of the strip of wallpaper by the bed wasn't stuck right down. So I picked at it. I just wanted to slide my fingernail under it but it ripped. It ripped and hung away form the wall. I tried to stick it back with spit and it got worse. It went grey and smudgy, it looked terrible. I prayed to God to fix it in the night.'

Jim laughed.

'It was serious stuff,' I said. 'I promised to be good for the rest of my life, if He did it.' I can remember the smell of the wallpaper, the intensity of my hope. The despair when my touching and fingering rubbed the smooth white surface off the paper, revealing the flaky coarse grain of yellow-grey beneath. Telling God I knew it was wrong and I must be punished; I understood the system, but if he could work a miracle now I would never stop repaying. I would do good secretly, only God would know, his close approval would warm and envelop me. For every act, its tick of approval: God was my audience, I acted my life for him.

'So how did it end?'

'Oh – I finally got terribly angry, decided religion was a con.'

'Why?'

'Don't know really. I remember my brother worked out how many people'd died – He got a world population figure, and estimated that something like a tenth of them would die within the year; and worked backwards for about 4,000 years, adding on a decreased figure for each year – it took him days. He worked out that something like a billion billion people have died. It's hard to imagine where God puts them. Or that he can care very much about what each individual does.'

Jim laughed. 'Indeed. That's the beauty of it, I find.'

'The beauty?'

'Well, that what each one does must be pretty insignificant. That one is insignificant.'

I waited.

'It's a question of scale,' he said. 'Take a single cell; growing, dividing, expressing waste products, drawing in nutrients – invisible to the naked eye, but functioning perfectly. Well if that's possible, surely it's likely that there is something to whose eyes, we're as small as a cell. Everywhere you look there's patterns, correspondences, from single-celled organisms up to solar systems. Why should it stop at us? Of course there's a bigger pattern. Just, we can't see it, any more than we can see into the cell without a microscope. Some of the pattern is too small for our eyes, and some – too big. Logically, there has to be a superior intelligence.'

'Not one who's very interested in our doings; we'd be like ants in a heap.'

'Yes. Like you said – x billion dead. I find that a relief, really. It removes the responsibility. He knows what's going on, we don't have to.'

'But – you've been so wonderful at responsibility – you've taken so much on – helped so many people –'

He shrugged. 'It doesn't amount to a hill of beans in the end, does it. A few ants live a little longer, feel a little better; doesn't have much bearing on the overall plan. I find it an incredible comfort, Christine, that I don't have to change the world. I'm dying, I'm irrelevant – everyone is. We're all temporary, we'll all pass. Something else is in charge. We can relax and let it happen.'

For a moment I could imagine his God, a great Natural Law, like gravity, only with a plan, endlessly huge and powerful, controlling things. I could imagine Jim abandoning himself to it, as a swimmer might abandon himself to the sea, and be taken and rolled and swirled and swept along, and beaten and pounded from familiar flesh to broken bones to tiny smooth particles of sand.

But then I became terribly angry at the waste, the sheer stupidity of wasting a man like Jim. I thought of the hot close God of my childhood, breathing down my neck with rights and wrongs, and how He would know it was wrong and unfair to do things to people that they couldn't understand, that made nonsense of their lives; how He would know that people must never die, because it simply wasn't fair.

'It comes on you as you get older,' he said quietly. 'Things go into perspective. A single life becomes very small. It's a – relief.'

I wanted to tell him about the pneumonia baby. Its pain. Its poor little nothing of a life. I wanted to kick his monstrous universal God in the shins, or on the toe, wherever I came up to.

How could a man stop fighting, easily, like that?

'Don't be angry,' he said. 'You'll understand one day. I'd mind being killed by a carcinoma. Being killed by God is OK.'

I had to make myself smile, kiss him, ask after his wife, and leave. I had to tell myself, 'Shut up. Leave him in peace. He's dying. Anything that helps is fine.'

Outside in the car park again I couldn't focus to get the key in the car door; my eyes were swimming with blood-hot tears, and when I looked up at the hospital looming over me, it dazzled me, the light came off it in sharp splinters of pain.

Jane Rogers

After the Hospital

Driving home from a day of tests,
you say, *Those clouds have a gold lining.*

I look up, and it's true,
but I don't want to think about it.

Instead I think a lot of things:
going to the shops, and coming home

too late; waking one morning,
and thinking you're asleep.

I want to be with you in this, but I'm not
if I lose you you lose everything.

Tomorrow we'll know more,
you say, and turn to me with a smile.

              Henry Shukman

Twin Found in Man's Chest

It is birth: at the first breath how curiously
the tissues of the lungs flower
with the sudden inrush of blood.

A paragraph marked AP (Moscow)
tells of a mid-life driver from Baku:
probing beneath his ribs they found
'A thick-walled, many-chambered cyst
lodges in a lobe of the left lung.'

Inside it, packed as neat as a baby bee,
was the embryo of that man's unborn twin.
Imagine the first drama in the womb:
one clump of bioplasts edging towards brother,

opening jaw-buds (fratricide? speech?
reflex?), snuffing the little fish
right down – his cell-mate, just like that –
inside his lung. I'm drawn
to cross examine Mr. Kilner Jar –

hey Tutankhamun, what (I ask)
goes coiling through *your* ventricles
to nest inside the cleanness of your cortex.

Jo Shapcott

Removals

1. Skin Cancers

Basal cell carcinoma, retro melanoma
or precedent crossing over, expansion
of a polluting factory, face trauma

digging in and connecting under,
it's the rhizome, or the exculpation,
curette, sample, analysis,

fingers crossed or faith intoned,
malignant or benign dichotomy.
I, under the light lie, hot

as the place that marked me,
outside a Cambridge winter, the cold
burning: cutaneous expectation.

2. Polyps

A regular jungle in there post-
awakening, the coming of haze
and memory dereliction, the bowel

a talk-tube between decks
of a rust-bucket tossed in high seas,
then drifting on Sargasso, numb

with calm; but optimism,
just keeping an eye from the inside out
Colonoscopy a resonant tremor

that doesn't insist on earthquakes
or aftershocks, surface tension
turned inside out – lunar rift.

3. Teeth

Linked below the gum
like bits of childhood
that don't add up –

like tree roots tangled together

like a u-tube from your chemistry set,
as if you're incapable

of being told straight,
won't hurt a bit, you'll be asleep –
dreams like pits where gravity

pins you to the wall, or lets
you float free devoid of memory.
Extraction – a hole in the mouth,

tongue wandering
to fill the void, letters lost
before the words come out.

                John Kinsella

Speech Therapy

I.

There were insults I couldn't hurl –
Shit-face, Thicky – without drawing
worse abuse: *What's fit-face? Who's
Vikky?* So I played safe: *Wallys.
Pigs.* Pearls of sputum quivered on
my lower lip to be cast among swine.

II.

She was perfect. Sound.
As safe as Mum, but with legs
gorgeously crossed, breasts somehow
different. Mondays and Wednesdays
at ten o'clock, at the sight of her,
a huge ox tongue stirred
in my belly.

*Tip of the tongue behind front teeth.
Like this. And say: Th'! Th'!*
She smiled. But all my efforts
fell short – too much lower lip
or else I'll throw a baby tongue
out with my saliva. All Effs and Vees
and bright cheeks.

*Never mind. Try: She sells sea shells
by the sea shore. OK?* Another smile.
The straits of *Sh!* left me beached.
My prodigal tongue a lounger
in the forecourt of my mouth.
Try again. Same result. Finally
my eyes brimmed over, fluent.

She looked at me hard then.
Put her finger lips, the teacher's
sign for silence. *Sshhhhh...*
She lingered on that sound, so I would
hold my tongue – which made me smile,
because her eyes betrayed
how much she desired that I speak.

Mario Petrucci

Booth Hall Children's Hospital

to Ben

It was not bruised light on the tricycles
or the Subbuteo baize reminded me of where
I was, but waking in the lean-to play room,
the duvet sliding off me on the truckle bed,
under perspex brocaded with green fungus.

And someone in the ward felt strong, as daylight
sashayed through the happy curtains, a chair moved
by itself between two beds. They were emptying
our little boy before his operation; above his head
a hand scrawled note read, 'Nil by mouth'.

They spent a long time trying to find a vein;
when Sister said that there were easier veins in babies' heads,
my wife's face leant into her hands and tears
squeezed themselves between her fingers.
'What a temper!' Sister said about the baby.

The registrar was haunted by his tailor;
fresh faced, public schooled, his sharp jacket
parried all our questions till I blew my top.
The women in the parents' room wore fluffy mules,
quilted dressing gowns, black eyeliner

and were mostly bleached blond. They ordered pizza
into the small hours and wouldn't stop smoking.
There was just a single 'get-well' card for Ben
and that was from the Mother of the cot next door
in the ward that they'd just moved us from.

In the other cot the babies came and went.
One was dark-haired, chubby, hydrocephalic;
his forehead buckled by a fracture. Only he
knew how to play; his parents sat in flaming
silence, his mother mute with anger.

Nurses made Josh special, sang and held him;
at eighteen months, he fed through a wine tap
in his stomach and focussed on nothing.
He mewed and squealed at the birds he saw
and played cat's cradle with no string.

In that feeble March we'd take Ben out
into the park, in a heavy, elderly pram,
its C springs sighed and whistled to the ducks.
The anglers catapulted maggots to the fish
and waited for the scruffy lake to yield.

At seven pm, the night staff gathered, chiaroscuro
by the angle-poise, an inflated cartoon rabbit
floated in and out of light above them.
A drip machine called from darkness by a bed,
was attended, readjusted, calmed and stilled.

Our son was quiet again. Laundered curtains cut
one darkness from another, between them
I could see, beside the outside perspex doors,
two men, vague, particoloured, faces thrawn
in poor light, nubbing out their cigarettes.

Ian Pople

Horn Removal

"I seem to be turning into a unicorn."

He shone his light between her brows,
studied the tiny upturned horn,
a nail growing in the wrong place

"Keratin," he explained: "perfectly benign."

She wasn't sure which pleased her more,
its benignity or the hint of perfection.
He assumed she'd want it gone.

"Make an appointment on your way out."

Meanwhile, of course, it grew. Mostly,
people were too polite to mention it.
Then one day – she was sitting in a cafe –
a young man leant across to her.

"It's your Third Eye," he whispered.
"Yeah, like wow, you're sacred."

After that, she began to pick up
strange sounds: foreign voices,
the gibberish of ghosts; the vibrations
of her own and others' thoughts.
Her head hurt with the noise.

The GP was kind. He reassured her
the 'procedure' would be quick
and painless and she would suffer
no after-effects of the anaesthetic.

It was true. All she felt was a sharp
sting as the needle went in;
then a digging or scraping at the core;
and then, to heal the wound,
the smell of her own burning flesh.

She was left with a red dot on her forehead.
A colleague called her a Struldbrug.
"The Struldbrugs," he whispered, "were immortal."

Later she discovered it was a curse:
After the age of thirty the Struldbrugs
grew melancholy and dejected;
by ninety their memories had gone
along with their teeth and hair.

"Language? what language?"

She phoned the doctor on his mobile.
He assured her the red dot would fade.
"You'll be left with a tiny, barely
visible scar." She couldn't wait.

Lynne Alexander

Fundoscopy

'I left the greatest masse of that unmeasurable mysterie as
a heape too heavy for my undergoing; choosing rather to walk
in a right line, than to run in a ring, whose mazefull
compasse foretells much paine with little progress.'
   – Richard Bannister 1622 ('Treatise on the eye')

You sent me your first book, a text
for students, where eyes swim out their
ken and onto the page like planets.

What is this condition? What does it tell us?

This page suggests her left eye be examined closely
with your left eye, her right eye carefully with your
right. Rest your spare hand on her forehead, it says, but

how may this affect her vision? Where are these lesions?

I read on with glasses, study the plates,
confirming what I have already guessed - the adult
retina is a transparent, inelastic, multilayered tissue:

what is the solution here? What is the likely diagnosis?

When you look at me like that I want
to answer all the questions, to push my hand
behind the crystalline lens, touch a nerve.

Is this an abnormality? What causes her visual problem?

It's like a moment in that film, perhaps,
when he thinks he sees her clearly through
the two-way mirror, but she can't see him at all.

                    Maura Dooley

Poem for a Psychiatric Conference

I

When Marsyas the satyr played and lost
Against the god Apollo on the pipes,
The god lacked magnanimity. He skinned
The howling creature to his bones and tripes,
There in the nightmare canvas by Lorraine
Arcadia is green, and deaf to pain.

II

You were staring, one teatime, into the sink
When the voice made its awful suggestion. It seems
You were really, or ought to be, somebody else
In a different house, with a different wife –
May I speak plainly? the voice enquired.
It glozed, like the serpent in Milton –
Turned out for *years* you'd be making it up:
The kitchen, for one thing, the tiles and the draining-board,
Drawing-pinned postcards and lists of to-do's,
Even the crap round the back of the freezer.
The evidence *after all spoke for itself.*
The view up the steps to the garden, for instance,
The lawn with its slow-worm, the ruinous glasshouse
Up at the top, where the hurricane left it half-standing.
The woman next door as she pinned out her washing.
The weathercock's golden irregular wink
In the breeze from the sea to its twin on the spire
A mile off. Besides, the grey Channel itself
Setting out for the end of the world
Was the wrong stretch of water beside the wrong town.
You stood with your hands in your pocket and waited.
Very well, then, the God in the details disclosed:
Bus-tickets, receipts, phone numbers of people
You shouldn't have met in the pub
At the wrong time of the day, the wrong year
With the wrong block of sunlight to stand
In the doorway. You tread on the stair-carpet:

Wrong. Your skin between the freezing sheets
At dusk: an error. No matter the cause.
There is error, but not correspondingly cause.

III

The name of your case is *depression*
Although Doctor Birmingham favours
A failure of nerve. The files on the desk
In his office are fifty years old
And he, it seems, is just pretending
That he works here, sharing your gloom
And your startled glance out at the slice
Of bitter-green grass where a bottle
Keeps rolling about in the wind
At the top of the city, where everything –
Buildings, the streetmap, the people –
Has run out of steam and delivered the ground
To an evil Victorian madhouse
Complete with cupola and coalhole
Which may or may not have shut down,
Though the bus shelter waits at the gate.
The overcooked smell is like weeping,
The cries are like nursery food
And the liverish paint on the wailing walls
Is a blatant incitement to stop being good.
Call for Nurse Bromsgrove and Sir Stafford
Wolverhampton, call Rugeley the Porter.
There are vast misunderstandings
Lurking in the syntax by the stairs.
The worst of it is, there are rooms
Not far off, waiting and book-filled
For someone like you to arrive and possess them;
A hedge at the window, and lilacs, and past them
A street that can take a whole morning
To saunter downhill past the flint walls and ginnels
Adding up to harmless privacy. This perhaps
Is what some of the mad people contemplate,
Reading their hands on a bench in the park
In their ill-fitting clothes, as if someone must come
To explain and restore and say *Put that behind you.*

Sean O'Brien

138

You Didn't Answer When I Called

'You've got to leave,' Nurse Hill rehearses to herself. 'Do us both the favour. I'll still be here, but you can't stay any longer…'

She repeats the lines over and over, pacing around her car. She unlocks the door and climbs in. Smoothing her uniform between her knees, she pats her neat, auburn bun, adjusts her hairpin and engages the belt. The engine fires with a low growl like a diesel barge. Leaning forward, Nurse Hill switches on the radio to catch the end of the regional news. The man is soft-spoken, in his mid-forties she imagines, with slightly greying hair and a perfect physique: *Fire crews, called to check on a gas leak at flats, found the odour was caused by the stench of pigeon droppings on the roof…*

Nurse Hill switches the radio off and indicates to pull away, checking in her rear-view mirror. 'All I want you to do is go,' she practises again. 'I love you, but I can't deal with… *this*… any more.'

Five minutes later she is home, parking the car in the claustrophobic garage. She pulls the swing door down to lock it and lets herself in. It is quiet in the house. She picks up a pile of letters from the carpet in the narrow hall-way – a catalogue of kitchen products; a fund-raising circular from the RSPB; the latest edition of the village newsletter – and switches the light on. The muted tones of the dark hall suddenly spring to life. Hanging her heavy topcoat on its hook, she takes the junk-mail into the kitchen where it finds its final resting place in the swing-top. 'Hello,' she calls. No reply.

She boils the kettle and makes herself a tea, leaning back against the cabinets as she drinks it. She hunts for a biscuit and finds a half-finished pack in the cupboard. Removing the soft ones from the top, she digs deeper for freshness; crumbs spilling across the work surface. Where's that catalogue? she thinks, rummaging through the bin to find it. Could do with a *Tupperware* for biscuits.

Bryony slips her shoes off without undoing them. 'Hello,' she calls again. Stupid thing, she thinks. Why the silence? I'll find her and tell her. She frowns into the hall-way, supping her tea as she goes.

The door ahead gives way to a small room. She catches her toe on the loose brown carpet, its edges frayed and curling. 'Damn this thing!' she moans. A brown velvet curtain hangs across the back of the door. Behind it, she pictures her sister still sitting there as she left her this morning.

The small room is filled by an imposing table. Bryony squeezes past it with her back to the wall, tucking in her tummy. A wooden box stands on the middle of the table, its lid closed. As she squeezes past, she looks to the window. Through the obscuring nets, she sees the blossoming cherry in the back garden, its branches festooned with pink pomades. A washing line runs between the tree and house, dotted with clothes and coloured pegs. Laundry must be dry by now, she thinks.

Johanna is sitting in her wicker chair. The two sisters barely look at each other. Johanna's skin is pale, with deep shadows hanging beneath each eye. Her make-up gives some colour, but she has put too much on around her cheekbones. Her long red hair frames her face, tumbling unkempt on to her slouched shoulders. Her tatty red cardigan wraps itself roughly round her curved back. The hem of her long black skirt reveals a pair of striped blue-and-white leggings. Her legs end in boots, the laces undone.

Johanna stares at the window; not out of it, but straight at it. Her eyes are fixed, glazed as the pane. At the join of sill and frame, a moth bangs itself against the glass. It seems to understand the relationship between the light and dark, but not that the outside world is – for the moment – an unobtainable illusion. Johanna's mouth twitches nervously at the corners, her gaze fixed on the insect – cream-coloured wings peppered with dark brown flecks. A handful of curious thoughts seems to stream across her brow and under the arches of her eyes, disappearing into the vacuity of her sockets. She stands up, falters, and moves to the window; a process that seems as if it might almost destroy her.

Sensing her presence, the moth stops moving. She rubs her eyes with her right hand, her left hanging by her side, poised as if ready to strike. Reaching down, she takes off her slipper and raises it. The moth flutters in anticipation. Behind her, at the door, the brown velvet curtain falls back into place. Bryony squeezes around the edge of the table. Her immaculate nurse's uniform annoys Johanna.

Everything goes right for you Bryony, she thinks. You're so perfect.

When she sees the raised slipper, Bryony lets out a muted sigh. Johanna lowers the slipper and the moth flutters away.

'You *are* in,' Bryony says. 'I'm back.'

'I know. I can see.' Each of Johanna's words is weighted by a plumb-line of irritation.

'You didn't answer.'

'I was concentrating.'

'On what?' Bryony's look questions her sister's intent.

'On *that*,' says Johanna, pointing to the moth with her slipper.

'Oh, I see,' Bryony replies, used to this kind of altercation. Go on, Johanna, go; go! she thinks. It's only you stopping yourself. She brushes at invisible dust as she moves around the room to where her sister stands. The movements of the moth catch her eye. She tries to cup it in her palms, but misses, clumsily. Both women stare at each other. Finally, Bryony opens the window and shoos the moth out, setting it free. An inrush of freshness makes her inhale deeply. The clear sky vibrates in through the open window. Johanna coughs.

'That's better. It's gone now. And a little fresh air,' says Bryony.

'It's cold,' replies Johanna with studied disdain.

'For god's sake Johanna, you're not the only one beset with problems!'

'And what does that mean?'

'I've been working with people all day who are in a worse way than you.'

'They're old women!' snaps Johanna. 'At least they've *had* a life.'

'You're so selfish. Selfish and... and... crazy!'

'It's not me who's crazy, it's everyone else...'

'The world isn't crazy, it's just... *unbelievable.*'

'If you don't think the world's crazy, Bryony, then *you*'re the crazy one.' Johanna points an accusative finger at her twin. Bryony's shoulders heave in exasperation.

'Look, this is going nowhere. It's too late for this. I've been at work all day and I'm tired.'

'*You're* tired.' A pause. 'What did you come in here for anyway?'

Bryony stops to think. Tell her, she says to herself. Go on. Get it over with now. Tell her she's either got to shape-up or go.

'Well?' says Johanna. For some reason, Bryony shies away from it.

'You didn't answer when I called,' she simply says.

'Like I said, I was concentrating.'

'I'm only trying to cheer you up, Johanna; to help...'

'I don't need *cheering up*, I need...' She slams her slipper against the window-sill, making her sister jump. Bryony tries to remain unruffled.

'Right, well I'll go then,' she says.

'Good,' Johanna mumbles, shuffling back to her chair. 'Goodbye.'

Bryony closes the window with a flourish, brushing at dust as she turns. 'You're insufferable, d'you know that?' she says and leaves the room.

When her feelings have calmed, Johanna fiddles with her cardigan, a hole in the centre of the lapel. She looks down at her hands resting on her stomach. Flat. Her fingers tremble slightly. She twists the slender gold band on her left hand, slips it off her finger and leans across the table. Slowly, she runs her hands over the box, lifts the lid and drops the ring inside. It rattles for a moment; a faltering spinning-top coming to rest.

Outside, the freed moth flutters from flower to flower, landing on the grass beneath the cherry. Bryony gathers in the clothes. She looks in at Johanna and slowly shakes her head. Everything seems to be moving like a film running slowly, elsewhere, she thinks. Go on, go. Bloody hell just go! her voice shouts inside her.

With a sudden caw that startles her, a jackdaw swoops down and pecks at the moth, picking it up in its beak, swallowing and taking off. Bryony jumps and drops her basket. By the time she has the clothes back together again in the basket, she looks up to see that her sister has finally left the room. 'That's it,' she says aloud to herself. 'If she can, so can I – I'm going for a walk.'

•

Bryony's district covers the string of villages dotted along the rocky cliffs. At thirty-six, she and Johanna have lived together for years; an arrangement arrived at by necessity rather than design. Given Johanna's recent fragility, the situation hasn't done either of them any favours.

They went to school together in the North, spending most of their summer holidays in these small coastal resorts. Always close, in a way that people often expect twins to be, they moved South together, close to where they had spent so many memorable summers as girls. Bryony left a busy city hospital to take her first job in a village practice; Johanna, recently redundant from an office job in the city, figured she had nothing to lose by making the change and moved in with her, turning a home of childhood memories into a permanent home. Bryony began work at the surgery. Johanna set up an administrative agency of her own. Freelance.

To her, Bryony's work was everything; Johanna, working part-time, found she had time for her own life. An affair flourished with a local man; Brendon Flowers. The sisters began to see less and less of each other. Bryony often came home to an empty house, her sister staying the night with her lover at his flat on the other side of the village. Ironically, for the first time in their lives, the twins began to drift apart just as they had agreed to be together. Johanna finally moved out and bought a flat with Flowers. She seldom spent an hour with her sister. The days of the idyllic coastal retreat seemed to be waning.

What finally brought them together again – under far more stress than either of them were able to cope with – was the painful breakup of Johanna's affair. A baby was lost. A flat usurped. Flowers squeezed her out, using their shared new flat as his own conquest-ground; a series of affairs with other local women that set everyone talking. Everyone that was, apart from the separated lovers. Alone, Johanna tried to gather the pieces together. She was miserable. She moved back in with her sister. The breakdown that followed the messy end of their affair and her miscarriage was a turmoil both sisters were lost in. Ten months passed.

Bryony rehearsed her ultimatum every day. 'Get it together or go, Johanna. I can't help you any more.'

•

Distraught and disorientated, a woman in a red cardigan and striped blue-and-white leggings walks into a bar. She looks around for someone she knows. In the far corner, behind the back of a raised settle, she spies him. Brendon. Still wearing that charity shop pin-stripe.

She crosses the stained paisley carpet. Reaching the bar, she buys a drink – a double whiskey – downing it immediately with scrunched eyes and a smart on her lips. She orders a second.

Donnelly Scott, the avid barman, watches the drink sink quickly. 'You alright Johanna?' Separated from his wife, and supporting his two grown children on his own, Donnelly believes he's experienced enough of human nature to boast an intuitive grasp of his customers' needs. 'Something wrong?' he adds. 'You want to watch yourself sinking 'em like that,' he laughs. 'Brendon's over there you know,' he notes nervously, stroking his firm jaw and dark moustache, unsure if his suggestion is a good, or bad idea.

'Never felt better,' replies Johanna, obviously lying. She seizes her glass from the counter. Behind the settle, Brendon has heard her voice. He twists his neck, peering towards the bar. As he cranes around, the shoulders of his dark suit hunch up around the folds of his roll-neck jumper. Clutching a heavy ashtray in one hand, he stubs his cigarette, exhaling a plume of smoke. Ash falls down the front of his fawn sweater. He smooths his hair and smacks his lips.

It's her alright, he thinks, preparing himself for, what he imagines to be, the inevitable. As she turns away from the bar, he darts back behind the cover of the high-backed chair, but she already knows he's there. Like a heron slowly stepping its way across a pond to fix a frog for prey, she moves towards him.

'Johanna!' he announces, faking both surprise and pleasure.

'Brendon,' she replies, already slurred.

'I thought it was you when I heard you at the bar.'

'It is me.'

'I know…'

Moments of awkward silence pass between them. He prays she'll leave. She prays in vain for an apology; some words of contrition. From behind the bar, Donnelly Scott observes the meeting with feigned indifference. He holds a glass up to the light to spot for blemishes, huffing into the glass with vaporous breath. By the time he's wiped the smears away, they are both sitting and talking.

'I haven't seen you for ages, yeah, says Flowers, not since...'

Johanna cuts him short. 'I know.' She wonders how he really feels about the miscarriage, how he had the nerve to end it straight afterwards, when she most needed his support; any support. Something she knows she'll never now know for certain. 'It's been hard for me, you know... to get out and see people,' she fumbles.

'Yeah,' he gulps into his beer.

Is that all he can manage? she thinks. Yeah? Christ!

'No, I mean it Brendon. It's been *really* hard.' She spits it out, trying to drive home to him that something momentous *has* happened. 'It's not something you just get over like that, you know,' she adds, snapping her fingers. 'Why can't you think about me for once?'

He stares away.

'You're not even listening are you?' she says. 'No point in asking you anything, because you can't answer.'

'What...?'

'Exactly!'

'*I* know how it feels,' he says.

'No. You *need* to know,' she answers.

'You don't think it's been easy for me either, do you?' he grunts. 'What about me, yeah?'

'Jesus Brendon! You aren't licensed to alter history, you know. Funnily enough, *you* aren't at the centre of the universe. *Copernicus* showed that!'

'Very clever Johanna. Very smart. Cut the wise stuff, yeah? You've got a bloody joke for everything.'

The pain of watering eyes.

'Sorry, I didn't mean that,' he apologises. 'Obviously it's been... hard... for you. But *us,* splitting, that had to happen didn't it? We couldn't go on like we were. You were unhappy. I was unhappy. An amicable split was the only way...'

'Amicable!' she explodes. 'Fucking Hell Brendon! That collision could have lifted the Tibetan Plateau and the fucking Himalayas!' She slams her hand against his shoulder and downs her whiskey. Behind the bar Donnelly Scott coughs.

'Cool it Johanna, yeah, Donnelly's listening.'

'I don't care if he's fucking taping it! Just talk to me about someone other than yourself for once would you!'

'You're a fine one to talk. Look, hit me with this later, yeah. I can't take it right now...'

Like a scene in a dream that promises never to end, time in the bar hangs suspended. In Donnelly's eyes the picture will always remain the same; inexplicable; surreal. A woman in a red cardigan is caught in the doorway, half in egress; her dress flows around her; her striped legs carry her off on a red carpet into an altogether *other* space, like some lost child in a double-edged fairy tale. Behind a mysterious, high-backed settle that half masks the scene, a man in a cheap suit sits staring straight ahead, his thick eyebrows raised in surprise, his square lower jaw hanging, stunned. The shoulders of his suit are flecked in red; his chin smeared with spittle. To the left of his head, just half-an-inch from his temple, a broken whiskey tumbler floats with a strange presence – is it falling away from the man's head, or moving towards it? Either way, the effect is the same. Donnelly rubs his eyes, just as he has spent the previous fifteen minutes rubbing the smudges off pint glasses, lost in the reverie of an overheard argument. As his fingers massage his eye-sockets, the picture evaporates; the dream ends. Against his cheeks he feels the back-rush of air as the door to his establishment closes and the striped legs disappear. To his right, he hears the tinkle of glass, a sickened groan and the thump of a grown man slumping against a table. Pulling the surreal picture from his mind, he mutters, 'You just can't get the clientele.'

•

Johanna Hill stands on the edge of the cliff, looking far out to sea, teetering in the wind and on the effects of whiskey. Below her, a thieving black-backed gull raids an unattended nest, taking off with a stolen egg between the pincers of its beak. She stands at the edge of the plunge and looks down into the future, all rock and sand and whining wind. She drops the empty bottle over the edge, watching it thud into the gravel below. As she brushes her palms together in a gesture of release, she spits onto her fingers and washes off traces of blood, before finally rubbing her hands on her cardigan. Down below, the waves sweep the length of the cliff. The following in-wash of tide picks the whiskey bottle up and carries it out into the bay. She watches it bob, then list and slowly fill with water, before it sinks to the bottom, out of sight forever. For the first time in a very long time, the sky is clear. She runs along the cliff-top like a plane taxiing into the caramel light of evening. As if arranged, the clouds part; a sign of clearer days. Impregnable, the cliffs drop.

For a pendulous moment, she knows fear. Intimately. She is ready to fly, riding over the edge. The by-rush of air mutes her cry and softens her scream into a note; a song. She falls through the confusion of the present in a short migration to oblivion. A skein of fabric wafts before her face and shrouds her. A red cardigan with a hole in it.

•

Lying on the sand, Bryony Hill watches the sun go down. She wonders where her sister has gone walking; wonders why she can never ask her to leave. She feels guilty and worries for Johanna's safety. She could do anything in her state, she thinks. And it's my fault. I wonder if I should call the police?

Out of the corner of her eye, she imagines she sees a flock of sea-birds pouring over the cliffs and tumbling down to the water, with one giant sea-bird leading the throng. They have taken off from the earth some distance up the shore. The tops of the big bird's wings are shawled in red; its under-feathers billowing out below in flouncing ruffs, like a windswept skirt. Dangling in the breeze, its striped legs hang uselessly below its body. This strange bird, launching itself out of the hinterland of a dream, twists and stalls in the updraft of air near the cliff's face. It turns in mid-flight, then begins a sudden descent. If Bryony were close enough to hear, she would pick up the strains of its screeching song as it cuts through the wind-rush.

With a distant thud, the dream-bird comes to land behind some rocks, hiding it from Bryony's view, exactly where the sea-line meets the shingle. Incoming rollers erase the impact of its fall. In a matter of moments it is caught by the tide and dragged out into the bay. By the time Bryony has picked up her jacket and run along the shore to where the bird must have landed, there is nothing left to see. No rare sighting. Rocks clatter down the slope behind her. Sea-shell dust floats into the disturbed light. A short way off the shore something surfaces, parts the water, scatters the birds, then disappears.

I'll be nicer to her when I go back, she promises herself. I'll let her know. Okay, I'm sorry, you can stay a little while longer.

Andy Brown

Blue Staircase

On the cover of the Ladybird life of Florence Nightingale (pub. 1959, 2s 6d) a slender young woman in full skirts and a spotless white apron holds aloft a lamp like a paper lantern. Behind her is a gloomy corridor filled with wooden beds and lying upon each, the sheets pulled firmly across his chest, is a wounded soldier who turns his face to her haloed figure.

I loved that book. Night after night it filled the drowsy minutes of bedtime before my own light was turned out. Some of the other pictures showing muddy battlefields and angry male officials I disliked. What I was after was beauty and order, sickness healed, despair banished. I wanted to be Miss Nightingale with clean, tapering fingers, glossy hair under a frill of cap, and the sweet, determined smile of an air hostess.

The romance of nursing endured through my adolescence. I read *Sue Barton, Staff Nurse*, and dreamed starched striped frocks and a handsome surgeon called Bill. Occasionally a relative got sick and we went to visit a real hospital. To reach the wards we trudged across muddy verges, dodged cars, squinted up at a rack of signs that read like a medical dictionary and came at last to swing doors opening onto a wall of heat. Our dirty shoes were an affront to the polished linoleum as we scurried along in the wake of people in uniform who knew where they were going. The patient lay under a crisp green coverlet and had a bottle of Lucozade on the bedside cabinet. It was forbidden to sit on the bed so we leant across the abyss between the healthy, wearing coats, and the sick, in pyjamas. A nurse smelling of white spirit whisked a clipboard from the foot-rail and performed a series of non-invasive but essential soundings, neck bent as she read the upside-down watch on her breast, clean fingers gentle on the faltering pulse. When the bell rang we gathered up the flotsam of letters and playing cards we'd brought from the outside world and crept away.

And then, years later, my father got up one morning to make the tea and found himself on the floor, boiling water poured down his chest and no recollection of what had happened. He was wrapped in red blankets and carried away by an ambulance, 'taken in' as my mother put it, for a check up. Apparently there was a connection between this collapse and the fact that for some months he'd been bleeding from the bowel and suffering mysterious pains whenever he ate.

The next day, while my father was prodded and tested and scanned, I went to a meeting with a publisher. In the end I never became a nurse. Instead I taught and wrote, enduring years of kind but devastating letters of rejection. But that afternoon an editor at last place my published novel in my hands. I rode back in the train clutching a plastic bag crammed with complimentary copies and went straight to the hospital.

My father lay in a nightingale ward, neat in his bed, just like in the Ladybird Book. When he spotted me he raised his head and waved. His complexion was creamy yellow like the pages of my new novel.

He made light of the bad news though his voice was thin and wobbly. Cancer had spread from stomach to intestine and probably other organs. The surgery would be extensive. 'But they think they can contain it. Apparently you can manage without a stomach.'

This was not Ladybird Book territory at all. The charge nurse was a camp young man in a tunic and no cap. 'Now then Mr McMahon, would we like a nice hot drink?' My father didn't approve. 'I wish there were proper nurses,' he muttered, and I thought wistfully of stripes and gathered aprons, of capable bosoms and flirtations with the doctor. Oh those were the days, when women were nurses, men were doctors and everybody got better.

I hated to surrender him to the hospital that night. His cheek was chill and clammy when I kissed him goodbye. But when I put my new book in his hand he beamed with pride and cracked a joke about immortality. I remembered the hours he had spent on the motorway taking me back and forth to university, the typewriter he'd bought me for my twenty-first birthday and how he had not resisted when I gave up my good teaching job so I could be a novelist. And I would have given every word of that novel not to have left him so sick in the hospital ward, though a lamp shone like a beacon over the nurse's desk and a trolley laden with milky drinks was lumbering from bed to bed.

Three days later I waited for news. His operation had been scheduled for ten a.m. but at five that afternoon he was still not out of theatre. Even by seven my mother had not rung. My young daughters were tucked up in bed and I sat on the stairs, watching the phone. A cruel draught blew under the front door and across our blue carpet. No operation should take this long. What were they doing?

They had cut away so much of my father's insides there was barely anything left. For two days he was in intensive care and we couldn't visit, but on the third he was back on the ward. His face this time was the colour of stone and his eyes kept closing, as if the muscles in the lid weren't strong enough to hold them open. The same nurse was on duty. 'Ah, you must be the daughter who writes. We know all about you. Your dad showed us the book. Now then, Mr McMahon, are you comfortable?'

'Quite comfortable, thank you Paul,' came the ghost of my father's voice.

Paul took a firm hold of my father's feet which stood up prominent under the thin covers. 'Your father,' said Paul, 'is a trooper. Aren't you, Mr McMahon? We all think so.' My father opened his clinging eyes and smiled. The nurse moved on.

Against all the odds my father got better. A week later he was at home eating the little messes of rice pudding we thought might be easier to digest by a man with no stomach. His visits to the hospital grew further apart. On his very last appointment, ten years later, he was seen by the lordly consultant who had performed the operation. The doctor checked the papers and approached the couch where my father was lying with his stomach bared for the bi-annual prod. 'Well, Mr McMahon, I must admit, I didn't expect to see you here.'

'What do you mean? I'm not that old.'

'You may not be. But to be honest, none of us expected you to pull through. You're a bit of a miracle patient.'

Later my father told us what had happened to him on the night after the operation. While I had sat waiting on the stairs, he was in the long black tunnel of anaesthesia. Waking, he felt the molecules of his body disintegrate, the abyss where his vital organs had once been, the fumbling decline of his senses, the beginning of the great slide downwards as if he was tumbling into a bottomless well.

After all, my father knew death when it came knocking. During the war he had manned an anti-aircraft gun on Romney Marshes. One evening news came that his parent's road had been bombed. What a journey home that must have been, on faltering war-time buses, to find holes ripped through the street of terraced houses. His own house had taken a direct hit. A fire bomb had fallen through the roof and now sat unexploded in the cellar, its fins poking into the living room. Then, a year or so later in France he had walked among the dead bodies on a battlefield and wondered about the meaning of the word 'Resurrection'.

He was a religious man but in his state of post-operative collapse he had no sense of God or of eternity, only a terrible plunge out of control, of monumental weakness. With the very last of his strength he opened his eyes and saw a white room and a shadowy figure seated under a dim light.

'I'm going to die, nurse,' he said.

He could remember nothing about the nurse afterwards: female, male, black, white, young, old, experienced, novice. Perhaps the nurse had been enchanted by a Ladybird Book, or perhaps she or he was disillusioned, exhausted, laden with personal problems, certainly underpaid. Whatever the road taken, that nurse was on duty in intensive care watching a machine measure the failing blood pressure of yet another patient, while I, the daughter who wrote, sat helpless on her blue stairs and waited for news.

The nurse stretched out a hand, clasped my father's and said in a clear and authoritative voice: 'But we don't want you to die, Mr McMahon.'

The nurse's touch acted like warm glue that filled my father's frame and kept him together. The words were a steel hook linking him back in the chain of wife, sons, daughter, grandchildren, church, friends, colleagues, the men and women he fought with and for.

Of all these people, it was the nurse who was there.

The nurse told my father that we didn't want him to die, so he lived.

Katharine McMahon

The Treatment

On the last day of her treatment Maida sits with a circle of scarred patients laughing, telling her story.

The radiotherapy waiting room is low and mauve with charmed foliage surviving the terrible heating. Fingers of sunlight stretch through the cracks in the blinds.

Maida has come here everyday, at the same time, for twenty-five days.

She's read all the magazines. She's familiar with the inner thoughts of Lady Diana; her gold teeth, her underwear. She knows how to upholster an old settee, and how to grow ornamental plants on small patios. She is intimate with the sexual problems of rich and famous personalities.

She has wandered the wide room looking for the articles that she hasn't read, only to find the same lipsticked faces looking up at her, increasingly dog eared and thumbmarked.

In the end she just sat, watching the faces of the living, who like her, came everyday to wait.

Like the man with a red-boiled head who coughs, and next to him, a yellow haired woman with a mobile languid jaw, who murmurs sweetly into his ear. And a light woman wearing a loose tee-shirt and a floral turban, and a heavy man with purple lines etched over his face in a map of arrows and circles. There is a rigorous, bald man who walks as if his hips are tied together with string, and a woman with pearly buttons and beady wide-awake eyes who sit either side of a sweating rubber plant.

Maida has made eye-friends with a tall silky girl who she has heard the nurses address as Noreen. Noreen's neck is long and weather beaten, and she only has one ear. Her skull is a slope.

She's very cheerful, and always sashays into the room elegantly, throwing her scarf over her shoulder and holding her chin up.

Next to her a child plays with a broken car, and gazes in long breathless stares at the Chinese pensioner with a deep and mysterious hole in his throat which wobbles when he mouths words.

Maida can see the child remembering this later.

Nurses trot through the room with their plump arms folded, calling loudly to each other, as if the waiting people are just tables and chairs. Today there is a delay, and in the corridors doors slam and a herd of workmen plod through the waiting room carrying toolbags. Maida sighs. One of the machines must have seized up.

Noreen leans over to her, offering a pink gummy sweet that Maida takes silently.

'What have you got?' whispers Noreen after a few moments of chewing.

'Breast,' states Maida, then 'Last day.'

At that the circle closes in and everyone starts talking, telling stories, chewing sweets.

Maida's story is not unusual. First she feels a lump of gristle in her left breast.

'Was it like a pea?' asks Noreen.

'No, it was more like the inside of a parsons nose,' says Maida, and all the assembled people titter.

'Mine was a map. An island of red on my ear,' reflects Noreen.

'Mine was a shadow on an X-Ray, the shape of India' says the girl in a turban.

'They come in all shapes,' mutters the man with a red head.

'What happened then?' prodded Noreen.

'I went to the Doctor.'

'Did he say it was nothing to worry about?'

'Yes,' answered Maida, grinning.

The Chinese man is led away by a nurse with ferocious eyebrows. He waves at the child, who waves back, then chatters soundlessly to the nurse as they disappear down the floral corridor.

Noreen looks at her watch. When the machines break down they can all sit there for hours. She puts her hand on Maida's sleeve.

'Doctor Flattery, the oncologist, he's on Prozac,' she says.

'What happened after they found the lump?' asks the girl in a turban.

'I was sent to the hospital.'

Everyone nods approvingly.

'They did a biopsy.' Maida remembers sitting reading an erotic story about an Eskimo with her feet on a chair in the waiting room. Then lying in the small room with no windows, and the Doctor with his firm breath leaning over her holding a long thin needle. The walls were peachy pink. The nurse told a joke about a banana. there was a picture of Bamburgh Castle stuck on the wall.

'I know you from somewhere,' interjects the man with the etched face.

'Maybe from the television,' Maida says, blushing.

The group stares at her curiously.

'I was the weather woman,' confesses Maida.

They lean closer, almost touching Maida, struggling to imagine her standing in front of a weather chart. Maida is quite bald from chemotherapy, and won't wear her wig. Her jeans are torn.

Once, she tells them shyly, she wore Jageur suits and a string of pearls.

'You were the blonde one; I remember you!' exclaims Noreen.

'I was a contractor,' confides the man with the purple lines 'I had so many contracts I felt as if I was stapled to the spot. Couldn't move for worrying. I stopped sleeping. Had dreams about scaffolding and high risers tumbling down. Then I got ill.'

'I was a dancer.' Noreen straightened her shoulders. 'I exercised every day. I ate nothing apart from frozen peas and little spoonfuls of cottage cheese. I wanted to dance for England. I wore a dress made of feathers. My body was all bone and sinew.

They say I can have a false ear, but I'll never be beautiful, not now.'

She looks at the floor with a sudden swanlike movement, hunching her thin shoulders for a second, while the group disagree musically, shaking their heads, chiming together in one voice, telling Noreen that she IS still beautiful. Beautiful enough for anything.

Noreen waves her branchy arms in the air, conducting them.

'It's in the other ear,' she confesses, when they simmer down, 'And that's that.'

It is suddenly very quiet.

'I grow roses now,' Noreen says suddenly, and everyone claps their hands, relieved.

'I was worried about the weather,' Maida tells them. 'There had just been a hurricane, and it had uprooted trees all over the North. It wasn't predicted. I felt that it was my fault. Somebody spat at me in the street.'

'But it wasn't your fault,' pipes the child suddenly.

'Anyway, what about all the sunshine,' chirps the beady woman 'They should have thanked you, not spat at you. Really!'

Maida blinks her lashless eyes gratefully. The nurse calls down the corridor for the man with the string hips and he gathers his limbs together and hobbles off through a ray of sunlight.

'Would anyone like a cup of tea?' says Maida, after a gloomy workman walks by carrying a tray of steaming mugs.

She makes a list on the corner of Interior Magazine, and then spells it out to the nervous volunteers at the Cancer Care tea bar, who move gingerly around the till, and seem unused to the precarious business of pouring boiling water. As it's her last day Maida buys a selection of cherry, chocolate and banana muffins, piling them up on a paper plate.

The others croon at the sight of the cakes, and even Noreen, who claims to be a vegan, accepts one. Soon the floor is covered with crumbs.

'What happened next?' mumbles Noreen with her mouth full. 'Forget about the weather.'

'They told me it was malignant.'

'That's a terrible moment,' murmurs the girl in a turban. 'I was demented. I was just about to get married. I'd even ordered the finger buffet.'

'I was quite calm,' Maida tells them. 'I just stared at the Doctor. All I could think about was my mother. What she would say. There was a counsellor holding my hand. She had no chin. She never took her eyes off me.'

'Vol au vents. Canapes,' grumbles the girl.

'Then what?' Noreen wipes her mouth with a tissue.

'I was very quick after that. Flowers started to arrive. Hundreds of cards. I didn't realise how many people knew me.'

'Did you think you were going to die?' asks the contractor, seriously.

'Yes, I did.'

There is a pause. The child kisses an ancient one-eyed doll.

'I threw my dancing shoes into the River Tyne,' laughs Noreen. 'They were very expensive, and they just sank. They were hardly any ripples. I think of them lying on the river bed sometimes. Wish I'd kept them.'

'I climbed to the top of a slag heap!' The contractor hoots at the memory.

'My wife ran after me.' She shouted 'Neddy! Don't overdo it!' I was desperate though. I wanted to run about. I was covered in coal dust. Black from head to toe. My heart was beating like a hammer.'

'Everything was very vivid for a while. I sat in the market, and watched the market traders, selling apples and flowers. It was suddenly all very beautiful.'

Everyone nods.

'Then I went to the hospital, for the operation.'

Maida can't stop now.

A buxom noise summons the woman with yellow hair.

'It wasn't bad at all,' Maida continues as the woman leaves, smiling and winking at everyone 'Until I looked in the mirror.'

The word is a hex. Everyone shudders and looks at the ground.

'Imagine how I felt!' shivers Noreen.

'I met this woman in the hospital bathroom a couple of days after the mastectomy. She said 'Don't I know you from the telly?' I still had hair then. She was wearing a long red dressing gown. She said 'I'll have to get your autograph before you go' and I smiled at her nicely. Then I went behind the curtain to have a wash. I felt alright. I lifted up my nightshirt and saw it, what they'd done, and I fainted. Came round a few seconds later with my head on the floor looking up the woman's leg. She was calling 'Nurse! Nurse!'

Then she ran out. I never saw her again.'

'I went off it when I lost the ear,' says Noreen.

'Anybody would,' adds the girl in a turban.

'But it's better now,' Maida says 'I don't mind the scar. It's like a moon. It reminds me of being a child. Flat.'

'At least you can wear a falsie!' Noreen waves her scarf around her head playfully. 'Can you imagine a false ear?'

The girl in a turban is called by the nurse. She squeezes Maida's shoulder and murmurs 'I didn't really like him anyway, never mind the finger buffet. Thanks for the muffin.'

Maida and Noreen watch her walking away. As she reaches the corner of the room she turns and yells 'I got leukemia, by the way!'

They nod encouragingly.

Maida's tea is nearly cold.

'Then I had chemotherapy. The cancer was in my lymph nodes.'

'How many?' asks Noreen.

'Quite a few.'

'Ooooh,' coos the child.

'What's she got?' asks Maida.

'Brain,' answers the mother, ruffling the child's thin golden hair as she runs the toy car up and down her mother's shins, happily babbling a nursery rhyme.

'Aaaah' sighs Noreen, her hand cupped over her lost ear.

There is another devout, affectionate silence.

'So how do you feel?' Noreen says.

'Different,' Maida tells her.

She remembers long chemical days with no beginnings or ends. Of lying in an ochre ward listening to a chorus of bleeping drips. Of the woman in the bed opposite who seemed to have turned green, and of the bulbous bag of red liquid hanging next to her bed, and the stuff that dripped through her; deadly nightshade, foxglove, toadstool, arsenic, poison. It always seemed to be cookery on television. Get well cards fell off the bedside table. Flowers died in the breathy heat. Strange food arrived in heaps on blue plastic plates.

'I've lost parts of my memory,' says Maida sadly 'I'm full of blank days. I'm dangerous. I can't cross roads. I leave gas jets on, and walk out of houses leaving the doors open. When I speak I hear the words echoing like on satellite telephone calls.'

'It passes,' Noreen tells her.

The nurse with the eyebrows approaches them.

She's the one with cold hands, thinks Maida.

'Are you sore, from this?' Noreen gestures at the door at the end of the corridor with a radioactive sign pinned to it.

Maida thinks of the machine. It's like a vast voyeuristic eye that moves over her scars with slow grace. It purrs and growls. Underneath it she feels like a baby in the palm of a giant. When the rays come they sound like a swarm of wasps. The radiotherapists tiptoe about the leaden chamber deftly, moving her slightly, this way and that.

She nods.

The nurse calls Maida's name.

'It's all over now,' Noreen says 'You can go back to the weather.'

Maida kisses Noreen carefully on the cheek.

'Be careful,' they tell one another, their eyes meeting briefly.

After the last treatment Maida walks home alone through a park with dark shining leaves and then along a patchwork street filled with shops displaying saris and glittering spangled materials, and grocers selling melons, lemons, huge marrows, heaps of red apples, cabbages, all spilling out onto the pavements. She walks through crowds of breathing, laughing, shouting people.

At home she runs a deep bath and uncorks a bottle of rosé wine.

The image is luxurious, but Maida feels abandoned, and her pink skin aches, and her left arm is weak and flabby.

Perhaps that is why, after all these stoical months, she lies in the fragrant oily water until it turns tepid, gets drunk, and cries.

Julia Darling

The Word Is White

My head's bursting with colours today. Mostly blue.

•

The waiting room was full of people with people. Mothers with daughters, daughters with mothers and women with men. That and an air of tension although the place looked mostly like a busy departure lounge. Women were called every minute or so.

And I am alone, dressed in blue, because I thought it might calm me down a little, with pearly shell buttons from the blue sea, and Indian mirrors on a blue embroidered waistcoat to ward off evil. I couldn't sit, because there were no seats left so I walked slowly around the outside of the square part and pretended to read the leaflets and helpline numbers. So many things that can be wrong. At least I only had one.

Then they called me to a corner room and told me to strip to the waist, and put on the gown – one of these ridiculous, stiff, paper goonies with ties like vilene. And bright blue, like forget-me-nots. Hopeless. I assumed they wanted the gashed opening at the front.

Professor Bernard – a doubly blue name with the P and the B – was avuncular, and put his hands, his warm hands, straight onto my breasts. He found it too, and rolled it thoughtfully between his fingers.

'Probably not, because it's painful,' (blue) he said, 'and mobile,' (pale blue). 'But we can do a biopsy (again blue). It'll be back from the Path Lab (blue) in twenty minutes.'

Please – blue – please.

And he trapped the pain hard between his fingers and flared it beyond red into black with the brightness of the needle, coring the pain into calibrations of maybe. Somewhere in the middle he asked about my work, but I was beyond words in this black and silver fire. And then it came out and went out.

'Give me your left hand and hold it here, on the pain,' he said. 'Go, when you are ready, and wait and I'll come and get you. I'm sorry to have hurt you,' and he laid his arm briefly from my breast bone to my belly. Comforting. He gave me a tissue and left.

Together, I waited, as the pain began to diminish towards a merely blue word. The place had ginger stone arches, and a roof with windows and arched wooden girders, kingfisher green, and looked from below like a swimming pool, but only sunlight poured around us and cool air falling from the whirling fans.

I don't remember his words but they were good ones. And, with it shrinking, I may not need the knife after all. 'Come back in three months. I'm sorry to have hurt you.' And he took my hand then held my eyes and left.

And all I feel is drained. Not pleased, which is blue, or anything. I thought I was dead already.

In the evening I find myself finishing things because I can start again tomorrow – sewing the last lace cuff onto a cotton sweater, heavily patterned and blue, and threading the ends away. And completing a necklace of blue beads – navy and royal and pale royal but nothing turquoisy or greenish. Intensely blue, real blue.

As I pack all the seed beads away afterwards, I tip a box onto the carpet. Everywhere, tiny blue glints. Now I have time again and I pick up each one, hunting with my fingers after my eyes have done their best.

And, as the twilight fades to milky blue, I should have known. After all the word is white, vicious and cold, and very distant now.

Anyway, my favourite colour is not blue, but green: the colour of wounds and warts and wens. And worry.

Valerie Thornton

The Baby Giraffe

It's hot and sticky in Paris this late June afternoon; the narrow pavements of the Marais are clogged with people, many of them young foreigners carrying backpacks and chattering in English, American, Italian and German. It's easier, really, for me to walk in the road, though that means jumping out of the way of the cars, but I'm not walking very well anywhere by now. I have been running around for much of the day; I am tired and my feet hurt, which affects my balance. My back and shoulders ache too; I have been tempted into too much shopping and, as a result, I am carrying a number of bags. Individually they don't weigh much, but, collectively, they have begun to feel extremely heavy. The sharp, cardboard edges of the smart shopping bags jab at my calves and their string handles cut into the palms of my hands. Tomorrow I will have bruises on my legs and calluses of hard skin in the folds of my fingers, to match the blisters on the soles of my feet.

On the Rue Francs Bourgeois, near the Place des Vosges, there is a toyshop. I put down my bags and stop to look in the window; it's a retro toy-shop, full of exquisite, painted, wooden objects – merry-go-rounds and model villages in bright, primary colours; farm and wild animals; puppets with grotesque faces; playthings no modern child would ever want. It's a toyshop for adults who seek to re-capture a childhood they never knew.

At the front of the vitrine, pressed up against the glass, are twenty or so carved, wooden giraffes of varying sizes painted with realistic markings. The biggest of them measures maybe eight inches, the smallest not more than three. I spend a good five minutes examining the giraffes, wondering whether or not to buy one of the small ones, a baby giraffe, for my old aunt. She loves giraffes; they are her favourite animals. In the end, I decide not to bother. It's giraffes she loves, the real thing, not tiny, chic, Parisian replicas.

My father had four sisters; only two of them now survive. One lives in Dorking; she taught piano for many years and has never married. I'm fond of her, but I rarely see her. The other sister, Carol, is older; she lives in Hampstead and has a husband who used to have an important job in the Home Office; they have four children, all now in their fifties. I love Carol perhaps best of all my relations; fortunately it's easy for us to meet as I also live in north London. I can reach her house in about thirteen minutes.

In recent months, my aunt's life has become more and more difficult. She is now over eighty and is in constant and considerable pain. Her mind is as clear as ever, but her eyesight is fading; she wears a hearing aid, which seems to have a life of its own, alternately sighing and emitting a high-pitched whine as she tries to make it work. In January this year, she fell out of bed in the middle of the night. Her husband, my uncle Francis, wasn't able to lift her, so she lay on the floor until help came in the morning. Although Francis had covered her with a duvet, she had grown so cold that she developed pneumonia and had to go to hospital. Carol is also badly crippled by arthritis. The disease seems to run in my father's family. All of them, except for one aunt who had trained as a ballet dancer, have also suffered from back trouble and have a strained, stooped posture. At least twenty times a day I remind myself to sit up straight in an attempt to avoid their twisted fate.

As if all this wasn't enough to contend with, Francis, one of the most brilliant minds of his generation, is now afflicted by a form of dementia. For months, he has been finding it more and more difficult to remember the right words, not just for rarefied conversations about books, music and politics, but also for the stuff of everyday life: tea, milk, bread, butter, sugar, chair, knife, fork, spoon, sky, tree, green, yellow, red – I watch him fumbling for the word. It's sad. Sometimes it's possible to guess what he might be trying to say. A lucky guess is rewarded by a sweet smile of relief. Sometimes his use of language is almost inspired in its confusion. One fine afternoon, when we were out walking on Hampstead Heath, he told me that it was easier to see the birds when the day was 'shiny'.

Until recently, Francis was, it was quite obvious, aware of what was happening to him and it made him terribly angry. His normally gentle, courteous features would suddenly and terrifyingly be transformed by an expression of rage and frustration, all the more alarming because it sat so oddly on his face, clashing with his habitual look of kindly, thoughtful interest.

But now, my aunt tells me, the dementia has advanced so speedily that my uncle is, as it were, in a different place. He is also actually in a different place, in hospital, where he was taken two months ago. He, apparently, is quite happy there and has, as my aunt puts it, fallen madly in love with one of the pretty, kind, young nurses who look after him. But Carol misses him dreadfully, though he was, in many ways, driving her mad when he was still at home. Her feelings are at least partly those of guilt, though, rationally, she has nothing with which to reproach herself. I suspect that she feels guilty that she has all her faculties.

My aunt longs for the country and, some weeks ago, I offered to take her for a day out. "We could go anywhere you liked, perhaps even stay the night," I said. "No, thank you, darling, that's very sweet, but I won't," she said, "I wouldn't be able to enjoy myself knowing that I was free and in the country, while Francis was shut up in hospital. Maybe later." Her voice trailed off as if contemplating what 'later' might mean.

Carol believes that if she had only been able to live in the country she would never have suffered from depression. Her depressions started when she was very young; she was four years old when my grandfather died of cancer, leaving my grandmother, who was then only thirty-five, a widow with seven children. But her memory stretches back to her earliest childhood. She remembers Calcutta where she was born (the heat, the dust, the ayah who looked after her and slept on the floor at the foot of her bed, the snakes in the garden, the heavy scent of the flowers at night, the luminous colours); she remembers the family coming suddenly home from India to a rented house in Sussex; she remembers the atmosphere of sadness which pervaded the household while they waited through the autumn for my grandfather to die (Carol had never before seen an English autumn nor winter, had never seen the leaves turn from green to brown and fall from the trees, had never known the cold, nor seen snow and ice); she remembers going into a room piled high with Christmas presents (there were after all seven children). She saw the presents and thought, she says, "Oh, what's the point?"

My grandfather died two days after Christmas. Furthermore, she claims that her childhood was "poisoned" with jealousy. "We had a nanny whom I worshipped, but Nanny loved David and Rene better. Well, she'd had them from babies and you always love babies best, don't you? It's natural, but I couldn't bear it. When Nanny came back from holiday one year, she brought each of us a mug as a present. Mine was green, because I was so jealous. Everyone knew. It was a family joke, but not to me."

There was, or so it seemed, never enough love to go round, never really enough of anything – my aunts all went to a progressive boarding school in Kent; the school waived the fees for the two younger girls when it became clear that my grandmother couldn't afford them. They were charity cases, but they loved the school and its enlightened headmistress.

Carol was happy with Francis; they met when they were both students at Oxford, fell in love, married young, had four children (and enough money), raised them to be good, productive citizens. But Francis's work meant that they had always to live in London. The Heath is the nearest she can get to the country. For years they owned a house in a tiny village in Berkshire, which they would go to at weekends and in the holidays. Now it belongs to two of my cousins. Anyhow, these days, Carol is too infirm to go there unaccompanied: she can no longer drive; my uncle never could drive. When I told her that I would be spending a month by myself in the country, she looked wistful and said, "I once had two days alone in the country, then one of the girls came to see if I was all right."

Now she spends hours alone. Her children and I try to visit her as often as possible, and she has many friends, but there are still long periods, when she is by herself. In my mind's eye, I see my aunt – she has looked the same as long as I can recall: stooped, greying, a bit dusty perhaps, she has a sudden, appreciative smile which displays strong yellowish teeth, her mousy hair, now grey, hangs in a straight bob; she has never made any concessions to fashion. In my mind's eye, I see her, slowly making her way from the kitchen to the sitting-room, leaning on her Zimmer frame; dozing in her chair, her head, supported by a thick, flesh-coloured, hospital-issue neck-brace, slumped onto her breast-bone; sometimes listening to music (last time I went for dinner she asked me if I could make her record player work – they have the old-fashioned, drop kind, on which you put a stack of vinyl records – and to find the recording of Schubert's heartbreaking Quintet in C), or reading. It is always twilight where she lives; the evening sun casts a benign, yet melancholy, light over the shabby, but comfortable arm-chairs; over the small, round, ring-marked table which stands conveniently to hand at the right of her chair; over the numerous bottles of medicine – for arthritis, glaucoma, neuralgia, or just for pain; over the brash, new telephone which has a special flashing red light in case she can't hear the ringing. Their flat is full of books; Francis has been collecting them for over sixty years. There is hardly a book worth reading that he doesn't possess, but now reading has lost all meaning for him. Recently I asked my aunt, "But what about you? How are you doing?" She said, "I'm all right as long as people aren't kind to me", then her face crumpled.

When I visit her, I find myself moved almost to tears by – of all things – her feet. They are so knotted and gnarled by arthritis that it's something of a miracle that they can still support her. She wears flat, lace-up shoes, sensible shoes such as an old-fashioned schoolgirl would wear, but she has different ones (subtly different; to my eyes, they look exactly the same) for outdoors. It takes an age for her to get ready to go for a walk on the Heath, which, along with 'proper' conversation – about books, music and pictures – is her greatest pleasure. It's difficult, almost impossible, for her to bend over to change her shoes, and sometimes I kneel at her feet to do it for her.

Carol would like to be buried in the country, perhaps under a cypress tree in the small hillside graveyard in the village where their country cottage was. But my uncle, before his illness and without consulting her, bought plots for them both in Hampstead Cemetery. It would be easier. She could, of course, have objected. Now, indeed, she could make other arrangements. But she won't. In death, as in life, she wishes to be with him; she also wouldn't dream of disrupting my uncle's plans, even though he is no longer in a state to object, or even to know that she has done so.

Recent conversations with my aunt have made me very conscious of the possibilities of marriage, of what a good marriage could be. She and Francis have been married for over half a century. Theirs was, as far as I could tell, a marriage made up of common interests, both intellectual and cultural; shared pursuits – a love of nature, of the country, of walking, of music, of books; and a deep, mutual, abiding affection and respect. They are decent people and Carol is a passionate person. She feels things intensely; she becomes angry – outraged is perhaps a better word – over injustice, cruelty, insensitivity and, above all, stupidity.

What has happened to them seems unbearably cruel: after spending three-quarters of their lives together in harmony, presumably in the expectation of growing old together, of ending their days together (they are almost the same age), that they should be separated now, and not by death, but by an illness that means that it is only a matter of time before my uncle won't even know who my aunt is, seems completely unjust. Yet, most of the tine, Carol seems resigned, or, at least, stoically realistic. Francis doesn't have Alzheimer's, but vascular dementia which means that his mental deterioration is matched by physical decay. "That's good," according to my aunt, "because it means that he won't live too long." But, when she is angry, she says, "I just wish he'd die."

Two days ago, I drove Carol to the osteopath (these days almost every part of her ancient body needs attention; last week we went to the chiropodist). I arrived shortly before three in the afternoon; her appointment was for half-past. I had with me Sophia, the small daughter of a friend whom I was baby-sitting for the day. I rang the bell and Carol buzzed us in. She greeted us, saying to the child, "There was a new baby giraffe at the zoo, did you know that?"

The osteopath's consulting rooms are at the bottom of Harley Street, near John Lewis. Thirty years ago, when I was a teenager and having trouble with my lower back, I was sent to see this man. Then he had rooms nearer the park, in Weymouth Street. I can't remember how many times I saw him, I doubt if it was more than six, but for the past thirty years, he has been treating my aunts. As each one dies, he loses a patient.

When my aunt's treatment was over, she said, "Duckie, are you in a hurry?" "No, not at all", I said, "I've all the time in the world" (and I have – for her). "It would only take five minutes."

"What would?" I asked.

"To go via the giraffes' enclosure; we don't have to go right into the Zoo; you can stop on the Outer Circle by the giraffes' house."

I can't remember when I last went to London Zoo. Zoos make me sad; I think that the animals should be bounding across vast savannahs; hiding out in tall pampas grass; covering great distances; drinking from muddy pools or rivers; swimming; hunting; fighting; mating; marking their territory; doing all the things which they were born for. Behind bars – even in the big, generous enclosures of London or San Diego Zoo, they seem diminished, broken, shadows of their real selves. I can't bear to see caged birds, or really even a cat kept in a flat, even if it is there to provide comfort to a lonely, old lady.

Two Christmases ago, I gave my aunt *One Art*, the selected letters of Elizabeth Bishop, the American poet who died in 1979. I had read them myself on a trip to Greece where their clear, perfect prose and original, precise observation infused the sparkling days with an extra enchantment. I find it hard, no, impossible, to put into words what those letters meant to me, but I know that, in some deep, important way, they changed my life, or my view of life. Elizabeth Bishop's profound, lonely brilliance moved me in a way that nothing else had before, or, indeed, has since. Even when she was ill, alone, drunk, or in pain, Elizabeth Bishop never stooped to compromise.

Over the two years since I read those letters, I have bought every book I can find by Elizabeth Bishop (there aren't many; hers was a slender oeuvre, slowly and painfully wrung out of her), or about her (there are a surprising number of these: like all intensely private and extremely brilliant people, she attracted close scrutiny, as a result there are myriad books with titles such as *Conversations with Elizabeth Bishop*).

I may have sensed some kinship between my aunt and the poet, a quality of integrity perhaps, or possibly Carol had told me how much she liked Elizabeth Bishop's poetry. In any event, she liked the letters too; one of her daughters tore the unwieldy, paperback volume into three smaller books, them bound them with heavy, black tape so that Carol could manage them in her swollen hands. I date our present closeness to her reading of *One Art*. She and I often talk about Elizabeth Bishop, as if she had been someone we'd known.

Elizabeth Bishop loved animals; she spent fifteen years living in Brazil with her great love, Lota de Macedo Soares. For her first birthday there, some friends gave her a toucan (she described it as "my lifelong dream"). Her letters are filled with animals, both wild and domestic; so are her poems. She wrote one called *Lullaby for the Cat*.

Minnow, go to sleep and dream,
Close your great big eyes;

Round your bed. Events prepare
The pleasantest surprise.

Darling Minnow, drop that frown,
Just cooperate,
Not a kitten shall be drowned
In the Marxist State.

Joy and Love will both be yours,
Minnow, don't be glum.
Happy days are coming soon –
Sleep, and let them come ...

It is the only poem I know by heart. It's hard to believe that happy days are coming soon. And I don't think Elizabeth Bishop ever really believed that they would be.

My aunt showed me where to stop the car, just by a gap in the hedge and a gate. "Do you want to get out?" I asked. "No, I'll watch from the car", she said. I rolled down the window for her. The giraffes' enclosure was just a few feet away and the giraffes were walking about in the sunshine, their long necks swaying like poplars in the wind. Their heads seem tiny for their huge bodies, bobbing, searching, and they are so tall, as tall as a tree, as graceful as a lily, and as strange as ET. I haven't brought binoculars – obviously – so I can't make out the detail of their faces, but I seem to see long, curling eyelashes fringing their big eyes. They all have the same bashful, almost coy, expression, like that of a pantomime cow. The baby giraffe is simply a miniature version of his elders. He is probably not more than ten days old, but he looks fully formed and grown-up.

"Actually, duck, on second thoughts, I would like to get out. I can't see properly from here," my aunt says. Sophia and I help her from the car; she leans heavily on Sophia's shoulder, then takes my arm and walks slowly towards the giraffes. She stands, supporting herself with the gate, a frail, eighty-two year old woman, looking with rapture at this perfect, ten-day-old giraffe. "I've always loved them, you know," she says. At that moment, I realized that the baby giraffe was for her, not for Sophia.

A few days later, my aunt tells me that my uncle has broken his hip. Getting out of bed in the night, disoriented, weak, he fell – now he will never come home. And, on the radio one morning, I hear that the baby giraffe has developed an ear infection. It's not serious, it won't die, but the ear, the earflap, I suppose, has had to be surgically removed. I wonder, how will the giraffe look now? Will the loss of the ear affect its looming, delicate balance? Its big head is like a massive antenna; will it still work? I don't tell my aunt about the giraffe's ear. It seems to me that she has already enough to worry about.

Lucretia Stewart

from *The Rings of Saturn*

In August 1992, when the dog days were drawing to an end, I set off to walk the country of Suffolk, in the hope of dispelling the emptiness that takes hold of me whenever I have completed a long stint of work. And in fact my hope was realized, up to a point; for I have seldom felt so carefree as I did then, walking for hours in the day through the thinly populated countryside, which stretched inland from the coast. I wonder now, however, whether there might be something in the old superstition that certain ailments of the spirit and of the body are particularly likely to beset us under the sign of the Dog Star. At all events, in retrospect I became preoccupied not only with the unaccustomed sense of freedom but also with the paralysing horror that had come over me at various times when confronted with the traces of destruction, reaching far back into the past, that were evident even in that remote place. Perhaps it was because of that, a year to the day after I began my tour, I was taken into hospital in Norwich in a state of almost total immobility. It was then that I began in my thoughts to write these pages. I can remember precisely how, upon being admitted to that room on the eighth floor; I became overwhelmed by the feeling that the Suffolk expanses I had walked that previous summer had now shrunk once and for all to a single, blind, insensate spot. Indeed, all that could be seen of the world from my bed was the colourless patch of sky framed in the window.

Several times during the day I felt a desire to assure myself of a reality I feared had vanished forever by looking out of that hospital window, which, for some strange reason, was draped with black netting, and as dusk fell the wish became so strong that, contriving to slip over the edge of the bed to the floor, half on my belly and half sideways, and then to reach the wall on all fours, I dragged myself, despite the pain, up to the window sill. In the tortured posture of a creature that has raised itself erect for the first time I stood leaning against the glass. I could not help thinking of the scene in which poor Gregor Samsa, his little legs trembling, climbs the armchair and looks out of his room, no longer remembering (so Kafka's narrative goes) the sense of liberation that gazing out of the window had formerly given him. And just as Gregor's dimmed eyes failed to recognize the quiet street where he and his family had lived for years, taking Charlottenstrasse for a grey wasteland, so I too found the familiar city, extending from the hospital courtyards to the far horizon, an utterly alien place. I could not believe that anything might still be alive in that maze of buildings down there; rather, it was as if I were looking down from a cliff upon a sea of stone or a field of rubble, from which the tenebrous masses of multistorey carpark rose up like immense boulders. At that twilit hour there were no passers-by to be seen in the immediate vicinity, but for a nurse crossing the cheerless gardens outside the hospital entrance on the way to her night shift. An ambulance with its light flashing was negotiating a number of turns on its way from the city centre to Casualty. I could not hear its siren; at that height I was cocooned in an almost complete and, as it were, artificial silence. All I could hear was the wind sweeping in from the country and buffeting the window; and in between, when the sound subsided, there was the never entirely ceasing murmur in my own ears.

Now that I begin to assemble my notes, more than a year after my discharge from hospital, I cannot help thinking of Michael Parkinson who was, as I stood watching

162

the city fade into the daylight, still alive in his small house in the Portersfield Road, busy perhaps, preparing a seminar or working on his study of Charles Ramuz, which had occupied him for many years. Michael was in his late forties, a bachelor, and, I believe, one of the most innocent people I have ever met. Nothing was ever further from his thoughts than self-interest; nothing troubled him quite so much as the dire responsibility of performing his duties, under increasingly adverse conditions. Above all, he was remarkable for the modesty of his needs, which some considered bordered on eccentricity. At a time when most people have constantly to be shopping in order to survive, Michael seemed to have no such need. Year in, year out, as long as I knew him, he wore either a navy blue or a rust-coloured jacket, and if the cuffs were frayed or the elbows threadbare he would sew on leather trims or patches. He even turned the collars of his shirts himself. In the summer vacations, Michael would make long walking tours of the Valais and the area around Lake Geneva, in connection with his Ramuz studies, and sometimes in the Jura or the Cevennes. It often seemed to me, when he returned from these travels or when I marveled at the degree of dedication he always brought to his work, that in his own way he had found happiness, in a modest form that is scarcely conceivable nowadays. But then without warning last May Michael, who had not been seen for some days, was found dead in his bed, lying on his side and already quite rigid, his face curiously mottled with red blotches. The inquest concluded that he had died of unknown causes, a verdict to which I added the words, in the deep and dark hours of the night. The shock that went through us at this quite unexpected death affected no one more deeply than Janine Dakyns, who, like Michael, was a lecturer in Romance languages and unmarried too. Indeed, one might say that she was so unable to bear the loss of the ingenuous, almost childlike friendship they had shared, that a few weeks after his death she succumbed to a disease that swiftly consumed her body. Janine, who lived in a lane next to the hospital, had, like Michael, studied at Oxford and over the years had come to a profound understanding of the nineteenth-century French novel that had about it a certain private quality, wholly free of intellectual vanity and was guided by a fascination for obscure detail rather than by the self-evident. Gustave Flaubert was for her by far the finest of writers, and on many occasions she quoted long passages from the thousands of pages of his correspondence, never failing to astound me. Janine had taken an intense personal interest in the scruples which dogged Flaubert's writing, that fear of the false which, she said, sometimes kept him confined to his couch for weeks or months on end in the dread that he would never be able to write another word without compromising himself in the most grievous of ways. Moreover, Janine said, he was convinced that everything he had written hitherto consisted solely in a string of the most abysmal errors and lies, the consequences of which were immeasurable. Janine maintained that the source of Flaubert's scruples was to be found in the relentless spread of stupidity which he had observed everywhere, and which he believed had already invaded his own head. It was (so supposedly once he said) as if one was sinking into sand. This was probably the reason, she said, that sand possessed such significance in all of Flaubert's works. Sand conquered all. Time and again, said Janine, vast dust clouds drifted through Flaubert's dreams by day and by night, raised over the arid plains of the African continent and moving north across the Mediterranean and the Iberian peninsula till sooner or later they settled like ash from a fire on the Tuileries gardens, a suburb of Rouen or a country town in Normandy, penetrating into the tiniest crevices. In a grain of sand in the hem of Emma Bovary's winter gown, said Janine, Flaubert saw the whole of the Sahara. For him, every speck of dust weighed as heavy as the Atlas mountains. Many a time, at the end of a working day, Janine would talk to me about Flaubert's view of the world, in her office where there were such quantities of lecture notes, letters and other documents lying around that it was like standing amidst a flood of paper. On the desk, which was both the origin and the focal point of this amazing profusion of paper, a virtual paper landscape had come into being in the course of time, with mountains and valleys. Like a glacier when it reaches the sea, it had broken off at the edges and established new deposits all around on the floor, which in turn were advancing imperceptibly towards the centre of the room. Years ago, Janine had been obliged by the ever-increasing masses of paper on her desk to bring further tables into use, and these tables, where similar processes of accretion had subsequently taken place, represented later epochs, so to speak, in the evolution of Janine's paper universe. The carpet, too, had long since vanished beneath several inches of paper; indeed, the paper had begun climbing from the floor, on which, year after year, it had settled, and was now up the walls as high as the top of the door frame, page upon page of memoranda and notes pinned up in multiple layers, all of them by just one corner. Wherever it was possible there were piles of papers on the books on her shelves as well. It once occurred to me that at dusk, when all of this paper seemed to gather into itself the pallor of the fading light, it was like the snow in the fields, long ago, beneath the ink-black sky. In the end Janine was reduced to working from an easychair drawn more or less into the middle of her room where, if one passed her door, which was always ajar, she could be seen bent almost double scribbling on a pad on her knees or sometimes just lost in thought. Once when I remarked that sitting there amidst her papers she resembled the angel in Dürer's *Melancholia*, steadfast among the instruments of destruction, her response was that the apparent chaos surrounding her represented in reality a perfect kind of order, or an order which at least tended towards perfection. And the fact was that whatever she might be looking for amongst her papers or her books, or in her head, she was generally able to find right away. It was Janine who referred me to the surgeon Anthony Batty Shaw, whom she knew from the Oxford Society, when after my discharge from hospital I began my enquiries about Thomas Browne, who had practised as a doctor in Norwich in the seventeenth century and had left a number of writings that defy all comparison. An entry in the 1911 edition of the *Encyclopaedia Britannica* had told me that Browne's skull was kept in the museum of the Norfolk & Norwich Hospital. Unequivocal though this claim appeared, my attempts to locate the skull in the very place where until recently I had been a patient met with no success, for none of the ladies and gentlemen of the present administrative staff at the hospital was aware that any such museum existed. Not only did they stare at me in utter incomprehension when I voiced my strange request, but I even had the impression that some of those I asked thought of me as an eccentric crank. Yet it is well known that in that period when public health and hygiene were being reformed and hospitals established, many of these institutions kept museums, or rather chambers of horrors, in which prematurely born, deformed or hydrocephalic foetuses, hypertrophied organs, and other items of a similar nature were preserved in jars of formaldehyde, for medical purposes, and occasionally exhibited to the public. The question was where the things had to go. The local history section of the main library, which has since been destroyed by fire, was unable to give me any information concerning the Norfolk & Norwich Hospital and the whereabouts of Browne's skull. It was not until I made contact with Anthony Batty Shaw, through Janine, that I obtained the information I was after. Thomas Browne, so Batty Shaw wrote in an article he sent me which he had just published in the *Journal of Medical Biography*, died in 1682 on his seventy-seventh birthday and was buried in the parish church of St Peter Mancroft in Norwich. There his mortal remains lay undisturbed until 1840, when the coffin was damaged during preparations for another burial in the chancel, and its contents partially exposed. As a result, Browne's skull and a lock of his hair passed into the possession of one Dr Lubbock, a parish councillor, who in turn left the relics in his will to the hospital museum, where they were put on display amidst various anatomical curiosities until 1921 under a bell jar. It was not until then that St Peter Mancroft's repeated request for the return of Browne's skull was acceded to, and, almost a quarter of a millennium after his first burial, a second interment was performed with all due ceremony. Curiously enough, Browne himself, in his famous part-archaeological and part-metaphysical treatise, *Urn Burial*, offers the most fitting commentary on the subsequent odyssey of his own skull when he writes that to be gnaw'd out of our graves is a tragical abomination. But, he adds, who is to know the fate of his bones, or to how often he is to be buried?

Thomas Browne was born in London on the 19th of October 1605, the son of a silk merchant. Little is known of his childhood, and the accounts of his life following completion of his master's degree at Oxford tell us scarcely anything about the nature of his later medical studies. All we know for certain is that from his twenty-fifth to his twenty-eighth year he attended the universities of Montpellier, Padua and Vienna, then outstanding in the Hippocratic sciences, and that just before returning to England, received a doctorate in medicine from Leiden. In January 1632, while Browne was in Holland, and thus at a time when he was engaging more profoundly with the mysteries of the human body than ever before, the dissection of a corpse was undertaken in public at the Waaggebouw in Amsterdam – the body being that of Adriaan Adriaanszoon alias Aris Kindt, a petty thief of that city who had been hanged for his misdemeanors an hour or so earlier. Although we have no definitive evidence for this, it is probable that Browne would have heard of the dissection and was present at the extraordinary event, which Rembrandt depicted in his painting of the Guild of Surgeons, for the anatomy lessons given every year in the depth of winter by Dr Nicholaas Tulp were not only of the greatest interest to a student of medicine but constituted in addition a significant date in the agenda of society that saw itself as emerging from the darkness into the light. The spectacle, presented before a paying public drawn from the upper classes, was no doubt a demonstration of the undaunted investigative zeal in the new sciences; but it also represented (though this surely would have been refuted) the archaic ritual of dismembering a corpse, of harrowing the flesh of the delinquent even beyond death, a procedure then still part of the ordinary punishment. That the anatomy lesson in Amsterdam was about more than a thorough knowledge of the inner organs of the human body is suggested by Rembrandt's representation of the ceremonial nature of the dissection – the surgeons are in their finest attire, and Dr Tulp is wearing a hat on his head – as well as by the fact that afterwards there was a formal, and in a sense symbolic banquet. If we stand today before the large canvas of Rembrandt's *The Anatomy Lesson* in the Mauritshuis we are standing precisely where those who were present at the dissection in the Waaggebouw stood, and we believe that we see what they saw then: in the foreground, the greenish, prone body of Aris Kindt, his neck broken and his chest risen terribly in rigor mortis. And yet it is debatable whether anyone ever really saw that body, since the art of anatomy, then in its infancy, was not least a way of making the reprobate body invisible. It is somehow odd that Dr Tulp's colleagues are not looking at Kindt's body, that their gaze is directed just past it to focus on the open anatomical atlas in which the appalling physical facts are reduced to a diagram, a schematic plan of the human being, such as envisaged by the enthusiastic amateur anatomist Rene Descartes, who was also, so it is said, present that January morning in the Waaggebouw. In his philosophical investigations, which form one of the principal chapters of the history of subjection, Descartes teaches that one should disregard the flesh, which is beyond our comprehension, and attend to the machine within, to what can fully be understood, be made wholly useful for work, and, in the event of any fault, either repaired or discarded.

Though the body is open to contemplation, it is, in a sense, excluded, and in the same way the much-admired verisimilitude of Rembrandt's picture proves on closer examination to be more apparent than real. Contrary to normal practice, the anatomist shown here has not begun his dissection by opening the abdomen and removing the intestines, which are most prone to putrefaction, but has started (and this too may imply a punitive dimension to the act) by dissecting the offending hand. Now, this hand is most peculiar. It is not only grotesquely out of proportion compared with the hand closer to us, but is also anatomically the wrong way round: the exposed tendons, which ought to be those of the left palm, given the position of the thumb, are in fact those of the back of the right hand. In other words, what we are faced with is a transposition taken from the anatomical atlas, evidently without further reflection, that turns this otherwise true-to-life painting (if one may so express it) into a crass misinterpretation at the exact centre point of its meaning, where the incisions are made. It seems inconceivable that we are faced here with an unfortunate blunder. Rather, I believe that there was deliberate intent behind this flaw in the composition. That unshapely hand signifies the violence that has been done to Aris Kindt. It is with him, the victim, and not with the Guild that gave Rembrandt his commission, that the painter identifies. His gaze alone is free of Cartesian rigidity. He alone sees the greenish annihilated body, and he alone sees the shadow in the half-open mouth and over the dead man's eyes. . .'

W.G. Sebald
Translated from the German by Michael Hulse

Interment

We walked from the lych gate,
The undertakers' men
Shuffling like a centipede
Professionally solemn
While we, the amateurs,
Followed on behind
Learning by doing,
Actors trying not to act
True feeling and propriety
In uncertain harmony.

They led us past the graves
Of those who had themselves
Shuffled off this world
Graves aslant
Like copperplate
On the page
Telling us
What we would not
Hear

We were too few
To sing the songs we knew
Too many
To claim the privacy we craved.
There, where my own birth
Was inscribed,
And memories were stirred
My mother,
Our Sister,
Was summoned unto God
Sung to her rest
By a boy
Whose voice
Was light
Turned
Into
Sound

Then to the
Cheap theatrics
Of the crematorium
With its perfunctory prayers
Synthetic tunes
And velvet curtain
Gliding oh so reverently
On silent motors
As if you might expect
The departed to appear
Once more
To take a bow

Then on into the air
With two more funerals ahead
And one behind
And other strangers shedding tears
For other years
Come
To
Nothing

And the drive back
Like a family when the bride has left
Laughing, even, remembering
But ultimately bereft.
The ceremony complete
We claim her back
From those who carried her
Those who committed her
Those who burned the past.
For now she is ours again
At last

Christopher Bigsby

The Goose

I

When Hermes gave that bit of a goose to the goose-farmer
it laid not only an egg
packed with gold but its leg
was a scaled-down version of a knight's in armor,

its beak done in a pinch
of gold so fine it might have been beaten by some master gilder
described by Pliny the Elder,
give or take a thousandth of an inch.

II

About as deep, then, as the melanoma
they diagnosed in one old friend, so taking it upon themselves to dig
a hole in her as long as the main street in Omagh.

III

As if they hadn't already made enough room –
for *whatever* it is – when they went after another's ovaries and womb.
Yesterday she drove down to Newry to buy a bit of a wig.

Paul Muldoon

Zen Sang at Dayligaun

As a' we ken o the sternless derk
is the warld it fa's amang
a' we hae o the burn and birk
is thir broon or siller sang

Each pair o een in lift or yird
micht hae them by anither
tho' the birk chants t' nae baist or bird
nor burn tae human brither

For the lyart sang's no' staneyraw,
thon gowden sang's no' stane
an' there's nae burn or birk at aw
but jist the sang alane

Don Paterson

dayligaun – twilight; *sternless* – starless; *derk* – dark; *birk* – birch; *siller* – silver;
een – eyes; *lift* – sky; *yird* – earth; *chants* – sings; *baist* – beast; *lyart* – silvered;
staneyraw – lichen; *gowden* – golden

L'Anguilla

after Montale

Northern muscle the eel
– greyblack all slimy
it flexes through our warm sea
our rivers and estuaries
then licks their bottoms
with its tongue its slime
tongue threading each muddy bum
– it likes shifting labyrinths
but it aims for the red granite
flicking its slick inches
snaking and thinning
an oiled slippy whip
cracking up and up
as the chestnut blossoms
burst white over its worm's
eye view inside the bosom
of dead water where this sperm
– tail and fins fletched
like love's arrow
in a ditch
in that dry or wet –
either way hairy – slit
where this sperm always fits
– a wee tiny bomb
kissing the ovum
then going *boom!*
in the palmy womb
this wet spark
burns green in the dark
only to break
and chitter in the wind dog's arc
over cities made desolate
– burnt out by hate
till its glister
coils moistly in the iris
like brother and sister
joined in perfect vision
– then bolts again
your fleshy slate
pencil – turns itself and nat-
ure around
warming the muddy ground

Tom Paulin

171

A Study of the Nude

Someone naked with you
will rarely be a nude.
A nude is never with just one.

Nude looks back at eveyone
or no one. Aubergine or bluish rose,
a nude is a generalization.

Someone has given their name
and face to be face all over,
to be the face of something

that isn't for caressing
except with the mind's hand.
Nude is the full dress of undressing.

At University

Puritans reckoned the cadavers
in Anatomy were drunks off the street;
idealists said they were benefactors
who had willed their bodies to science,
but the averted manila-coloured
people on the tables had pinned-back
graves excavated in them
around which they lay scattered in the end
as if exhumed from themselves.

Les Murray

Song of the Jewish Princess

My thunderer blew in through the door, autumn leaves swirling behind him, green and brown scraps of the fading year barbed on the frayed strands of his wild woollen cloak, dry twigs pinned on his shoulders under the wide strap that held his bag, one lone leaf poised like a dancer on the brim of his hat.

Today, he who was always on time, he who always closed doors behind him, he who held himself carefully in his own space, today he was tousled, windswept, his cheeks red, his nose glowing and bulbous, his eyes wrinkled against the winter wind, his mouth taut with hurry and cold against the grin that I knew could warm his face. Well, he said, what are you waiting for?

I hushed my body's desire to rush to him, and began to play.

I am the original Jewish princess. The authentic article. The instrument on which the real music, according to the text, can be played. Play me. I shall sound true to you.

It was a long day, stopping only for wine and bread, and the bitter goats' cheese Carlos had brought with him. He worked himself and us hard and did not talk to me, except to make points about the music. By early evening, I was shivering with tiredness and expectation. As we all walked through the cold stone halls to the Hall of Mirrors, I huddled into my own deep blue woollen cloak, the colour of the evening summer sky. Coming from the cold, the wave of heat in the Hall hit me full in the face. The guests hardly noticed our arrival, and scarcely nodded an ear in our direction as we began to play. As usual, Ferdinand and Isabella talked throughout, though I knew that any flaw in the performance would invoke sarcasm the following day.

Halfway through the evening, some late guests arrived, and as the huge wooden doors were opened to admit them, the gusting wind blew out all the candles – except for two; one behind me and one behind Carlos. Momentarily the Hall was in silence, and without any sense of pre-planning, Carlos and I began playing our star piece of the evening; strings, wind and voices flashed into the dark, and between verses Carlos and I improvised. For the first time that day he and I looked full at each other, our eyes, so alike, green flecked with brown, flashing across the Hall, each lured by the pool of light behind the other's head. I swear that we invented fire that night. Flame spiralled and pirouetted between our notes, and for those few moments, the chatterers were silenced.

At the end, the ripples of music bowed their way into the corners of the Hall, and we were applauded. Carlos nodded his head at me, in approval and desire.

I can pick up any instrument and bow or pluck or blow and it will speak. My mother was the same. The bow cuts deep and springy into the string and I curve my body in reply.

When Carlos came into my room, he shut the door quietly and carefully. We still did not speak. Under my blue woollen cloak, his body felt as familiar to me as my own. His green eyes held mine and as we deepened into each other, our movements fitted easily, as they always had.

Play me. I shall sound true to you.

Later we lay, my face nuzzled into Carlos's armpit, smelling cloves and camomile mixed with the acrid savour of satisfaction. There is something I must tell you, he said. I caught my breath. You're going back to her, I said, I knew it. It was only a matter of time.

He flipped himself over on top of me so that he could look at me. It isn't that, Isabella, he said. I began to cry. Every time I see you, I said, I feel it's for the last time. She won't let go. You can't leave the children. I hate goats' cheese.

He put his hand over my mouth. I bit his fingers. Isabella, he said, you must listen. And then he whispered. He was late this morning because he had heard that before very long all infidels would be banished from Spain. I am Jewish, Isabella, he said softly, and you know what that means. I must leave before I am killed.

I stroke him. I knew you were Jewish, I said. Not just because of this - many men are circumcised in this world of mixed races. I just knew. You couldn't know, he said. Not in the way the Inquisition will know, not in the way – I interrupted: I am coming with you, I said. No – he began. This time I put my hand over his mouth. Then I told him about my mother.

Never have an affair with a musician, she said. A scribe, a soldier, a goat farmer if you must, but not a musician. When I was tiny, she let me pluck the strings on her fiddle, showed me how she tightened the tension, let me hold the bow in my fat hand and promised that one day I would be able to play as she did.

She was right about that, although she did not live to hear it. She also didn't live to see me disregard her advice about musicians. No doubt she would have smiled. My father, you see, was an itinerant musician, a man from North Africa, a Jew, a wandering minstrel who probably left behind him as many children as musical memories. He came to our village one night, in the height of the summer. My mother's husband was away in the mountains, with the goats. It was late, no-one saw him arrive. My mother gave him shelter. He played to her. The next morning he wrapped his Ud, the instrument which is so like the courtly lute that every amateur plays here, and he disappeared. My mother described his fingers like spider's webs, trailing and caressing the strings, no frets to hurdle the fingers, allowing him to bend their tunes to his will. He was dark skinned. With green eyes.

My mother told me all this the night before she died. The soldiers came, looking for infidels. My mother was Jewish, but she thought no-one knew. She told me the story about my father, gave me her blue woollen cloak, and made me go and hide with the goats. Her charred body was flung on the ground some days later. I think about her often. I wonder how long it took for the thick earth to rot her flesh. I prefer to think about that than to wonder what the Inquisition did to her. I also worry, because I cannot remember the colour of her eyes.

When a string is ready to snap, it plays sharper and sharper. It cries for attention that can do it no good. My life is fraying at the edges. I begin not to sound true to myself.

The following afternoon, two musicians, carrying instruments, strolled towards the town walls. Carlos and I also each carried a small phial of poison. His alchemist friend assured him that anyone who took it would fall asleep long before the poison began to eat them away. We promised each other through our tears that we would die rather than be subjected to torture.

The soldiers on guard by the town walls laughed and applauded as we cavorted with our fiddles, mad court musicians aping their wandering minstrel brethren, a lower caste, vulgar and uncertain and despicable. So harmless and silly were we, that they allowed us to wander through the gates and serenade a flock of goats herded on a hill opposite.

I have left my texts behind me.

We slept in a field. Next day, lulled by the quiet of the countryside, we were reckless. A small town, sleepy in the early afternoon haze, suddenly came alive with shouts and screams. Soldiers and locals chased a small group of people, men, women and children. An old man tripped and fell, just beyond the entrance to the alley in which we hid. The crowd kicked him bloody and limp. Then they hurtled past us, knocking us aside and when they had passed, Carlos was no longer with me. I waited, huddled in an abandoned house, hoping he would come back. When it was dark I searched a little. The streets were strewn with dead and wounded. No-one dared to touch them. I dared not stay.

I have to learn how to improvise all over again.

Memory can be kind. I remember endless roads and fields, green streaked with brown, brown and green. I could not eat. I felt sick all the time. My fiddle opened doors to me, gave me beds and food. I took it all, and more often than not gave it to the next beggar I met on my way. I searched every face for the familiar mouth, for the green eyes. I learned that northern Italy, Mantova, Ferrara, Venezia even, were the places to go. I hardly noticed that my periods seemed to have stopped. The road changed everything. In any case, the real me was somewhere else, with a man whose hair curled over his collar, whose crooked nose could wrinkle in glee, whose eyes were like mine.

When I finally cried, my imagination flooded out of me. I bled for four days as I had never bled before. Now I knew that Carlos and his child were gone from me for ever. To the rest of the world, he had never been. To me, he could never be again; neither cloaked in rage, nor clear in love. Just misty in my music as I played.

My text comes from the heart. Nothing can be more authentic.

Giovanni has brown eyes. He is kind. He is good. He is my rock. He is calm and decisive, and he waits for me to love him. I should love him. I am grateful to him. After all, he picked me out, a grubby, weary, wandering minstrel, travelling round Italy, playing anywhere, and he made me into the highest in the land – in the region, anyway. I am the Duchess. Of course, no-one knows that I am Jewish. Merely that

I am Spanish. I speak Italian impeccably, but with a soft, sibilant accent. When I am asked when I left Spain, I say 1490; if I told them the true year, 1492, they might associate it with the expulsion of the Jews and wonder.

Musical Chairs

Curled up in the snow. Firm and snow. Warm inside and warm outside. His body cradled   in a white shape, his head curled comfortably on a slightly higher mound, his arms folded across his chest, hands bunched inside his gloves, legs curled upwards, his knees touching his elbows. The watery sun glazes the snow, a translucent, bluish light seen through the curtains of his eyelids. His whole body is smiling. This, he thinks, is the garden of Eden. He could float for ever, weightless, free. No need to know whether he is in the air or on the ground, indoors or outside, in day or night, in silence or in sound. Moving or still. Asleep or awake. Voices or silence. F sharp or B flat. Whatever they are. Pussy cats or monkeys. A bubble of laughter tingles. Did he say these things out loud? It doesn't matter. No one can hear.

At first they thought I was dead. The doctor didn't want to loosen my clothes in the sub-zero temperatures. Speed was of the essence. They worked swiftly and silently, their boots scrunching in the snow, small grunts, tiny clouds of steam, warm air as they breathe out, evaporating as it cools rapidly. They laid me on a stretcher, a nod from the doctor and I was winched up to the helicopter. The rescue team strapped on their skis, ready to go back down the mountain. Under the top sprinkling of new snow, one of them found an empty whisky bottle. Lucky devil, they smiled, this probably kept him alive.

Arcs of sound criss-cross space, filaments, trajectories stringing through the pure air. The sounds are clean and white and sweet and have distance between them, as though they are being played by an invisible orchestra spread out in a gigantic semicircle, across an arctic continent as far as the eye can see, some of the players below the curve of the earth's horizon. How on earth can the conductor see them at all? As he strains to see, the players appear, scattered, wearing their prescription black and white. The white of men's shirts and the women's blouses is different from that of the snow, faint timbers, pink, lilac, peach, blue, as if reflecting the vibrancy of the living skin, the bare faces and hands, none of them affected by the cold.

In the helicopter, the first thing I said, even before I opened my eyes was, 'That Sibelius is a fucking great composer.' Someone laughed out loud in relieved hysteria.

Now he sees the conductor, wielding the baton, long hair swirling, head nodding and shaking in rhythm, long, flowing hair catching the light as it swirls and sways. Delicate hands hold the baton firmly. The conductor's back was towards him. Who was it? He ran through the names of all the conductors he knew. None of them had quite that combination of firmness and delicacy. Who could it be? There was something about the angle of the head, something – no. Impossible. It was no one he knew.

In the hospital I was crazy with impatience. 'I'm filming next week. I've got a thousand things to do. When can I go home?' They soothed me, muttered things about a hairline fracture on my collarbone, pulled the sheets more tightly round me, tucked them in, kept the bed neat and contained me in a white cocoon far more dangerous than the snow. The newspapers covered the story with appropriate headlines: 'Film director saved from avalanche.' I didn't see them. I didn't care.

The conductor disappeared. Now there were just the musicians, playing. Then the sound went. He can see them bowing and fingering and blowing and plucking but he cannot hear anything. Then, suddenly, the conductor is there, facing him. She is smiling. Jane stands before him, slim and exquisite in tie and tails, smiling. Smiling.

Be careful, they said. No coughing, no laughing, no vigorous exercise. If you promise to look after yourself, you can go home.

Damn her. She raises her arms, the baton held loosely in her right hand. She begins to conduct. She is facing him. She is conducting him. Common time, she says, this is in common time. Four in a bar. Four what in a bar? Come, now, you know what four in a bar is. Four men getting pissed out of their minds in the pub at the end of the road while I have to get the kids to bed and get ready for the concert. He screams. She turns away from him, back to the orchestra, raises her arms gently and leads them sweetly into the Adagio.

Back to London there were endless meetings. The composer's widow, retained as an advisor on his music, knowledgeable to a fault about his intentions. After all, hadn't she copied it all out for him in her own fair hand, so much more legible than his? Had he not entrusted her with the task of protecting his traditional airs and modern graces from any inappropriate interpretation after his death?

He screams again. The orchestra has gone. The vast expanse of snow is smooth and untouched. A white sheet crumpled and curled round two small bodies, their limbs flung easily and carelessly over his. God, what a flat. One large room, painted white, a kitchen area at one end, barely room for a table and chairs, certainly no room for even an armchair. The older two staying Saturday nights with him. Not the baby, of course. There they were, the three of them, cuddled under the blankets in that double bed. He fought Jane against their coming to stay, and ten minutes after they arrived, he knew he didn't want them to go away again. Ten minutes after he had delivered them back to Jane, he had flung himself back into work.

This project took off like a dream. I'd wanted to make a film about the composer for years, and when he died suddenly I thought I'd blown it. His widow, whom I knew well, told me about the last symphony. No one else knew he had been working on it. She asked my advice. She offered to play it through on the piano to me. I refused. No,

I said. I'll hear it when they rehearse it. What do you mean, she asked? I've got this marvellous idea, I said. I will raise money for a film, a co-production, with German television, with American television, with Japanese television, and I will make a film about his life, the film I always wanted to make, and the world premiere of his posthumous symphony will be on film. How about it? Crazy, eh. But not as crazy as I was for the whole of last year, sweet-talking the men with the money, with no more aesthetic sense than a rubbish bag, into believing they were a cross between James Agee and Dilys Powell. I was exhausted by the end of it, but successful. As always.

Their last holiday together was in Scotland. Their last family holiday. Caught the car-train, arrived in Perth and spent the first night in a bed and breakfast in Blairgowrie. The town bleak and desperate, full of bleak men. The local canning factory shut down six months before. On the window of the careers office a notice pleaded, 'Does your drinking cause you and your family problems? We don't ask you to give up your drinking, just come up and talk it over a cup of coffee.'

Supper that evening; there was reconstituted Scotch broth, darkened with an Oxo cube, salmon surrounded by salad and swamped with chips, a bottle of Heinz salad cream. Afters, thawed strawberries and cheesecake. The sound of a Hammond organ drifted into the dining room.

Later, the kids asleep, down in the bar, a nightcap whisky, and the lady of the house sits at the organ, her back to the room, the colour telly on, with the sound turned down. She plays 'Beautiful Dreamer' and 'Home on the Range'. Next morning, as they drive away, on a hill stands a lone piper, playing 'Scotland the Brave', the tone lifting the landscape, the tune drifting high above the fumes and the drizzle.

When I know what I want to make a film about, I find the form. I puzzle and puzzle and one day it all begins to come clear. I hate films of concerts, the audience sitting there, the players shiny, stuffed; I don't mind when I am at the concert myself, one of the audience, glorying in the excitement of the living music. I just can't stand seeing it on film. So I puzzled away for a long time about the best way to take responsibility for the world premiere of a symphony by a Scottish composer whose work had not been sufficiently appreciated during his lifetime. No concert, I thought. Then how play the music, how be seen to play the music for the first time, and the first time which would last forever, because it would be recorded on film? Rehearsals. That was the answer. I would film all the rehearsals, then I would intersperse the biographical stuff with the rehearsals for the posthumous symphony. There would be no need to hear the complate work, because by the end of the film, the complete work would have been heard. Brilliant. I love rehearsals, people turning up in any old clothes, the conductor making a mixture of esoteric musical jokes, sarcastic jabs, putting his whole body into the music, shaping it, guiding it, attacking it, and then standing back and letting the orchestra simply flow with what they have learned.

Jane had brought two scores with her. He didn't say anything, but she knew he didn't like her working on scores when they were together. Learn to read music, she'd say, then I can explain what I'm doing. I'll teach you. No need, he'd answer. He hated those lines and squiggles and splodges.

What instruments do you play, they asked me on chat shows? I don't play anything, I'd answer. I'm musically illiterate. How can you make films about musicians, then, they asked? Easily, I'd say. You don't have to be a soldier to make films about war. What is music, they'd say? I can't tell you, I'd answer. It's beyond words. It has nothing to do with anything else in my life. It has nothing to do with the words through which I try to make sense of the world and control my life. Music can be inappropriate to an occasion, it can be played out of tune, it can be boring, but it has the supreme virtue of being beyond words and that is why I like it. It is as simple as that. It sits in your head, like the most recent Boy George hit, or an advertising jingle or a string quartet. It inhabits you. Sort of like the music of the spheres, they'd say? Yes, I'd say, something like that.

Jane didn't understand. He didn't know how to explain it. Sooner or later people alwyas wanted your soul. Music simply had it. He gave it freely, voluntarily, willingly. He was Faust and the music was his Mephistopheles. The deal was simple. His soul, in exchange for the time it took to play a piece of music. Unlimited borrowing, with no fines for anything overdue. Or, if you preferred it, a bank full of time stored up in it, with interest paid gently, even with pleasure. The best sort of investment. Better than people. They always wanted your soul, sooner or later.

We spent the main part of the holiday in the hotel complex at Aviemore, ideal for the kids, and handy for walking. The baby bounced on my back or Jane's and the other two alternately moaned or looked forward to the treats of lunchtime miles away from everywhere, with a view totally lost on them. Sprigs of heather plucked from the summit of summer Cairn Gorm. On each stem, a full nine bells of pale purple flower, each bell pouting to a narrow opening, the hood protecting the delicate interior from the mist. Walking through the drizzle, carrying sprigs of heather. Small, spiky leaves, dark green, littering the stalk to its strong base.

One day we took a chairlift up to the middle station of Cairn Gorm, the kids screaming with excitement and fear as we floated above the burn, thrilled to bits as the chairs slowly came down to earth. Two parallel lines of rocks marked the path to the summit. Signs warned climbers to beware of sudden mists. I wondered what it would look like in the snow.

When he was three, some unnamed tragedy drove him to bed in tears. A toy music box, clutched in his hand, played "Baa Baa Black Sheep". The first hymn he ever heard in school, "Oh God, Our Help In Ages Past", stayed in his head for the whole week, carrying him through the strange newnesses. When he passed the eleven plus, "The Lord Is My Shepherd" (Crimmond) sang him through the summer holidays, tune and descant together. Buddy Holly rode by his side on a bicycle through university, and in early married life, Mozart made friends with the late Beethoven quartets. Then Jane took up her music again.

We didn't need to talk to each other much on holiday. Mostly we were sorting out the logistics of the day, dealing with the kids. Only there were some evenings when we faced each other across the dinner table, having sorted out the arrangements for the following day, when the little silences interrupted us. How was it that two people who were so closely related, who never lost the desire to touch each other, even after they had stopped touching each other; how was it that we couldn't make it work? We knew the obvious problems: Jane hated my world, the world of high-powered hustlers, a world peopled with acquaintances and not friends, a world I loved. And yet she liked my films. Always. And wanted me to make them. Me? I don't know. But every time she took out a book about music, or opened her manuscript book, I froze. I was always too busy to go to concerts with her, even before she started working again. Genuinely busy. With work like mine, there is always something important to do.

He can't take his eyes off the ground. He knows that if he looks up, he will be swirled away, the sky will whirl him into its vortex, the evil in him dragging him round and round, swinging his body by the head, gashing his flesh on the rocks, ripping his skin away.

We went to Loch Ness to look for the monster. We had tea in Inverness. We watched the salmon leaping obediently in Pitlochry. We climbed the steep path to Arthur's Seat. I held the kids' hands tightly, but I was more scared than they were. I couldn't take my eyes off the ground.

He remembers a joke told at a ceilidh. On the day of judgement all the men in the world get together to go to heaven, and when they get up there, St Peter says, all the hen-pecked husbands go to one side and all the non-hen-pecked-husbands go to the other. So there's a huge queue of hen-pecked husbands, and only one chap on the other side. So St Peter says to the one man, you must be a brave chap, and the man says, Oh no, I'm standing here because my missus told me tae.

We loved the ceilidh; the piano so sharp it was almost flat on the next semi-tone up. The kids clapped and stamped. The next morning we drove back to London, the kids tired, ready to go home. I took in the luggage while Jane made the tea. When the kids were in bed, we sat opposite each other in the kitchen we'd both planned, with the clock ticking quietly. We looked at each other. It was beyond words, this. I said, I'm going. Yes, said Jane, if you hadn't said it, I would have. So I packed some things and went to stay in the flat. I was a danger on the roads that evening, driving my car, crying and playing Dusty Springfield. I wanted her, I wanted me, I wanted us.

He knew exactly how he was going to do the film. All worked out. First all the biographical stuff would be shot, on location, of course, in Scotland. Then the rehearsals would be filmed in London, and then the wonderful process of editing would begin, the bit he loved more than any other, because it was in the editing that the world was finally built, and everything would fall into place. He had a week's holiday before it all started. He went skiing. On the last day, he caught a glimpse of the Arts page of an English newsaper. "Conductor sacked," it said. There it was, in black and white. The orchestra lined up to play in the film, had risen as one and rebelled against the conductor. Discontents that had been rippling for years finally came to a head. Crisis. The orchestra's work had to continue. "First Woman Conductor," said the subtitle, and there she was. Jane, slim and exquisite in her tails, holding her baton delicately, her arms raised. Smiling.

When I got back from holiday, I dumped my luggage in the flat and took a train straight to Scotland. I bought a bottle of whisky. I hired a car and drove to Cairn Gorm. The sun was bright on the bluish-white snow. I took a chairlift up to the middle. My head was empty. Nothing. No song, no music, nothing. I got out of the chairlift. Signs warned climbers about sudden mists. I took the top off the bottle and drank as I walked. When I found comfortable spot, sheltered from the worst of the wind, I sat down and finished the whisky. I was almost asleep before I got to the end. I was cosy, comfortable. I slid down in the snow, curled up and waited for the music of the spheres.

At first they thought he was dead. He was still, he didn't seem to be breathing. Then, when they realised he was alive, they worked swiftly and silently. When he had been put on the stretcher and winched up to the helicopter, the rescue team began strapping on their skis, ready to go back down the mountain. One of them nearly fell over something half-buried in the top sprinkling of new snow. Lucky devil, he said, this probably kept him alive. He's going to have one hell of a hangover.

There was really only one thing to do, and I found myself doing it almost without realising it. I phoned Jane. Did she know what a bastard I was on the set? She didn't doubt it, she said. Under the gentle, artistic exterior, I was as big a shit as anyone else. Yes, but did she mind, I asked? Of course she bloody minded, but I had to remember that she was a professional (as was I) and this was a job. She would give as good as she got if I treated her badly. Do we hate each other, I asked? I shouldn't think so, she said. We just can't live together. We get in each other's way. So what else is new? The music will be wonderful, she said. The orchestra is great.

When the committees nominated the film for its various awards, they always chose the same extract: in it an orchestra, dressed in its customary black and white, played the entire symphony, spread out in a gigantic semi-circle, scattered as far as the eye could see, some of the players below the curve of the earth's horizon. The white of the men's shirts and the women's blouses picks up timbres different from those of the snowy landscape: pink, lilac, peach, blue. Before them stands their conductor, slim, in tie and tails, her baton moving precisely, her long flowing hair catching the light as her head dips and sways.

Just before the film's premiere, I bought myself a book on the rudiments of music.

Michelene Wandor

From Eydon to Moreton Pinkney

He had no idea where he was, not a clue. The road, narrow and unmarked, was dark before and behind him with no trace of houselights or any other sign of human habitation. The verges were lush with undisciplined sloe, hawthorn and bramble, waving skeleton fingers against the darkening winter sky. This, and the total absence of signposting, suggested he was at least in Northamptonshire at last.

Visibility was dwindling dangerously, though it was only four o'clock: there were traces of fog drifting in the beam of his lights. Despite his desperate sense of urgency, therefore, he flipped on the hazard- and fog-lights, sat resignedly where he was, and prayed.

Some time later – hours? days? aeons? he glimpsed the friendly glow of headlights behind him: a muddy, aged four-wheel-drive loomed out of the darkness. The other driver, to his inexpressible relief, drew up.

'Y'allright, mate?' He rolled down the window and leaned out eagerly, incoherent with relief. The raw chill, prickling with moisture, slapped him in the face.

'Thanks for stopping. I'm totally lost. Where the hell am I?'

'Just outside Eydon.'

'Eden? Oh, *Eydon*. Look, d'you know how to get to Moreton Pinkney from here?'

'No problem. You're not far wrong.'

'Thank God for that. I'm so late –' the words burst out, but he was able to keep himself from saying more.

'Got 'em all waiting for you, have you?' said the voice in the dark, genially.

'I hope so', he said icily, intending to deflect further enquiry, but the man was incurious.

'Just keep on the way you're going. Go up to the crossroads. Turn right for Canons Ashby. When you get to Canons Ashby, turn right again. That's the road to Moreton Pinkney.'

'Right, and right again. That's marvellous. Thank you so much.'

'Any time. Hope you don't get stick when you get in, mate.'

Right, and right again. He stuck the key in the ignition, let in the clutch, and moved off as the red tail-lights of the Land Rover vanished round the next bend. Right. He was beginning to feel slightly ill with apprehension. He had a vision of Barbara's face, as he had last seen it: past anger, past anguish, merely looking through him with blank, tired eyes which conveyed a weary sense of his total irrelevance. As the car began to move, and his lights roved across the space where he had been waiting, memory suddenly caught him, triggered by the shape of the three tall trees caught in the beam. It was *the* layby. They'd just agreed to buy Over End House at Moreton Pinkney, more than they could really afford, but they'd loved it, and they'd decided to take the gamble. After a euphoric lunch in the pub, they'd gone off grinning like a couple of kids. As he drove back towards Bicester, they kept glancing at each other, then Barbara had reached over and squeezed his knee … and a minute later he spotted the layby, and parked the car. He could still remember her breathy giggle. 'Brian, we *can't*! don't be silly …' then he'd got his hand up her skirt, and she decided maybe they could … How old had they been then? Thirty two- or three, maybe? Jessica was about three, and Simon was still a baby. Barbara's mum had them for the day while they househunted, another reason he'd felt so frisky. Funny. When in your life do you stop doing things like that? He'd got so busy in the years after the move. More responsibilities. He'd got involved with the Düsseldorf partnership. More money. His worries about paying for Over End House had vanished, but so had any chance of making love to his wife, even at sensible hours, and in the matrimonial bed.

Right again ... the big house at Canons Ashby loomed up at the side of the road like a beached Cunarder, a few lights shining yellow and friendly. It receded behind him, and though it was dark, and foggy, he felt a terrible unease. You know the road home, even after years, and even in the dark, and it did not feel like the road to Moreton Pinkney. Not at all. Hedgerows, the powerful beam of his headlights picking up the road-surface, one little road looks much the same as another, but it was wrong, he could tell. Had he missed a turning? Had one of the farm-gate gaps in the bushy hedges actually been a road? There was a village coming up. Adstone. He must have overshot.

There's a pub at Adstone, he remembered, the Cross Keys. A charmless, barnlike affair in classic Northamptonshire style, the stone laid as alternating thin and thick courses so that the structure was longitudinally striped like a liquorice allsort. Pathetic hanging baskets totally failed to cheer it up in summer, the beer was terrible and the chips came out of a packet. He pulled the Rover up in the forecourt, and eyed it with misgiving. Light spilled from the small windows, fighting through the mass of cheery Christmas tinsel and artificial snow, accompanied by a dreadful, pulsating racket.

He pushed open the door. Karaoke night at the Cross Keys. My God. The room was full of people, jeering good-humouredly. There was a little stage at the end, dimly visible through trailing wreaths of cigarette smoke, surrounded by a battery of amplifiers and electronics and a tangle of Christmas decorations. A sweaty farmhand, a great bullock of a man in jeans and a Massey Ferguson teeshirt, was doing his Noddy Holder number to ironic applause.

Brian fought his way to the bar.

'Plain tonic water, please', he yelled. 'And –'

'AND HEERE IT IS, MERREE CHRISSMASS, EV'RYBODY'S HAVIN' FUN', blared the yokel. Some total bastard had turned up the amplifier.

'Can you tell me –'

'LOOK TO THE FUCHURE, IT'S ONLY JUST BEGU-U-UN!'

'*CAN YOU TELL ME THE WAY TO MORETON PINKNEY*!'

The barmaid, a stout, pudding-faced girl whose ponytail was decorated with tinsel, looked at him with bovine incuriosity.

'Yerwhat?' she mouthed. Looking at the change he handed her, she took out the price of his drink, and returned the rest, selecting out a couple of coins. She leaned across the bar to shout in his ear. 'These ain't legal tender no more!' she shouted, handing them to him separately. He shoved them all in his pocket, regardless.

'Can you tell me –' She had already turned away.

A burly, elderly man in a heavy fisherman's jersey touched his elbow, and, when Brian looked at him, he swallowed down the last of his pint and jerked his head meaningfully. Leaving his untouched drink on the bar, Brian followed him out. The older man opened the door, and they passed together from the warm fug of the bar to the cold fog of the car park.

'I'm more than grateful', he began.

'Don't give it no mind', said the other. 'I bin comin' to the Cross Keys for my pint this twenty year, and I'll go on comin' till I ain't comin' nowhere, but I kin do without that karaoke. It was Moreton Pinkney you was after, wasn't it?'

'Yes, that's right. I must've missed the road in the dark.'

'It's easy done, in these parts, if you don't live round here.' But I do, he wanted to say, yet the words stuck on his tongue. Was it still true?

'Look', said the old man. 'You see that road off the green? Go up there, and turn left. Then right at the next crossing, and that's the road to Moreton Pinkney.'

'Thanks very much.'

'Don't mention it. 'S nice to see family at Christmas, ain't it?'

Brian started the car, and set off again, following directions. The powerful engine purred obediently; he was held in a smooth cradle of hydraulic suspension. Walnut fascia, real leather upholstery. That had mattered a lot, once (though he had long been able to take it for granted), though Barbara could never see why. Another memory came welling up irresistibly: the first time he had a proper car. He'd kept the news to himself; laid plans from the office. Coming home in it triumphantly on the first of August, he remembered the intoxicating smell of newness, the smug, expensive crunch of brand-new wheels on the gravel. He opened the door and sat in the car, waiting for Barbara to come out and exclaim.

She had come out, he remembered, a tired, shabby-looking woman in a denim skirt and a plain cotton jumper, and stood looking at him as he sat, half in and half out of the car. And, the memory continued uncomfortably, after a half-minutes' slow burn, she had exploded.

'I don't believe it. What's *happened* to you, Brian?'

'But –'

'You went and bought a car. And I suppose you'd totally forgotten it was Simon's Sports Day?' He had. He had forgotten completely. He'd been in so late all that week, he hadn't actually seen the kids since the previous weekend. He sat silent, furious; furious with himself, furious, above all, with Barbara for making him feel guilty when he was the one who supported the whole pack of them. 'Can you even remember what the child looks like? He's up in his bedroom, trying not to cry. Just go to hell, Brian. And take that bloody car with you.' Then she had stalked back into the house, and slammed the door.

He turned right. That was a bad moment, God, it was a bad moment. He hadn't wanted to remember it. He had been so angry, and so hurt, they had barely spoken for a month. He'd been offered a long trip to Düsseldorf, six weeks, and he had jumped at it. And in Düsseldorf, he had met Liesel … and for a while, Liesel had seemed like the answer to the whole mess … This was not the road to Moreton Pinkney. A few minutes later, he saw the sign for Weston: he had gone wrong somewhere. He kept going. There was little traffic on the road so near Christmas, but he could see headlights flashing as they breasted a distant hill. He slowed, and flashed his lights; the other driver stopped.

'Sorry to trouble you, but can you tell me the way to Moreton Pinkney?'

'No problem. You're headed for Helmdon. Get yourself turned round, and go back the way you came till you get to the t-junction. Turn right, and at the next junction, turn right again.'

'Cheers, mate'. The voice from the dark wound up his window, and drove on.

Brian drove on cautiously, looking for a turning-place in the pitch dark which was not a farm-track, afraid that if he got off the tarmac, the heavy car would stick fast. It was too big to attempt a three-point turn on so narrow a road without getting into the verges. It was raw-cold, and when he let it into the car, the fog caught in his throat, but it was not freezing: the sticky Northamptonshire clay would hold fast if it got half a chance. Half a mile further down the Helmdon road, he found a turning point which looked reasonably safe, and headed back towards Weston. He was beginning to lose his temper. What had happened to the bloody roads? They were winding, countrified and difficult, but he couldn't remember them being this bad.

Liesel had laughed at him for living in the country. 'It is your English fantasy', she said, 'but it is so inconvenient, and there is no culture.' Liesel had been a big mistake, looking back. And she had got to be a habit, so when she chucked him for bloody Hansi, he'd been all softened up for that evil little cow Michelle. Michelle saw the point of living in the country, oh, yes. You could always find the latest *Country Living* somewhere in the flat. The trouble was, she saw herself as the second wife with the old house, the new Aga, and the Smallbone of Devizes kitchen. His second wife, to be precise. Barbara never knew about Liesel – he was pretty sure about that – but Michelle had made damned sure she knew about Michelle, the conniving bitch.

He was desperate to see Barbara again. Michelle worked out in a gym; her stomach was lean and flat, her toenails immaculately polished; she attracted admiring glances wherever she went. Barbara was his own age, and looked it; she hadn't risked a bikini for years. But unlike Michelle, she'd always seen him as a man, not a means to an end. Not always a good man, not always the man he would have liked to be, or the man she would have liked, but a man. And he was so tired, so lonely. He'd swop all the tapas and designer water in the world for fishfingers and chips with his own wife and children, and he knew he'd pissed it all away.

There was a car moving up on him, a big car, fast, its driver arrogantly failing to dip his headlights. Brian's anger stirred. Two could play at that game. He accelerated, his own lights still on full beam; they raced each other down the narrow country road. He could see nothing of the vehicle behind him; his rearview mirror was blinding with white light, but he could sense its power. It picked up speed smoothly, and in a moment, it was by his side, a lethal overtake; they raced neck and neck, then the other pulled ahead of him, and slid triumphantly in front. A t-junction was coming up; without slowing, the big car slid majestically leftwards, and as it did so, Brian, braking for the junction, caught a glimpse of its numberplate.

X registration. X? But there weren't any X registered cars; they only went up to V. His own headlights caught the signpost at the junction: Canons Ashby. Somehow, he had missed Moreton Pinkney again, while his mind was preoccupied with the other driver. Surely it was illegal, even for vanity plates ...? Some new thought was tapping at the back of his mind; with vast, dismayed reluctance, he let it in. There *were* X registered cars, and he would never get to Moreton Pinkney. He would never get anywhere, because he had finally and definitively gone to hell in his big car.

Jane Stevenson

Remember This Moment, Remember Us

It is nearly Christmas and Rick is getting quite drunk at a party in a friend's clothes shop. It is a vast shop in a smart area of West London, and tonight the girls who work there have got dressed up in shiny black dresses, white velvet bunny ears and high shoes. When Rick and Daniel arrive the girls are holding trays of champagne, mulled wine and mince pies. Has there ever been anything so inviting? The girls help Rick's son Daniel out of his pushchair, remove his little red coat and show him to the children's room where remote-controlled electric toys buzz across the floor. There is a small seesaw; several other local children are already playing. Rick sits on the floor and Daniel, though it is late for him, chases the electric toys, flings a ping-pong ball through the open window and dismantles a doll's house, not understanding that all the inviting objects are for sale. Rick began drinking an hour earlier. On the way to the party they stopped at a bar nearby where Rick used to go when he was single. There, Daniel, who is two and a half, climbs right up onto a furry stool next to his father, sitting in a line with the other early evening drinkers. 'I'm training him up,' Rick says to the barmaid. 'Please, Daniel, ask her for a beer!' 'Blow-blow,' says Daniel. 'Sorry?' says Rick. Daniel holds up a book of matches. 'Blow-blow.' Rick opens it and lights a match. 'Again,' Daniel says, the moment he's blown it out. He extinguishes two match books like this, filling the ash-tray. As each match illuminates his face, his cheeks fill and his lips pucker. When the light dies, the boy's laughter rings out around the fashionably gloomy bar. 'Ready, steady, blow-blow!' 'Blow-bloody-blow,' murmurs a sullen drinker. 'Got something to say?' says Rick, slipping from the stool. The man grunts. Rick persuades the kid to get into his raincoat and put on his hat with the peak and ear-flaps, securing it under his chin. Rick slings the bag full of nappies, juice, numerous snacks, wipes and toys over his shoulder and they go out into the night and teeming rain. It has been raining for two days. News reports state that there have been floods all over the country. The party is about ten minutes walk away. Rick is wet through by the time they arrive. His successful friend Martin with the merry staff in the big lighted shop full of clothes Rick could never afford, embraces him at the door. Martin has no children himself and this is the first time he has seen Daniel. The two men have been friends since Martin designed and made the costumes for a play Rick was in, on the Edinburgh fringe, twenty years ago. Rick congratulates him on receiving his MBE and asks to see the medal. However, there are people at Martin's shoulder and he has no time to talk. The warm wine in small white cups soon cheers Rick up. Rick hasn't had an acting job for four months but has been promised something reasonable in the New Year. He has been going out with Daniel a lot. At least once a week, if Rick can afford it, he and Daniel take the Central line into the West End and walk around the shops, stopping at cafes and galleries. Rick shows him the theatres he has worked in; if he knows the actors, he takes him backstage. Rick's other children, who live with his first wife, are in their late teens. Rick never not wants to have a child in the house. When he can, he takes Daniel to parties. Daniel has big eyes; his hair has never been cut and he is often mistaken for a girl. People will talk to Rick if Daniel is with him, but he doesn't have to make extended conversation. As the party becomes more crowded and raucous, Rick chats to the people he's introduced to while drinking steadily. Daniel is given juice which the girls in the shop hold out for him, crouching down with their knees together. Quite soon Daniel says 'home dadda'. Rick gets him dressed and manoeuvres the pushchair into the street. They begin to walk through the rain. There are few other people about, and no buses; it is far to the tube. A taxi with its light on passes them. When it has almost gone, Rick jumps into the road and yells after it, waving his arms, until it stops. As they cross London, Rick points at the Christmas lights through the rain-streaked windows. Rick recalls similar taxi rides with his own father and remembers a photograph of himself, aged six or seven, wearing a silver bow-tie and fez-like Christmas hat, sitting on his father's knee at a party. At home Rick smokes a joint and drinks two more glasses of wine. It is getting late, around ten thirty, and though Daniel usually goes to bed at eight, Rick doesn't mind if he is up. They eat sardines on toast with tomato ketchup; then they play loud music and Rick demonstrates the Hokey-cokey to his son. Anna has gone to her life-drawing class but is usually home by now. Why has she not returned? She is never late. Rick would have gone out to look for her, but he cannot leave Daniel and it is too wet to take him out again. When Rick lies on the floor with his knees up, the kid steps onto him, using his father's knees for support. Daniel begins to jump up and down on Rick's stomach, as if it were a trampoline. Rick usually enjoys this as much as Daniel. But today it makes him feel queasy. Yesterday was Rick's forty fifth birthday, a bad age to be, he reckons, putting him on the wrong side of life. It is not only that he feels more tired and melancholic than normal, but wonders whether he can recover from these bouts as easily as he used to. In the past year two of his friends have had heart attacks; two others have had strokes. Time is rushing at him. He guesses that he passed out on the floor. He is certainly aware of Anna shaking him. Or does she kick him in the ribs too? He might be drunk, but he has to inform her immediately that he is not an alcoholic. However, Rick feels strange, as if he has been asleep for some time. He wants to tell Anna what happened to him while he was asleep. He finds some furniture to hold onto, and pulls himself up. He sees Daniel running around with a glass of wine in his hand. 'What's been going on?' Anna says. 'We went out,' Rick says, pursuing the boy and retrieving the glass. 'Didn't we, Dan?' 'Out with dadda,' says Daniel. 'Nice time and biscuits. Dadda have drink.' 'Thanks Dan,' Rick says. Rick notices he has removed Daniel's trousers and nappy but omitted to replace them. There is a puddle on the floor and Daniel has wet his socks; his vest, which is hanging down, is soaked too. Rick shakes himself into some kind of animation. Sometimes Anna tells him how much she envies the way father and son get along but he can see she isn't in the mood to repeat this tonight. He says to her, 'You think I was asleep but I wasn't. I was thinking, or dreaming, rather. Yes, constructively dreaming...'. 'And you expect me to ask what about?' 'I had an idea,' he says. 'It was my forty fifth birthday yesterday and a good time we had, too. I was dreaming that we were writing a card to Dan for his forty fifth birthday. A card he wouldn't be allowed to open until then.' 'I see,' she says, sitting down. Dan is playing at her feet. 'After all,' he continues, 'like you I think about the past more and more. I think of my parents, of being a child, of my brothers, the house, all of it. What we'll do is write him a card, and you can illustrate it. We'll make it now, put it away and forget it. Years will pass and one day, when he's forty five with grey hair and a bad knee, he'll remember it, and open it. We'll have sent him our love from the afterlife. Of course, you'll be alive then but it's unlikely that I will be. For those moments, though, when he's reading it, I'll be vital in his mind. What d'you say Anna? I'd have loved to have received a card from my parents on my forty fifth birthday. All day I thought one would just pop through the door, you know.' He is aware that she has been drinking, too, after her class. Now, as always, she begins to spread her drawings of heads, torsos and hands out on the floor. Daniel ambles across the big sheets as Rick examines them, trying to find words of praise he hasn't used before. She is hoping to sell some of her work eventually, to supplement their income. She says, 'A card's great. It's a good idea and a sweet, generous gesture. But it's not enough.' 'What d'you mean?' he says. He goes on, 'You might be right. When I was dreaming, I kept thinking of the last scene of Wild Strawberries.' 'What happens in it?' 'Doesn't the old man, on a last journey to meet the significant figures of his life, finally wave to his parents?' 'That's what we should do,' she says. 'Make a video for Daniel and put it in a sealed envelope.' 'Yes,' he says, drinking from a glass he finds beside the chair. 'It's a brilliant idea.' 'But we're quite drunk,' she says. 'It'll be him sitting in front of it, forty five years old. He'll turn on the tape at last and -' Rick says, 'There won't even be tapes then. They'll be in a museum. But they'll be able to convert it to whatever system they have.' She says, 'My point is, after all that time, he'll see two pissed people. What's his therapist going to say?' 'Well,' he says. 'I don't mind that. I'm not ashamed. Don't we want him to know that you and I had a good time sometimes?' 'Okay,' she says. 'But if we're going to do this, we should be prepared.' 'Good,' he says. 'We could -' 'What?' 'Put on white shirts. Does my hair look too flat?' 'We look okay,' she says. 'Well I do, and you don't care. But we should think about what we're going to say. This tape might be a big thing for little Dan. Imagine if your father was to speak to you right now.' 'You're right,' he says. His own father killed himself almost ten years ago. 'Anna, what would you like to say to Dan?' 'There's so much... really, I don't know yet.' 'Also, we've got to be careful how we talk to him,' he says. 'He's not two years old in this scenario. He's my age. We can't use baby-voices or call him Dan-the-Noddy-man'. They dispute about what exactly the message should be, what a parent might say to their forty five year old son, now only two and a half, sitting there on the floor singing 'Incy-Wincy Spider' to himself. Of course there can be no end to this deliberation: whether they should give Daniel a good dose of advice and encouragement, or a few memories, or a mixture of all three. They do at least decide that since they're getting tired and fretful they should set the camera up. While she goes into the cellar to find it, he makes Daniel's milk, gets him into his blue pyjamas with the white trim, and chases him around the kitchen with a wet cloth. She drags the camera and tripod up into the living room and gets it ready. Although they haven't decided what to say, they will go ahead with the filming nonetheless, certain that something will occur to them. This spontaneity might make their little dispatch to the future seem less portentous.Rick lugs the Christmas tree next to the sofa where they will sit for the message and turns the lights on. He regards his wife through the camera. She has let her hair down. 'How splendid you look!' She asks, 'Should I take my slippers off?' 'Anna, your fluffies won't be immortalised. I'll frame it down to our waists.' She gets up and looks at him through the frame, telling him he's as fine as he'll ever be, too. He switches the camera on and notices there is only about fifteen minutes worth of tape left. It will be sufficient; it will have to be. With the camera running he hurries towards the sofa, being careful not to trip up. They will not be able to do this twice. Noticing a half-eaten sardine on the arm of the sofa, he drops it into his pocket. When Rick sits down he knows this will be a sombre business for he has been, in a sense, already dead for a while. Daniel's idea of him will have been developing for a long time. The two of them will have fallen out on numerous occasions; Daniel might love him but will have disliked him too, in the normal way. Daniel could hardly have anything but a complicated idea of his past, but these words from eternity will serve as a simple reminder. After all, it is the unloved who are the most dangerous people on this earth. The light on top of the camera is flashing. As Anna and Rick turn their heads and look into the dark moon of the lens neither of them speak for what seems a long time. At last Rick says 'Hallo there,' rather self-consciously, as though meeting a stranger for the first time. On stage he is never anxious like this. Anna, also at a loss, copies him. 'Hallo Daniel, my son,' she says. 'It's your mummy.' 'And daddy,' Rick says. 'Yes,' she says. 'Here we are!' 'Your parents,' he says. 'Remember us? Do you remember this day?' There is a silence; they wonder what to do. Anna turns to Rick then, placing her hands on his face. She strokes his face as if painting it for the camera. She takes his hand and puts his fingers to her lips and cheeks. Rick leans over and takes her head between his hands and kisses her on the cheek and on the forehead and on the lips, and she caresses his hair and pulls him to her. With their heads together, they begin to call out, 'Hallo Dan, we hope you're okay, we just wanted to say hallo -.' 'Yes, that's right,' chips in the other. 'Hallo!' 'We hope you had a good forty fifth birthday, Dan, with plenty of presents'. 'Yes, and we hope you're well, and your wife, or whoever it is you're with.' 'Yes, hallo there...wife of Dan -' 'And children of Dan,' she adds. 'Yes,' he says. 'Children of Dan - however many of you there are, boys or girls or whatever - all the best!' he says. 'A good life to every single one of you!' 'Yes, yes!' she says. 'All of that and more!' 'More, more, more!' Rick says. After the kissing and stroking and cuddling and saying hello, and with a little time left, they are at a loss as to what to do, but right on cue Daniel has an idea. He clambers up from the floor and settles himself on both of them, and they kiss him and pass him between them and get him to wave to himself. When he has done this, he closes his eyes, his head falls into the crook of his mother's arm, and he smacks his lips; and as the tape whirls towards its end, and the rain falls outside and time passes, they want him to be sure at least of this one thing, more than forty years from now, when he looks at these old-fashioned people in the past sitting on the sofa next to the Christmas tree, that on this night they loved him and they loved one another. 'Goodbye Daniel,' says Anna. 'Goodbye,' says Rick. 'Goodbye, goodbye,' they say together.

Hanif Kureishi

New Year's Diary

On New Year's Day I have stomach pains but put them down to over-indulgence, nothing more. They're a little worse next morning but I try to ignore them and struggle into the office: my boss is away, and it's up to me to get the week's work done. Only when I start sweating, and realise I've been reading the same paragraph for half an hour, do I concede defeat. From home, in Greenwich, I call my parents, who're GPs in Yorkshire. 'Sounds like appendicitis,' they say as I describe the symptoms. 'Best check it out at the local hospital.'

Most of us, if we're lucky, see little of hospitals, until old age. But thirty years of television soaps make the place seem strangely familiar. My admission, from A & E, passes in a drama-documentary haze. I'm put in a gown, a sort of paper toga, which tears in half almost at once. I'm addressed by the wrong name, despite the name-tags round my wrist and ankle, and this seems normal, since I'm not myself. I have my possessions ticked off and put in safekeeping, though no one will take responsibility for my wallet, which I have to carry round, miser-like, for the next two hours, while I'm wheeled about for various tests and x-rays. The porters carry two-way radios, like dockers loading cross-channel ferries: the height of efficiency, it seems, though for long periods I'm left sitting about in empty corridors, along with unoccupied wheelchairs, empty trolleys and laundry-baskets.

No one seems sure what's going on, least of all me. But things begin to happen nonetheless. Round midnight I'm wheeled into surgery to have my appendix out. A routine operation, though I don't feel very routine when I wake next morning, dehydrated after the general anaesthetic, two drips in my arm, and all stitched up below my navel, at the spot they call MacBurney's Point.

The ward I'm put in is all-male – six beds, whose occupants are matey and attentive. A nurse attaches my drip to a pole on wheels, a kind of mobile lamp-post, so that, once I'm fit enough, I can walk around (like Gerard de Nerval going round Paris with his lobster on a lead). There's a cheery hospital radio to listen to, though no one does. There's food three times a day, but no one's much interested in eating: the baskets of fruit which visitors bring lie untouched, fruit suddenly seeming too acid, not bland enough. (Only the healthy care about healthy eating.) There isn't much appetite for reading, either, which is just as well since none of the reading-lamps seem to be working. Are these lamps victims of cutbacks, or has no one bothered change the bulbs? I ought to ask someone. But for now I prefer to lie there.

It's a cruel time of the year to be in hospital. The new year sun shines in like a promise but this isn't a place for resolutions or fresh starts. Most of the patients are old and, as the Larkin poem has it, 'here to confess that something has gone wrong'. Mornings are the worst. We have our drugs, wash, breakfast and newspapers, yet it's still only nine o'clock and the prospect of a ward-round – and the chance to discuss things with a doctor – looks as remote as the world outside the window. 'Long day ahead,' someone usually says around now. Or: 'How you feeling?' 'Worse, if anything, today.' Still, those past pension age seem to agree that they're 'better off in here', where it's warm, than they would be at home or braving the streets. 'Snow's all right for kiddies. But when you get to my age...'

For some, spending winter in hospital has become a way of life – the poor man's equivalent of wintering in the Bahamas. Mr McMahon, in the corner, is here with an unspecified chest complaint. An ex-rag and bone man (he even looks like Steptoe), he has come from a North London hostel – 'I got a room there, with three radios and twenty shirts' – and this seems to be his migratory pattern: a shuttling between hostel and hospital. 'Ten London hospitals I bin in. There's Guy's, University College, the Temperance, the London Hospital...' Outside, he spends his pension and social on horses; in here he can't, and funds accumulate: 'Last time I come out of University College, I had over two hundred quid to spend.' Unlike the rest of us, who're happy to be bed-bound, he spends his day in an upright chair ('better for mi chest') and twice a day demands his 'nibble-iser', clamping a green mask on and inhaling deeply. There are endless squabbles with the nurses over this piece of equipment, about how often he's allowed it and whether it's doing him any good. 'Tell me, John, how long can a man live if he's always constipated?' he says, as though to settle the argument. 'John' is his name for everyone, even the nurses.

Mr McMahon, it becomes clear, is working himself up to a big row, after which he'll leave and go back to gambling. In the meantime, his ranting Pinteresque monologues help us through the day. Addressed always to John yet directed at no one in particular (he sits hunched, avoiding our eyes), they often circle back to a woman called Mary: 'Tell you how I met her, John. There was this hole in a fence, see, which I nips through into the park to have a kip. Only when I try to stretch out on a bench, there's this couple on it, having a shag. 'Clear off', the woman says. So I do. But she gets a glimpse of me, see. And two days later I run into her and she asks can she come and live with me. Oh, she were a wicked woman, that Mary. Tell you how it finished, John. We wus at the dogs, see, with two mates of mine and their wives, and I went to buy four coffees for them and two teas for us. When I gave her her tea, she says 'Is that all you think I'm worth, then, a filthy cup of tea?' – and she throws it over me and then rips me shirt down the front. Well, I kicked her out after that, kicked her out I did.' These monologues continue all day – selling tips at the dogs, working a fiddle with soap at East End markets, being nicked for stealing a bundle or rags in Leyton. We are a captive audience of four. Mick works at Smithfield and has torn his back muscles while lifting sacks. Harry has trouble 'down below' and sits on a rubber cushion bleeding gently into his pyjamas. Steve works in the wine cellar of a central London hotel and after one operation on a ruptured appendix has now had a second to remove blood clots from his legs (lucky me, who had mine caught before it perforated). Is it politeness or fascination that keep us silent? Whichever, no one tells Mr McMahon to shut up.

Only the nurses interrupt him, with their four-hourly routine of temperature, pulse, blood pressure and banter. 'Good day, gentlemen,' is the usual greeting, followed by 'Gawd, you're a miserable bunch today.' 'And how are you, young man?' is reserved for the elderly. There's a pressure to respond: not to be cheery looks like ingratitude. When one nurse accuses me, 'I've not seen you smile since you came in,' I assure her I've never been happier in my life. The day nurses are young and inexperienced, the night staff Irish or Afro-Caribbean and much tougher. Morale is high, despite the low rewards (us lot) and appalling pay. Between tasks, the nurses gather round a huge tin of Quality Street, laughing and pigging themselves. Then there are the cleaners, who double as dinner ladies. They're friendly, brisk, mostly Italian and keep a close eye on our solids and fluids. Only once is there any unpleasantness. Mr McMahon's bedpan – a flat-bottomed bottle, like a Sicilian peasant's gourd – is left unemptied by his bed, and the cleaning lady steps on it, tipping it over her foot. Dabbing at her shoe with a tissue, she complains as bitterly as she dares: 'It's not nice.' Mr McMahon blames the nurses – 'They should have emptied it. I told 'em' – and eventually, with a show of gallantry, does the job himself. But it ruins both their mornings.

Few patients make it to the television room down the corridor. I turn up one evening and find it full of visitors watching Parkinson. VISITORS ARE NOT ALLOWED TO SMOKE IN THIS ROOM says a large sign, but they pay it no attention. The six of them seem to be together, all one family. Giving up on the person they're visiting, they settle in for an evening's viewing and chatter noisily between fags. Resentful, claiming priority, in need of convalescent quiet, I stand up and switch channels ('No one watching this especially...?'), to something on Channel 4 – archaeology, opera – that I hope will clear the room. It works.

The following evening, my last, a new patient is put in the next bed. He's 88 and has just had an operation for a stomach ulcer. There's one drip in his arm, another at his side, a third taped to his nose, an oxygen mask over his face, and a loud hissing noise. His wife (same age: married for 64 years) sits holding his hand, waiting for him to come round. Nurses try to wake him, without success. His wife points out that he's deaf but she can't remember in which ear. By the time they find the hearing-aid she has remembered and it's inserted in his right ear. 'Mr Willey...Mr Willey...MR WILLEY,' the nurses shout. Still no response. His wife is persuaded to leave and return next morning. Reluctant to go, she stand by his right ear: 'It's me, Jim. Good night, darling. I'm going to bed now, darling. Now be a good boy and I'll see you in the morning. Goodnight Jim, goodnight, goodnight.' As she leaves, a nurse notices that the tube from the oxygen cylinder is lying on the floor. Hence the hissing: for the past hour, it's us, not Mr Willey, who've been getting oxygen. The nurse quietly sticks the nozzle back on the cylinder. The doctor comes in at two and four but Jim doesn't stir till seven, and then only vaguely.

At nine, the hospital barber turns up: cropped hair, thick-lensed spectacles, white expressionless face – a bit like an executioner. Thank God we've all shaved already. But then the barber spots Mr Willey. No man has ever looked in less need of a shave, but hearing yet another person in a white coat ask him something he gives a grunt, which the barber takes to mean yes. The barber mixes his lather. It's too watery, and runs down Mr Willey's chin onto his chest, wetting his pyjama collar. It sploshes over the tube attached to his nose. It trickles into his open mouth. The barber moves with painful slowness: we all want it to be over. Finally, as the doctors arrive on their ward-round, the deed is done.

It's five days since my operation, and though the doctors insist I can't return to work for three weeks I'm allowed to go home. Hyper with drugs and relief, I dress, pack my bag, give Mr McMahon my four uneaten tangerines, and say goodbye. I'm in no state to reach a considered judgement on the National Health Service, but Greenwich District Hospital must have served me well or I'd not be leaving it so quickly. There've been moments in the past week when I've felt a Thatcherite fury at NHS inefficiency, and others when I've felt a sentimental wonder that something so utopian and free-to-all could have come into being in the first place. But mostly what I've felt has been a woozy affection for its mix of care and carelessness, management and muddle – an affection that makes me hope it will always be there.

Three days later, I go back to Greenwich District to have my stitches out, and in a fit of nostalgia revisit the ward. Mr Willey is out of bed and sitting in a chair. Mr McMahon, after an altercation, has discharged himself into the cold.

Blake Morrison

Just One Evening

Bob just sat propped up on his pillows. He wasn't in pain, didn't need food, medication, anything. He was there for observation. He'd haemorrhaged into the soft tissues in his thigh but luckily not into his hip joint. His blood pressure had dropped and they just wanted to keep an eye on him for a day or so. A and E was a strange place to be, but it had a bed free when he arrived, so that was that.

He had a room to himself, with its own washbasin, lavatory and television set. It was hot and they'd left the door open so that he could see the comings and goings in the main corridor and the nurses' station. He'd sat through a pleasant Friday afternoon, chatted with cleaners and nurses, been brought cups of tea and felt the usual warmth of being in a place where everything seemed geared to looking after him, taking away responsibility and giving him access to a sort of childhood dependence again. When he'd told Sandra, the little, brown-haired nurse who checked his temperature and blood pressure through the day, that it was like a four star hotel, she'd smiled and said, 'Just you wait.'

She was from Northumberland and, as she was tucking in his sheets and adjusting his pillows, she'd told him that she was heavily into slimming.

'What for? You look fine to me.'

'Ah, but I'm getting married in September.'

'So?'

'I've got to be measured for my dress in August. I want to be slim for that.'

'What, and then let yourself get back to normal again once you're married.'

'Yeah.'

She seemed not to notice the inconsistency.

'The physio'll be here tomorrow,' she said. 'You'll have to be careful, though. Don't want to start bleeding all over again.'

'Aye, it's a nuisance.'

'Think yourself lucky.'

'Why?'

'You're not on Warfarin for fibrillation, are you?'

'No.'

'The ones who are have to keep their levels much higher than yours. This happens to them all the time.'

Bob smiled at the matter-of-factness of her tone. She was talking about conditions that could erupt into people's lives and play havoc with everything and yet she gave it no more stress than her need to slim. He supposed she had to; there was too much mayhem around. If you let yourself get caught up with it, you'd go mental.

He heard the swish of wheels and saw a bed appear in the corridor. In it was an old man. He was either sound asleep or unconscious. His wild grey hair and beard spread around his face and a nurse was leaning over him as he was trundled along calling his name loudly and shaking him.

'James. James. Come on, love. Talk to me.'

There was no response. As the bed disappeared into one of the rooms off the corridor, Bob heard her voice insisting, still loud, still urgent. Sandra had taken no notice of it all.

'Not like "Casualty", is it?' said Bob, knowing that she must have heard the same remark hundreds of times.

'Wish it was like "E.R."', she replied, giving his blankets a final pat.

'Why?'

'George Clooney,' she said, doing a knee-trembling, fainting mime as she spoke the name.

'You'll have to make do with me,' said Bob.

She smiled, looked at him, cocked her head on one side and said, 'Bob, you're a fine-looking man. But you're no George Clooney.'

'I make up for it with my personality,' he said.

'I've noticed. Now, I've got work to do. See you later.'

She walked away down the corridor and Bob watched her. She was pretty and, in his eyes, had absolutely no need to slim. The sway of her hips and the bonus of her uniform gave A and E a distinct edge over any four star hotel.

The nurse calling for James to wake up had been joined by another but they were still having no luck. Apart from their voices, he heard only the background hum of quiet machinery – heating, air-conditioning or something. There was little movement; doctors and nurses strolled through the corridor, unhurried, carrying notes, stethoscopes, blood pressure monitors and things hidden under towels that Bob preferred not to speculate about. Each time he found himself inside a hospital, whether as patient or visitor, the ordinariness of it all surprised him. In rooms all over the building people were suffering, dying, having babies or being dragged back from the brink of some physical disaster. It was mysterious, magical, and yet those responsible for it went about their work as if they were stacking supermarket shelves. Their functions interlocked and overlapped. Cleaners brought the meals and the jugs of water and swept the floors; nurses nursed, physios physioed and doctors doctored. Most of all, it was the cleaners who brought it home to Bob. Whatever traumas and tragedies were going on, they quietly, patiently brought the drinks on time, pushed their mops over the floors and anchored the impossibilities in a dependable normality.

From the things the nurses were now calling to James, it was obvious that he'd woken up. They were asking him, still loudly, what he'd been drinking or taking.

'We need to know so that we know what to give you, sweetheart.'

James seemed as uncooperative as he'd been when he was unconscious but, patiently, the nurses repeated their questions over and over again and gradually seemed to be accumulating the information they needed. Bob put down his book and listened. It struck him that they were talking to James as if he were some sort of pet.

'There. That's a good boy. Yes. Good boy, James.'

He was surprised when he heard them repeat the man's date of birth. He worked out that he was just forty-three years old. When he'd arrived, he'd looked to be in his sixties.

Bob's mind drifted off as he listened and the monotony of the words and the heat in his room combined to make him drowsy. Before long, the book had slipped to the floor and he was asleep.

When he opened his eyes again, he seemed to be in a different place. He'd been woken by voices; loud, complaining, protesting voices. James was standing in the corridor right outside his door arguing with two nurses. He was stark naked but, from what he was saying, Bob realised that he was determined to discharge himself. There was blood on his chest and face. It seemed to have come from a head wound. Both nurses were wearing gloves. James was pushing them away, swearing and making the familiar throat-cutting gesture, presumably to frighten them into giving way. Somehow, in the face of all this, they still managed to speak sweetly to him, encouraging him, reasoning with him, trying to ease him back to his room.

'I'm wanting fucking out of here. You've no fucking right to keep me. Like a fucking gaol, so it is.'

'James, James. You can go when the doctor's had a look at you. You were very poorly when you came in and . . .'

'Fuck off, bitch.'

The other nurse took a different tack.

'OK, OK. Tell you what, James. You can't go out like that, can you?'

'Course I fucking can.'

'No. You'll be arrested. We need to get your clothes on.'

'Fuck off. Nobody dresses me. I'm not a fucking kid.'

'No, no, you can dress yourself. We'll leave you in your room to put your clothes on. Then we'll . . .'

'No. Fuck off. I don't trust any of you bastards.'

And so it went on. Bob recognised the stalemate as the nurses' seemingly boundless patience was met by James's aggressive obstinacy. Short of sedating him, there was no way out. It needed something unusual to break the deadlock. And it duly arrived.

The evening shift was coming on and, in charge of it was a woman well into her fifties. She was tall, slow of movement and wore a uniform different from that of the other nurses. The most surprising thing about her, however, was her accent. Her voice was low, caring, but she sounded as if she spent most of her time in Buckingham Palace or at Hunt Balls.

She came along to where James was still swearing and protesting. She seemed not to notice his nakedness as she pulled on her gloves and reached for his arm.

'Now, you've decided you'd like to leave us, have you?'

Even James sensed that something different was happening.

'So what?' he said.

'Well, I think that's very thoughtful of you. It's true that we are rather busy and the fewer patients we have, the easier it is for us.'

'Aye . . well . . .'

'It's very kind of you to help us, especially since you've had rather a lot to drink today. Shall we just put our clothes on and then we'll see what can be done.'

'Aye. Well, as long as these bitches here leave me alone.'

'They're not bitches, James. They're nurses.'

'Well, I'm sorry but . . .'

'I accept your apology. Now, I'd like you to co-operate with us. I think you should just go and have forty winks and then we'll see, eh?'

James looked around him, disorientated by the woman. He caught the eye of one of the nurses, made his throat-slitting gesture again and nodded, before turning to go back to his room.

It was the beginning of a long night for Bob. The position of his bed and his open door gave him the perfect spot from which to witness the Friday night activities. The quiet normality of the afternoon was replaced by scurrying nurses, a stream of patients in various drug or alcohol induced states, with wounds of all sorts, transfusions, drip feeds and a relentless clamour. When a nurse came to check his pulse and blood pressure, he got the impression that it was something of a relief for her. Sandra's place had been taken by Gemma, a mother of two, originally from Ireland, whose gentle accent was therapy in itself.

'Ah, you've a lovely, laid-back pulse there,' she said as another bed was wheeled past the door. In it was a young man, hooked up to a saline drip. The nurses were calling him Francis and asking the same things they'd been asking James earlier.

'Fuck off,' he said.

'How do you put up with it?' asked Bob.

'What?'

'This lot. The swearing, the ingratitude. I mean, these buggers are totally reliant on you to survive but they treat you like . . . well . . .'

'Shit?' said Gemma, smiling as she supplied the word for him.

'Yes.'

'You stop noticing it. No point in getting upset. Anyway, it's the drink talking. Or the drugs.'

Two police officers arrived and stood in the corridor; one male, one female.

'Who called us then?' asked the woman.

'Well, it wasn't the girlfriend, it was a male companion,' replied her colleague.

'Ah,' said the woman, as if that explained everything.

'But it's so personal,' said Bob. 'I mean, they're calling you a bitch, effing and blinding all over the place.'

'Yes, but then there's the charming fellas like yourself to make up for it all.'

Bob smiled and nodded towards the police officers.

'What're they here for?'

'Could be anything, but I think it's James,' said Gemma.

'Oh?'

'Yes, he's a regular. We've phoned the psychiatric hospital. He'll need to go there. But he won't be happy about it. I think they're here to help us.'

'What happens when he arrives there?'

Gemma's shrug was very expressive.

'He'll shout some more. They'll maybe give him something to quiet him. But they won't make a difference. Poor soul.'

On cue, James started shouting in his room again. The policeman and woman strolled along to his door. Bob saw that they, too, were wearing gloves. As they went into the room, a huge 'Fucking Hell' from James confirmed that he'd noticed their arrival.

'There,' said Gemma, hanging Bob's notes at the end of the bed. 'Now I'll go and get your neighbour settled.'

'Who's that?'

'Francis. Just admitted. Full of God knows what. Been drinking since lunchtime and taking all sorts of pills, so his pals told us. Dead to the world. He won't be bothering you.'

She went out and Bob listened as she joined the nurse already with Francis and began asking for the information they needed to bring him back from his oblivion.

The gulf separating the nurses from people like James and Francis seemed vast and it was easy to dramatise it. On the one hand, there was compassion, selflessness, concern; on the other, brutish egocentricity. It was the classic confrontation between good and evil. And Bob smiled as he realised his own place in it. He admired the nurses, was grateful for their caring, and yet their uniforms made them part of his fantasies. In some obscure oedipal way, his libido responded to having them settle him into his pillows, hold his wrist, smile at him and give him their full attention. It was like receiving maternal affection from someone almost young enough to be his daughter.

He felt a slight shudder as the thought came to him. At least with James and Francis the nurses knew where they were but his fantasies were more subtle violations. It was another reminder that this was a real A and E department, with none of the artificially concentrated drama of the television, but with layers of unspoken tension. As James swore his insults at them and the anxiety levels in all the other patients rose at his terrifying threats, the nurses continued calling him darling, speaking softly and offering tea and toast. They managed to preserve the balance. But, all the time, in the minds of some of their 'respectable' patients, their uniforms were being peeled from them and they were satisfying different appetites.

Another drunk staggered past his door, supported by a nurse. He, too, was bleeding. She was wearing gloves.

'What the fucking hell . . .' he began.

'Language,' said the nurse.

'Sorry. What the hell would somebody be bad to a nurse for when all she's doing is trying to help him?'

'It's the way of the world, darling,' said the nurse.

'Fucking awf . . . Ooops. Bloody awful world,' said the man.

The procession continued. Bob wasn't sure whether things had quietened down in James's room or whether the voices were just being lost in the rest of the hubbub. Derek, a patient in one of the other rooms nearby had been plugged into a heart monitor. Bob could hear the regular beeps that indicated that he was still with them. As the evening wore on, he began wishing that Derek would die so that the irritating noise would stop.

Gemma came in again just after ten; not for any specific reason, just for 'a breather' as she said.

'You wouldn't if you knew the things that go on in my head,' said Bob.

'Like what?'

'Fantasising about your uniforms,' he said. 'It's disgusting.'

Gemma laughed.

'Everybody does it,' she said.

She patted her stomach.

'You wouldn't like what you saw underneath anyway. I've had two kids. It's like a war zone down there.'

She talked about her kids. The six year old wanted to be a doctor, the eight year old a presenter on MTV.

'She's got her priorities right,' said Gemma.

A shout from James's room made them both look out into the corridor.

'No. Fuck you. That's it.'

It was James. He came out of the room, still naked but carrying a basket full of clothes. He sat on a chair and began pulling on the trousers.

'Oh God, no,' said Gemma.

'What?' said Bob.

'That's not his clothes. He's nicked them from another room.'

She went out and joined the others who'd come out of his room and gathered round him. It made quite a group; Gemma, two other nurses, two police officers and a hospital security man.

The effects of whatever had rendered him unconscious were wearing off fast. His language was even worse than before and the presence of the police had ratcheted up his aggression. He'd pulled the trousers on and everyone obviously thought that that was preferable to him being naked. But they still had to get him back to his room until the psychiatric nurses arrived.

'I'm not fucking going,' he shouted. 'Make me, you bastards. Go on. Make me.'

The policewoman reached for his arm.

'Don't touch me, you cow,' he said, his face jutting out towards hers so that he was just inches from her. Bob noticed the involuntary movement as she pulled her head back from the smell of his breath.

'Yeah,' said James, and, once more he slid his finger across his throat, slowly, with his eyes fixed on hers.

'OK,' said the policeman. 'Leave him with us. You get back to your real patients.'

Gratefully, the nurses went away down the corridor. The security man left too, to find out whether the psychiatric people were on their way. The two police officers and James stood just outside Bob's room. In the surprising silence that followed, Bob noticed that the beep of the heart monitor had stopped. Before he had time to wonder what it meant, Derek appeared in the corridor.

'Hiya,' he said to the police. 'Just off for a fag.'

'Good idea,' said the policeman.

'Fucking head off, that's all,' said James. 'Clean off. The bastards. Just the body there.'

'Don't get excited again,' said the policewoman.

'Listen, cow. Just fuck off.'

Again, he stared into her face and made the throat slitting gesture.

'I want to go home,' he said. 'I'm alright now. Better. Why can't I go home?'

'The doctors still need to check you out. You've had a knock on the head and we...'

'I'll knock you on the fucking head, pal.'

'Yeah, yeah. OK,' said the policeman, wearily.

'What d'you mean, "yeah, yeah",' said James. 'This is my fucking liberty we're talking about. You're stopping me doing what I fucking want.'

'Look, just calm down,' said the policewoman.

James turned to the policeman.

'Tell this fucking whore not to speak to me,' he said. 'She can keep her fucking mouth shut.'

'It'd be better if you did, too, sir,' said the policeman.

James lunged forward, jabbing his finger into the policeman's chest.

'Yeah? You fucking think so, do you? Fucking pigs. You're all the same. Just want to put me in the cells, don't you? That's it, isn't it? You blue bastards.'

And, to Bob's surprise, he actually slapped the policeman across the face. Astonishingly, the young man just shook his head.

'That's not a good idea,' he said.

'OK, do something about it, then. Come on. Fucking arrest me. Come on, you fucking coward. That's what you want, isn't it? I know you only . . .'

Moving more quickly than Bob would have thought possible, the policewoman suddenly produced a pair of handcuffs and clipped one of the bracelets on James's wrist. The other was already round her own.

'OK,' she said. 'You've got it. You're under arrest.'

'I thought so,' said James, somehow pleased that he'd been proved right. And, with another throat-slitting movement, he added, 'I'll have you, you fucking dyke.'

For the first time, the policeman seemed to notice that Bob was watching them.

'It's what he's wanted all along,' he said.

And, suddenly, they were gone.

After that, the blood, the swearing, the ingratitude continued but seemed more generalised, part of the fabric of the place. The episode with James had frightened and saddened Bob. The thought that this probably happened every week was depressing. When the matron, or head sister or whatever she was, came in to see him, he couldn't resist mentioning it.

'I know,' she said, her modulated tones once more sounding incongruous amid the curses and yelling of the patients. 'But one gets used to it. They don't mean it; it's the drink talking. It's just dissatisfaction really.'

'Dissatisfaction?'

'Yes. The week's work's over and they're just going out to find some sort of relief, a little pleasure to counteract the drudgery. And all they find is the same thing that they found last week, and the one before, and so on.'

'But how do you put up with the attacks? I mean, forgive me, but you don't sound as if you're used to this sort of language.'

The woman laughed.

'You'd be surprised. No, no. I do what I can here, then I go home and just close a door on it. My husband always pours me a huge gin and tonic and we listen to music and talk about other things.'

From the room next door came the sudden, urgent noise of Francis being violently sick. At last, his body had started to reject all the things he'd poured into it. He coughed, moaned and spluttered. Even the cough was a complaint; a cough which felt sorry for itself.

The woman stood up.

'Better get him cleaned up,' she said. 'At least he's coming round again.'

'Don't they disgust you?' asked Bob, marvelling at the contrast between her refinement and the coarseness that she was about to confront.

She smiled and shook her head.

'Certainly not. You're just seeing the effects. We know some of the causes.'

'I don't see . . .'

She held up a hand to stop him.

'James, the chap who was in here earlier.'

Bob nodded.

'The first time we saw him was two days after his brother was killed in a car crash. A lorry shed its load as he was overtaking it. It decapitated him. James has been here on and off ever since. He needs to come.'

Gemma was hurrying down the corridor. She came in.

'Sorry to disturb you,' she said, 'but there's a call. They want to know if we've got any beds?'

'Yes, there's one in bay seven.'

'Can we take him then?'

'Yes. What's the problem?'

'Guy called Kevin Foster. Bottle in the face.'

The woman looked at Bob and smiled.

'No rest for the wicked,' she said.

Bob tried to return her smile but it didn't feel right.

'Could you shut the door please?' he said.

Bill Kirton

Waiting

Been waiting a long time?
Yes, I know. Me too, actually.
But don't even think of getting up
and leaving this waiting room,
this long corridor that twists
over months, over gaps
in the floorboards that twice
you've fallen through
and had to be helped back up
to your place in the queue
that shuffles forward at a pace
of one step daily – but one step,
nevertheless, nearer to that end
you've reached in your mind often.
Here, listen to this music
that means so much to me,
and try this book – I think
you'll love it enough to read
a second time – and maybe
I'll bring a bottle of wine
to share with you, standing
under the portraits of poets
that we might just toast
because they knew about waiting.

Matthew Sweeney

Exile's End

You will do the very last thing.
Wait then for a noise in the chest,
between depth charge and gong,
like the seadoors slamming on the car deck.
Wait for the white noise and then cold astern.

Gaze down over the rim of the enormous lamp.
Observe the skilled frenzy of the physicians,
a nurse's bald patch, blood. These will blur,
as sure as you've forgotten the voices
of your childhood friends, or your toys.

Or, you may note with mild surprise,
your name. For the face they now cover
is a stranger's and it always has been.
Turn away. We commend you to the light,
Where all reliable accounts conclude.

Michael Donaghy

A Gull

A seagull stood on my window-ledge today,
said nothing, but had a good look inside.
That was a cold inspection I can tell you!
North winds, icebergs, flash of salt
crashed through the glass without a sound.
He shifted from leg to leg, swivelled his head.
There was not a fish in the house – only me.
Did he smell my flesh, that white one? Did he think
I would soon open the window and scatter bread?
Calculation in those eyes is quick.
'I tell you, my chick, there is food *everywhere.*'
He eyed my furniture, my plants, an apple.
Perhaps he was a mutation, a supergull.
Perhaps he was, instead, a visitation
which only used that tight firm forward body
to bring the waste and dread of open waters,
foundered voyages, matchless predators,
into a dry room. I knew nothing.
I moved; I moved an arm. When the thing saw
the shadow of that, it suddenly flapped,
scuttered claws along the sill, and was off,
silent still. Who would be next for those eyes,
I wondered, and were they ready, and in order?

21 June

Fade then, light; but longing never will.
Midsummer makes the west spectacular
and even gives its last glow a show
of reluctance, as if it had postponed
midnight. But midnight is too faithful.
You're back among the black, the black,
you're down and fit to drown, to drown,
you're padding into nightmare town.
You haven't got a house, a bed-light,
there are no clocks or telephones out there,
you are on your own, you have a large panic
waiting to break through your chest, you are panting,
you count, as it arrives, each brimming pang.
What a clutch of sheets! What a parody of pain!

The longest day, the night is not so long.
You fling back the curtains, the morning sky
is like a meadow. What is it you want?
I don't know. You cannot walk there. No.
So what do you want? The morning, perhaps,
and then I want the day, another day.

Edwin Morgan

To My Father

Pausing in your Gibbon at the passages you marked –
the noble spirit of Aurelius,
the salutary balm of Boethius,
the fortitude of Julian –

I see you reading in a pool of light,
a studious young man in Singapore,
with six good volumes named for Everyman;
so shortly after Belsen and Treblinka

restoring, by the scruple of the act,
the faith that words can say what living means,
can name the spirit in our brief machines –
calm and intrepid in the barbarian night.

We walked at Brothers Water
when your words were mostly blotted by a stroke,
and hazarded at what on earth you meant,
more than a pantomime but past a joke,

parading an imaginary cross –
a priest? – till in the end,
associating Marlowe's lines,
we got the word you wanted: caterpillar.

All winter long your own decline and fall.
Till all the words of all the histories
had come, on a certificate, to these:
Bronchopneumonia. Cerebrovascular disease.

[II]

What would I give to stand with you again
before that boar that thundered across a clearing towards us once,
standing as high at the shoulder as the shoulder of a man,
making our stunned bones jump and thud with every running thump.

What would I give to hear you tell again
(your table-talk) of red-hot irons up King Edward's anus
or William's bloated body, like a blown-up football bladder,
pricked and deflated to fit it in its coffin.

What would I give to see you laugh again
at Stan and Ollie malarking their lives away
or another repeat of another repeat of *Only Fools and Horses*,
half knowing, half remembering that what you saw was funny.

What would I give to know you in your bed,
your reassuring breathing rising steady, falling, rising,
a tide-line soughing in the Babylisten at my side:
in, out, in, out, in, out, in . . .

– Instead I'm reading what the nurse from Allied Medicare recorded:
Bill was very tired today. He managed a glass of water,
a glass of Build-up. Bill has had a bowel motion.
He has not eaten any lunch. He is not feeling well.

[*III*]

Salt & Son have goldfish in a tank,
a box of tissues placed for customers,
the saviour on his cross, and photographs
of older Salts and hearses drawn by horse.

I made my way out back, through stacks of coffins,
looking for the room they call the chapel.
Someone unseen was whistling at his work,
someone else lay zippered on a trestle.

How did you get in here? he asked, embarrassed,
a beef-complexioned foxy youth
with bottlebrush hair and a ring in one ear.
I've come to see my father. William Hulse.

So this is it. The chapel. What a place.
Plastic flowers. A cross. Consoling light.
Two straight-backed chairs. The coffin lid
stood upright in the corner.

That charcoal suit was never really you,
and after all the weight you lost of late
you seem so little in it. Like a boy
in granddad's clothes. There's nothing left of you.

You're not yourself. Your face is solemn, waxy,
gone angular. Your glasses fit all wrong.
You smell of something strange. You're cold and hard:
I touch you, and you're terrible to touch,

and on my neck the hairs rise up in ice,
stiff with death, like when I was a boy
and you read 'Danny Deever' to me. And
his soul passed overhead.

[*IV*]

Come to thy journey's end with a good grace,
the stoic wrote, *just as an olive falls*
when it is ripe, praising the earth that bare it,
grateful to the tree that gave it growth.

Dad, I'm afraid you'd approve of this churlish priest,
saying the requiem for his friend deceased,
damning as pagan the passage we asked him to read,
dismissing as hopeless the Roman's natural creed,

his human love of this life, not the next,
preferring Newman, as he must,
and preaching his afterlifing text
over your coffin'd dust.

You know I feel he treads you in the dirt.
The anger chokes me. Dad, he does you hurt.
Your lifelong friends Aurelius and Christ
gave equal measure to your mortal heart.

What does he know of hope, what has he known,
who tells us there is hope in Christ alone?
What does he know of hope, who will not see
the wisdom of the olive and the tree?

And yet: he was your Father. And your friend.
And in my heart I know you'd say he's right
to guide us to the way, the truth, the life.
So, Dad, for your sake, at your journey's end,

I'll kneel to him, and to your god, today.
But, where no priest can hear, to you I say:
I shall not look upon your like again.
To that, amen.

Michael Hulse

Burning

Almost a year ago now that you left us,
and today the news of Francis Bacon's death
reminds me of your stay in the hospice,
how like his paintings you looked.
It's taken so long to miss you,
longer to stop the hurt that surprises.

The wind's howling outside,
and I've struggled to write of the artist,
of how his paintings move me.
Fashionable now to label his works
'horrific', but he clearly said
he just painted life the way that he saw it.

Both bohemian and nihilist,
but somehow telling awful truths
about how we've lost our way,
about power and lust and hate,
that awful *nothingness*
that most of us just drift through.

My father's the only person I've ever known
so sure about salvation, so *assured*.
We're far too full of the joys of life,
or worried and scared as we run about.
We're simply smears of dark pigment,
but Francis, Dad, you both burned bright.

Rupert Loydell

Ward Seven

(for Bill Cooper)

Lurching out of anaesthetics
On tubular Health Service beds,
Some will now require prosthetics
Or bags that drip to keep them fed.

Counting trains and feeding pigeons,
An amputee can still react
To the world that once he lived in
Before he signed the standard pact:

More years, less pain, terms understood
For his abridgement at mid-thigh;
No clause, though knives and wills are good,
Can guarantee that no one dies.

Each beyond his own salvation,
Their democratic suffering breeds
A politics of supplication,
To each according to his needs...

Douglas Houston

Reading Pascal in the Lowlands

His aunt has gone astray in her concern
And the boy's mum leans across his wheelchair
To talk to him. She points to the river.
An aged angler and a boy they know
Cast lazily into the rippled sun.
They go there, into the dappled grass, shadows
Bickering and falling from the shaken leaves.

His father keeps apart from them, walking
On the beautiful grass that is bright green
In the sunlight of July at 7 p.m.
He sits on the bench beside me, saying
It is a lovely evening, and I rise
From my sorrows, agreeing with him.
His large hand picks tobacco from a tin;

His smile falls at my feet, on the baked earth
Shoes have shuffled over and ungrassed.
It is discourteous to ask about
Accidents, or of the sick, the unfortunate.
I do not need to, for he says 'Leukaemia.'
We look at the river, his son holding a rod,
The line going downstream in a cloud of flies.

I close my book, the *Pensees* of Pascal.
I am light with meditation, religiose
And mystic with a day of solitude.
I do not tell him of my sorrows.
He is bored with misery and premonition.
He has seen the limits of time, asking 'Why?'
Nature is silent on that question.

A swing squeaks in the distance. Runners jog
Round the perimeter. He is indiscreet.
His son is eight years old, with months to live.
His right hand trembles on his cigarette.
He sees my book, and then he looks at me,
Knowing me for a stranger. I have said
I am sorry. What more is there to say?

He is called over to the riverbank.
I go away, leaving the Park, walking through
The Golf Course, and then a wood, climbing,
And then bracken and gorse, sheep pasturage.
From a panoptic hill I look down on
A little town, its estuary, its bridge,
Its houses, churches, its undramatic streets.

Douglas Dunn

Post-Mortem

This is my body, me on the slab,
lying in the sun which burns
as if to melt the etched frost
from the man-tall windows.

In this swelter, how can flies
resist the game, the deep red
sweetmeats in the cavern of me,
vascular stamens of a Venus trap?

My three skin-petals gape,
one from each shoulder to waist,
and one up from my chest,
which covers nose and mouth.

She wears a mask too,
a plastic face-shield, gloves,
blue shiny gown; armour of life
against the seeds of where I've been.

She feels ice-spores of marble
in my pulse-less arms.
She pictures, on my tight shut eyes,
the exile's distant glaze.

She heaves huge jars down from a shelf,
unscrews one, lifts my gut-coil
from its marinade of formalin,
gently shakes the drips onto the floor.

She weighs it on a grocer's scales
and slips it into me. It's cold,
but her assistant settles it
and stitches it in place.

Liver, stomach, lungs, each cradled,
slid and sewn; painstaking work.
They lift my sawn ribs like a lid,
plant the heart, and close its cage.

They take out the wood brick
that propped my shoulder-blades
and arched me open. I sink onto
the metal slab as though I'm sighing.

My viscera complete, they fold in
all three petals, cauterise and seal
with thread the Y-shaped wound.
I am all of a piece, but lifeless.

My skin sticks to the stainless steel.
They hose me down, under and over,
yanking me up with a leg or an arm
to drench me, peel me from the slab.

Water gutters over earth-brown tiles
and chokes into a central drain.
She scissors free my mouth and eyes
from stitched serenity.

She bows down to my dry lips,
kisses them – passionless –
and waits for my first gasp,
then points to a mustard-coloured door:

'It has been longer than you think',
she says, 'In the next room you will find
some simple clothes and food. You will
be hungry. We have work to do.'

Michael Symmons Roberts

Wasp

They found you cold, fists jammed on each other,
Arctic on Antarctica. And between them,
paper, scrawl: a crumpled note signed and sealed.
To release it meant prising a wrist,
cheating the knot of rigor mortis.
Then a policeman picked it with a jemmy…

Just once, this once, make sense of me?
Her words, questing, tightened their wire
across my chest. The car where they found you,
shut windows weeping with monoxide,
was hauled away; sold off to strangers
at a cut price they never fathomed.

Lies. All of it… a first, final readership,
hostaged to your death, in a coroner's office.
You should have shared. You didn't.
All this time… all that time, *you knew.*
Your parents bunched, stark as witnesses;
made for the door. You'd cut the ice.

•

Solstitial visitor, always the wasp
in your quick-fire combing along my shelves.
Were those books your pollen?
or the excuse for returning them
unread, spurning discussion
with a thrumming whisper, *bed*?
All reasons for talk squandered, unheard.
Only fear of love unsheathed your sting.

Quick – it's me. I unclenched the lock.
Snapdragon, campion: the flowerbed
no flower-bed, but a furnace of wasps
sizzling, dangerous. And you, waiting,
your shoes treading pollen,
gold-dust, haloes,
through brindled grass. And the trees
flexed over you like surgeons.

•

Ice. Our first winter: a glassy hive.
Honey in jars – bottles, sidelong,
whispered KILNER, KILN. . . KIL. . .
I dipped a spoon in the first of the year,
tugging the surface to a muscle of lava;
slipped it, neat, in your bowl of coffee.
Half-love, your love's language:
you stirred its black spiral.

Charred stubble in fields. The winter's
burn-off snatched at your asthma:
a tantrum of breath
till I traced your inhaler.
That weekend, recovering, propped-up
with *Germinal*, you hauled one word
from your silted throat (*bed?*).
Winds outside made war on the aspen.

Snow. December; castanets of hail;
holly we brought in snared with hooks.
Taps betrayed us, a clanking mutiny
bursting a wall. We boiled snow:
snow on snow. Our windows, portholed
on a white atlantic, silently froze.
Bed, with the fire's dying collusion,
gave up its gift as we crammed for warmth.

•

Leaving unspoken what the doctor told you,
the clack of your step said: *Don't, don't,
don't*… I cut to the kitchen, jabbing
a kettle's thick, cool waist for coffee.
London in March. A second opinion
grudged the first. *Anything to be done?*
Nothing between us the train couldn't say,
hammering northward: *too late too late*.

•

Not now: your touchy, embattled cry
as I steered you from silence, hoping you'd walk
a little of the way. 'The woods perhaps?
a tree-creeper's nested'. But: *No – you
go*. I'd veer out, make eighty yards
before I stopped, stranded with wonder:
your seeping, last hours (minute by minute)
traduced to a bird on shrivelled bark.

That silence. I tried it.
An anchor scudding the sea-floor,
you were snared on a weightless sand;
for days you couldn't move or speak.
Then, a false Spring:
you asked for food; for your bed.
to be placed in the hall-way
as though you'd fledge.

Your silence was fear, furled like a sting.
Your dad called by to run you to hospital.
Wants me to go and get it over!
You swayed to the car where your father
sat smoking. *Cunt – I'll die
where I like*
    slamming to the bedroom,
snatching your things.

•

They found you cold, the car's drained engine
ticking to zero; you, flexed over yourself,
catapulted to that final wish: an Arctic quiet;
the sealight torching your eye like a mirror…
I came home to cupboards – their after-life, memory;
your clothes strewn-about, burgled from wardrobes.
And the garden: its hive, a Vesuvius of larvae,
fresh tenants of this frozen site.

David Morley

217

The Mighty Pen

In March 1983, when I was living on the edge of the desert in El Paso, living on the edge in some other ways, too, I got a bad cold that turned into pneumonia. It wasn't just bad luck. I was seven months pregnant and although I'd been eating right and sleeping right, my mind was another story. I'd been pushing myself too hard. I'd been trying to finish a novel. I had been working on it since my four-year-old son was an infant and was desperate to end it before the new one arrived. I wanted a clear head, by which I mean I didn't want to live inside it anymore, pulled this way and that by imaginary people and events. I wanted to put away my ghosts and live in the real world, instead of just pretending.

In the rush I forgot to pace myself. Or as my doctor put it, I didn't listen to the messages my body was sending me, until it upped the ante. I ended up in hospital, and when they sent me home I couldn't shake off the cough. The cough sent me into premature labour. My doctor sent me back to bed and put me on medication to stop the contractions. It was a new wonderdrug with only one known drawback: it made your heart race. It made you think you were about to die.

But I didn't let it take me over. I couldn't afford to. I had to think about the baby, who had stopped growing during my illness. I had to slow down to give her the chance to catch up. So I stayed in bed as the doctor ordered and took my pills and listened to the messages my body was sending me and waited. I lay on my left side and looked through the two slit windows at the grey stone wall that stood in the way of the sun. Then I lay on my right side and stared at the cheap brass knob on the plywood door that led into the bathroom. I stared at it until it disappeared and I was back in my book again, back in the middle of the last chapter, on the edge between what was clear and what was still too dark to imagine. I'd take one step forward. I'd wait until my eyes adjusted and I could see where I was. Then I'd take another step, and then another. I'd open my eyes again and see the cheap brass knob on the plywood door and I'd look at the clock and see I'd been asleep. Before my dream dissolved, I'd prop up my pillows and pick up my pen and write it down.

Two weeks before the baby was due, I found my way to the end. I felt stronger now, strong enough to take my notebook to my desk. I paced myself carefully this time. I travelled back and forth, between desk and bed, typing one line at a time, resting between paragraphs. I finished the clean draft with six days to spare. I handed it to Paul. He wrapped it up and sent it off. I came off the drug, which wasn't called Anxietron, but should have been. I packed away my typewriter and turned my desk into a changing table and went into labour on my due date, in the early hours of the first of May.

The nurses at the hospital picked up signs of fetal distress almost as soon as they put me on the monitor. But because it was Sunday and the first fine day of spring and all the surgeons of El Paso had gone off to play golf without their bleepers, it took them eight hours for them to organise an emergency Caesarean. Then there was another lost hour I spent with a clatter of orderlies, stuck in a lift. Or maybe it was shorter. I was back on Anxietron, a massive dose to stop the massive contractions, and when your heart is galloping you lose all sense of time.

By the time we got to the operating room they had tracked down the anesthesiologist. He had just left the ninth hole of the Coronado Country Club and was now on his way. The nurses rushed about getting me ready so that they could surge ahead the moment he walked in. This meant strapping me down less than gently on a bed shaped like a cross. Paul was there when they put me under. He was wearing surgical scrubs and his eyes flashed like the lights on an ambulance. They probably shouldn't have let him stay for the operation, because it turned out to be a rough job. The placenta was blocking the cervix and the cord was wrapped around the baby's neck so tight it came this close to strangling her. They had to yank the baby out, and my blood splashed everywhere, on their coats and on their shoes.

By the time I found all this out, I was back on the ward. I couldn't take it in, it was like listening to a story about someone else, because the baby in Paul's arms was not blue but perfect. And now it was my turn. Now I had her nestled in my arms, now it was the middle of the night, now my cocoon was thinning. An alien thought was trying to get in. And now it was the middle of the next night and I was alone with the baby and it had begun to sink in that she had almost died.

Now all I could think about were the what-ifs. What if I had not gone on the monitor, what if they hadn't fixed the lift in time, what if this had happened just a years earlier, when there were no monitors – would I have died, too? What if the fetal distress had been more serious than they were admitting, what if she hadn't recovered so fast, what if I had chosen the wrong doctor, what if she had taken risks she shouldn't have done, what if I had, too. What if I gone to bed when I should have done and kept that cold from turning into pneumonia. What if I took one step closer to the edge of the cliff. Would I lose my footing, would we fall? I had taken myself off painkillers because I couldn't bear the haze but I was still floating in and out of it. As I sat on the edge of the bed, holding the baby in the crook of my arm, staring into the dark, I drifted off to sleep. I woke up just as I was falling over. I wrenched the baby back so fast I tore my stitches. I was sure I had smothered her. When I saw that she was still breathing, I put her into her cot so that she'd be safe from me. I sat back into my pillows, watching the only thing that mattered, watching her little chest heave and fall.

•

I made myself a promise. I was never going to forget. Beauty was breathing, breathing was truth. That was all I knew and would ever need to know. But then we went home and the promise got lost. Life returned to normal. Which was not very normal by normal standards, life with Paul being the marital version of whitewater rafting. During our first eight years together, we had moved ten times. We'd gone from Greece to Boston to New York to Mallorca. After that it was London, then Lesbos, then London again, then El Paso, then San Francisco, then a small town in northeastern Connecticut called Pomfret and now El Paso again. We'd run out of money almost everywhere. There'd been a fair number of rash investments, smashed cars and unlucky nights at the card table. But just when it looked like it was all over, Paul would think up this amazing idea for a bestseller. He'd hammer out a first chapter and an outline and send it to his agent, and more often than not, he'd manage to sell it. Not for as huge sum he'd been seeing in his dreams, not enough to make up for the serious novel he would have preferred to be writing, but usually enough to pay for next adventure.

He was always coming home with surprises. Sometimes it was a car we couldn't afford, sometimes it was a house on the other side of the country, complete with tickets. Sometimes he stayed at home all evening, and sometimes he jumped out of his chair at eleven saying, 'I'm bored. I'm going out.'Sometimes I went to bed. Sometimes I stayed awake waiting for him to come back. Sometimes I decided I couldn't bear living like this anymore, not now that we had two small children, but where would I go? Sometimes he would wake me up at five in the morning, to tell me about this chase he'd had with the police, only to shake them off by turning off his headlights. Or his voice would wake me up, and he'd be in the next room telling someone other how beautiful his first wife was, or he was crying because he'd called her up and she'd hung up on him, or he was waking me up to tell me he had just read an incredible book. Or had read the page I had left in my typewriter and wanted to tell me it was incredible. Or else had decided the time had come to tell me the whole story about an indiscretion he'd committed years ago, because he would be sitting down the next day to turn the indiscretion into a novel, the serious one that had been through so many false starts, and that he had abandoned so many times, so that I could have the privilege to write whatever I wanted, at whatever pace.

Six months after Emma was born, he woke me up to ask me if I would take over his teaching job so that he could go to Mexico and work on his serious novel. I agreed, and so, strangely, did his boss, even though I had no experience and was only vaguely qualified. I had never planned to teach but it was like coming out of hibernation. It woke me up. It made me realise how much I had missed the company of other people. It made me ask myself why I had spent so many years cooped up in a room with my thoughts. At first I found it exhausting because Matthew was only in school for half days and Emma wasn't sleeping through the night yet. Then I worked out how to prop her on my arm in a way that made it impossible for me to roll over on her.

One night I woke up to find that her head had rolled off. I was only dreaming that I had woken up, but when I did wake up, I went into a panic, because I couldn't find the baby anywhere. Then I heard her crying in her cot. I picked her up and rocked her back to sleep but the dream was another story. I couldn't shake it off.

When we left El Paso for Mallorca that June, I took it with me. By August it was fading, but during the winter it came back. By now we were well into our next adventure, living a large sombre house just outside Oxford, on Boar's Hill. It owned by a mathematical biologist who was on sabbatical in Los Alamos, New Mexico. He was mad about gargoyles. He had framed photographs of them on every wall. In the great, grand study where I was meant to be writing a novel, the glassed-in bookcases were full of books about insects. I could not get my own beyond the first page. First pages had always been a problem for me. Of the ten years I had spent writing fiction, I had spent seven of them writing and discarding failed first pages. But this time, I had no time for such luxuries. Because now it was my turn to write the best seller, and Paul's turn to do something serious. The novel he'd been writing in Mexico had come to nothing, but while he was there he had decided that what he wanted was a postgraduate degree. This is why we were in Oxford.

We were financing the first year of his course with the proceeds of the novel I had finished before Emma was born. The bestseller I was to have ready by June. Of the many holes in our plan, the biggest was childcare, or rather, the lack of it. We couldn't afford it, and Paul couldn't help either because he had his course to do. And then there was my choice of subject. I had gone for one of those what-if plots that seem so funny when you first think of them. What if a man took over the care of his children, to let his wife go back to work? What if he was competent, but his wife's friends refused to believe it? What if, having battled it out with him, they came to accept him, and appreciate him, perhaps a little too much? I had not thrown away many first pages before I began to ask myself, what possessed me to think up such a story. What if it was my subconscious working? What if I had invented this plot because I was afraid it might happen? Or was already happening? Or had been happening for years? What if he was having affairs all along, and I couldn't bear to see it? What if this explained why I was writing in circles? What if we got to June and I was still writing in circles? What would become of us if we couldn't pay the rent? What if we couldn't eat? What if we had to sell the car, if we had to go back to America, if even there, we had nowhere to go? By the end of winter I was hardly sleeping at all and my heart raced every time I walked past the study. I came down with a cold that turned into pneumonia. I spent a month in bed.

One night, I woke up to find that Paul was not next to me. I could hear him on the phone, downstairs in the hallway. He was telling someone how badly I had failed him. He had been depending on me to keep us afloat, but now I had allowed myself to get ill and he couldn't give a moment to his studies because he was looking after the children all day long, so now he was going to have to leave his course, the first thing he had done in his adult life that had made him happy. He told his friend he would never forgive me for leaving him in the lurch like this. But the very next day he came up with the perfect salvage plan.

The idea this time was for an update of Love Story. He got so caught up in it that he decided to write the whole thing before sending it out. The hero was a Silicon Valley billionaire. He meets a beautiful young girl who has lost her way in life, and under his tutelage, she decides to get serious and do a course. She does not drop out when she gets pregnant, but then, two months before the due date, she walks in front of a bus. They keep her alive on a life support machine until the baby is viable. When they pull the baby out, the father is there in the operating room and is the first to hold him. In the final tearful scene, the hero takes the healthy newborn into intensive care to see the mother he will never know. Then he kisses her beautiful forehead and flicks the switch.

He sent it off saying it was money in the bank. But his agent thought otherwise, and so did his editor. They told him it was a male fantasy, and male fantasies weren't selling. They suggested a rewrite that included the female point of view. I cannot remember if I was the one who offered to do this, or if he was the one who first suggested it. I do remember that he said he would take full responsibility for the children while I did the rewrite, and that – strangely – I was surprised when he failed to do so.

What I remember best is the Sunday morning four weeks later. We had decamped to a more modest house in East Oxford by now. I didn't have a study, so I was working on a rickety sideboard in the sitting room. Paul had been out all night with his best friend, a Mercedes Benz dealer who had flown over from Chicago. They were now sleeping it off. Paul had woken me up in the middle of the night to impress it on me that I had to get this draft finished today or else we were ruined. I had closed the sitting room door with the idea of cutting down the noise. The children were pounding on it, but the end was in sight.

I had written a hundred and twenty pages of love story from the point of view of the woman. But now, as I approached page 121, I was facing a technical problem. My heroine had just walked in front of a bus. Now she was a vegetable. How was I to write from the point of view of a vegetable? Why had I ever consented to do so? Why hadn't I seen this coming?

What was the inspiration for this story? To what degree was it about him and me? What was he trying to tell me? What if he hated me? What if he wanted to turn me into a vegetable and then turn off the life support machine? What if he wanted me dead? A great surge passed through me as I wrote Paul a note on page 121: 'I'm sorry, but I'm not going to do this for you. *You* finish her off if you want to. But don't expect me to help.'

•

I remember how surprised I was when Paul did not take kindly to my postscript. He told me that I had damaged his book so badly that it would take years to repair. He was going to have to ditch the whole idea and move on to another rescue plan. The next day he flew off to Chicago, to work for his friend the Mercedes Benz dealer. He came back six months later but page 121 still loomed large. I had returned now to my own novel, which was finally working, because I was in control of the plot this time and had arranged for my hero to pay for his mistakes. On my new first page he is living alone, because his wife and children have left him. He has no idea where they are.

In real life, all I wanted was a temporary separation. Paul was trying to talk me out of it, usually by trying to convince me that I had lost my mind. Night after night, we'd argue about my mind and whether or not I had lost it, and my fear of being turned into a vegetable, and what this signified. If I went to bed without giving in to his version, if he asked me if I still loved him and I said no, he'd wake me up in the middle of the night to ask me again. I got more and more run down. I came down with more colds that turned into bronchitis or pneumonia. And then one night I found a lump in my breast.

It was a cyst, not a tumour, but they weren't sure it wasn't calcifying. So in January 1986 I checked into John Radcliffe Hospital for a biopsy. I went in the afternoon before my operation. Paul came in to keep me company and stayed at my side into the night. His eyes were like lights in an interrogation room. He began by telling me he had been into my computer and read everything I had written. He asked me why I was so angry, what he had done, how he could change. He told me I had to get better, he couldn't bear to see me so weak, couldn't bear watching me turn my anger against myself. He told me I had strengths I didn't know about, while I had nil by mouth.

In the morning they gave me my pre-op. When my operation was delayed, they gave me another. I spent the day floating in a morphine haze, listening to music. It does not seem plausible that the controllers of Radio 3 had decided to give over the entire day to multiple performances of Mozart's Don Giovanni. But that is what I remember hearing. The music got mixed up with all the other sounds. I kept hearing footsteps coming down the hallway. It must have been the heart patients, clattering to the smoking room at the end of the hallway. I thought it was the devil, coming for my soul.

Late in the afternoon, the orderlies came for me. They wheeled me off and parked me in front of a set of green swinging doors. A doctor dressed in green put me under, and next thing I was waking up to the chill of the recovery room. I could remember my name when they asked for it but only just.

They wheeled me back to my ward. I tried to help them help me onto my bed, but I couldn't. They propped me up in my pillows, because I couldn't do that, either. In the morning, when the consultant did his rounds, he explained that I had lost an unusual amount of blood. They had decided not to give me a transfusion because of the recent scare about blood supplies contaminated with the HIV virus. I was going to feel unusually weak for some time he said, and it was also going to be some time before my test results came back. 'I'm sorry to leave you in limbo, but there you are.'

There was one thing I could take comfort in. Things could be worse. All I had to do was look around the room. Begin with Mrs Miller, the woman next to the window. She was suffering from a wasting disease. Then there was Mrs Flynn across the aisle and Mrs Swallow, right next to me. Both had just had double mastectomies, probably too late.

You would not know to look at them though. They were dressed in chirpy pink nighties and aquamarine slippers and sky blue padded robes. They commented often on the loveliness of the floral arrangements and hallmark cards that surrounded them. They kept themselves busy with knitting and magazines and thank you letters, and when a nurse wheeled in the payphone trolley, they spoke to their husbands, sons, and grandchildren that they would have used if they were phoning from Marbella. They said things like, 'Oh, I'm having a whale of a time,' and 'Oh you shouldn't have!' and 'What a perfectly lovely thing to say!' They talked about clouds and silver linings, and everything being for the best at the end of the day. Even when the heart patients clattered down the hall for their smoking break, gaunt and grey and gasping, even when the smoke in the smoking room got so thick it rolled into our ward, the most they did was purse their lips. 'Oh dear, it's so sad, isn't it,' Mrs. Flynn would say. And Mrs Swallow would say, 'But some things can't be helped, can they?' If there was a nurse in the room checking pulses, she would sigh and allow a dark thought to cross her face and then she would brighten as she thought of yet another way to revive the charade.

The charade got more difficult after lunch, when we were joined by Mrs. Meadows, an elderly woman with a thick white beard and a serious incontinence problem who kept falling out of bed. At teatime, we were joined by a dwarf named Miss Mendoza. They put her into the bed right across from mine. She was conscious but only just. She lay flat on her back, her haylike hair splayed on the pillow, her glassy eyes fixed on the ceiling, her little chest heaving and rattling under the sheets.

I had never heard this sound before. I had stupidly assumed that it was just a figure of speech. The rattle got louder in the night. Every time it woke me up, I'd look over at her bed. I'd see a nurse there, whispering to her, patting her hand. She had no family, they explained in the morning. That's why they were filling in. Around lunchtime, when the rattle grew fainter, the nurse who was holding her hand called in two orderlies and had them wheel her away. Mrs. Flynn put down her magazine to watch her go and then turned sharply towards the window. Mrs Miller said, 'Oh dear,' and Mrs. Swallow said, 'It's so sad, isn't it?' The nurse who came in to change the sheets said not to worry, they had only taken her off to a private room.

Mrs Mendoza died that afternoon, just before smoking break. It was just as well, a nurse told us. She had so enjoyed the quiet of the private room. She had slipped away so peacefully. It was sad, but some things couldn't be helped, could they? Nods all around. And sighs. And here and there a pursed lip. Then the tea lady wheeled her trolley in, and that was that.

But that night I couldn't stop looking at the blank sheets on her bed. I looked at them until they were there again, Mrs Mendoza in her bed, the nurse in her chair. Mrs. Mendoza rattling louder with every breath she took, the nurse holding her hand.
I didn't want to die.
I couldn't stop myself.
I closed my eyes.

I woke up to the clatter of a trolley. 'Milk?' said the tea lady.

I tried to nod.

'Feeling a little low this morning, are we?' I nodded again. 'Let's prop you up then,' she said. 'There now. That's better then, isn't it?'

'Got some sleep, did you?' Now it was the nurse to check my pulse. 'Tell you what,' she said. 'I'm going to get you on your feet today.'

'You can't,' I said.

She shook the thermometer. 'We'll see about that.'

After she had finished her rounds she came back for me. She lifted me to a sitting position and told me to use her arm as a prop. 'Now put one foot down, very gently,' she said.

'I can't,' I said.

'Just try.'

So I put one foot on the floor, and then I put the other foot on the floor. 'Now walk,' she said. I did. I made it all the way to the end of the hall.

'Well done,' said Mrs. Flynn when I had made it all the way back.

Mrs. Swallow said, 'Now that wasn't so hard, was it?'

I sat down on my bed. I was short of breath and my stitches hurt.

'You did have us worried, you know,' said Mrs. Miller.

'But everything works out in the end, doesn't it?' said Mrs. Flynn.

'Sometimes you can worry yourself sick just by thinking too much,' said Mrs Swallow.

'My thoughts exactly,' said Mrs. Flynn. 'It does make you think, though, doesn't it?'

I'm sure I didn't cry, but I still ache when I think about it, even all these years later. I can't get it out of my head. I can't decide what I feel worst about – their dignity or my lack of it, my histrionics or their kindly acceptance of it or my sudden change of heart. No, now that I thought about it, now that I had seen it, I didn't want to die after all. No, from that moment on, I knew I wanted to live, no matter how much it hurt. I can't explain why. And perhaps I shouldn't. This is what I see when I try to find the words: the dwarf rattling in her bed, and the nurse holding her hand, saying nothing, saying everything.

Maureen Freely

The Package

I have to push at the door with the side of my elbow and there is a crackling sound; letters and leaflets and fliers are already stacked up behind it. I am putting the keys back in my pocket and repeating to myself, over and over, plants heating terrapin, plants heating terrapin. Then I stop thinking about that because the door swinging back releases a rush of air, and the air in the flat smells of her. As I bend to pick up her post, making my way down the corridor towards the kitchen, I feel as though I should be calling out, I'm here, I'm here, here I am. I've never been in her flat without her.

My girlfriend hates wearing tights. Too restrictive, she says, imagine having a band of elastic around your waist all day. She only ever wears skirts in summer. When I first met her she was wearing a long skirt down to her ankles, slit up the front to her thighs. The skin of her legs was smooth, slightly darker than mine. She had a tiny graze on one of her knees.

Her plants are all cacti – windowsills and windowsills full of them. Thorned, determined and waxy, they cluster like green sea urchins around the edges of her rooms. Beautiful, she says, but untouchable. I fill a jug of water at the kitchen sink. The silence of the flat is putting me off kilter, like the presence of a new person in a clique of friends. I tilt the jug into all the pots. Not too much because cacti have long, water-seeking roots and resinous cuticles that hoard water in case of droughts ahead. The terrapin is half-in, half-out of its brackish water, and has its head and legs retracted into its shell. Its case is synthetic-looking, as if a plastics expert manufactured it specially for this species – concentric green and yellow lines, symmetric, tepid to the touch. I cannot look at its shell without imagining the soft, skeleton-less body underneath. I sprinkle the dry, flaked food on the surface of the water, and wait for a moment. No movement. I switch on its bar of white UV light. One of its legs twitches. She says she doesn't like the terrapin much. That bloody thing, she calls it. But I've seen her with her cheek pressed up against the sealed, thick glass. Among the post I find on the mat is a white card. We tried to deliver a package, it reads, but you were out. There is a map on the back, showing me how to find the post office. I have half an hour before my first afternoon appointment, so I pull the front door closed behind me and set off. Frost cracks under the soles of my shoes and my breath moistens the inside of my scarf. It's late March. It's been warm. People had cast off their winter coats and the bravest had even sat – swathed in jumpers, scarves and incongruous sunglasses – on cafe tables in the street. Daffodils and violets are on sale in the florist at the end of the street, but the air today has that metallic coldness that presages snow. Her flat is in a slightly dilapidated Victorian block just off a main road. Weeds straggle down its damp-swollen red brick facade. But her area is smarter than mine – more restaurants, fewer corner shops, even a theatre. The houses I pass, the little map held out in front of me, are white stucco, blank-windowed, with steps

226

leading up to the front door. The man behind the perspex grille reads her name on the card and looks me up and down, frowning. She's away, I tell him, she's my girlfriend. I have to sign my name in a grey box on a piece of paper on a clipboard before he slides the parcel into the space under the grille, and I can pick it up and walk out of the doors with it held in both of my gloved hands. I am out on the pavement before I examine the parcel. It has brown paper, taped down at the ends with wide transparent tape. The width of a shoebox, it has a dense yet soft weight, and her name and address on the front in blue felt-tipped pen. Bold, confident capital letters. I turn it over in my hands. Then I am unaware of the cold, the street around me, the people passing, the post office behind me: on the back is a rubber-stamped name and address. Pierre Kant, it says, Faculté de Histoire, Universite de Paris. The impression of the stamp is darker on one side than the other. I imagine him pressing his stamp – his own, personalised stamp, made for him and him only – into the ink-sodden pad, then slamming it carelessly and unevenly on to the back of this parcel. He'd then toss it into the university mail system. He had probably never even considered the possibility of it ending its journey here, in my hands.

She always writes with a fountain pen. She went to a traditional primary school where people were still caned for talking and where they were all taught proper, joined-up, cursive writing. I imagine her, aged nine, serious, knee-socked, missing some teeth, labouring over the upward curves of Ls or the fiddly cross strokes of Fs. She fills her pen every night, dipping its gold, spiked nib into a slick of ink; she will then wipe off the excess ink on some item of her clothing. She always wears something black (underwear, she tells me, should always be black). She keeps her pen in the front pocket of her small rucksack. Other things she always carries with her include a computer disc, the contents of which are a mystery to me, a lipstick, a mobile phone, a penknife, a blue notebook with yellow elastic round it, and a compass on a purple string.

Iron wings of tension fan out from between the man's shoulder blades. I press the tips of my four fingers into the knots; circles of skin under my touch empty of blood, turn a yellowish white. Air expels from the man's lungs; the knots slacken, blood returns to his skin. Pierre Kant. I ask him questions. 'How often do you exercise? What do you do for a living? How long do you spend at a computer? Do you have any injuries I should know about? Do you have pain in any other part of your body?' He answers each in turn, and as he sits, legs dangling off the bench, I note his answers. I'm an osteopath. I am trained in the ways muscles and skeletons conspire, sometimes together and sometimes against each other. I know that the body works like the rigging of a ship: if a rope is pulled one way by some invisible force, another will take the strain. If you just look at the strained rope you're never going to solve the problem. What you have to feel for all the time is the strength, direction and reason for the invisible force. The parcel was heavy yet yielded to my touch. As if something had been wrapped for its postal journey. Something valuable. Something Kant had wanted to arrive intact. 'You've torn a ligament between your shoulder blade and spine,' I am saying. The man's face creases around the eyes, and he peers at me as if he can't quite see me properly. How long does it take to get here from Paris? Three hours, four at most, if you used the tunnel. Longer by ferry. 'Do you have any idea how this might have happened?' My pen is poised above my paper. Not a fountain pen. A fibre tip. Green ink. Makes a scratching noise as it moves over the surface of the paper. So you get to see people in their underwear, is what most people say to me when I tell them what I do. That, or: so do you give good massages? My girlfriend (who wasn't my girlfriend at the time, although the idea of her becoming so had crossed my mind as soon as I saw her but been rejected out of hand. Too glam for the likes of me), looked at me properly for the first time when I told her: I am in awe of anyone who can do that, was what she said. Awe. Her exact words. We were at a dinner party. Her hand made a concertina with the folds on the linen tablecloth. When I asked her why, she shrugged: makes what I do seem like a waste of a life. The man on the bed, shoulders crunched up round his ears because of the pain in his back, flushes, rubs the back of his neck with the palm of his hand. 'Er. I. Well ... I can't remember actually.' 'I see,' I say and write 'sex injury' in green fibre tip in his notes.

My girlfriend has green eyes. Except, just for a moment, after sex, they look blue.

When I leave the practice building, I'm expecting it to be gloomy and dull outside, but as I lock the door behind me the dark seems luminous, silenced. Then I see that a thin layer of snow lies on the path and the garden and the trees and the roofs of cars. My bicycle seat is crystallised with sharp white. But the roads are bare, slicked black. I leave no trace as I travel.

She phones later. There's a micro-second delay on the line which blizzards periodically with static: I imagine the signal of her voice and my voice, bouncing off a satellite suspended thousands of miles somewhere above the North Sea. She's in Amsterdam: it's full of men with drawstring-waisted leather jackets and moustache-less beards, she tells me. The hotel has a Turkish bath and a black rubber dildo in the bedside drawer. The canals are frozen over. She lost a glove earlier today. The producer is being overbearing, the translator pedantic. The camerawoman is getting flu. And how are you, Sam? she asks. There is, at that moment, a great cheer behind her and music starts to throb. She's in a bar, she says, sorry about the noise. I want to ask her who she's there with. But I don't. I tell her I'm well and that today it snowed, that the radio is saying it's the coldest spring on record for forty-six years, and that the buds that had been appearing on the trees will now get frostbite. Is everything OK with the flat? There is a pause. We listen to the sound of distance, of the North Sea, of satellites. Fine, I say, it's fine.

She has brown hair. Underwater, it acquires a life of its own, swirling around her like serpents. When we met, at the party, the music was so loud she had to lean towards me to hear what I was saying. Strands of it snagged on my jumper, brushed against the nape of my neck. Later that night, at home, I would find three hairs caught on my clothing. 'She's an AD,' my friend Paul told me in his kitchen. 'Documentaries.' I diced the dense, slippery orange flesh of a mango into geometric cubes with the tip of a silver knife. 'AD?' I asked without looking at him. 'Assistant Director. Pretty good, I'm told.' Paul tipped the mango cubes into a bowl full of crushed slivers of ice. 'Sam,' he said, 'she's a tough nut to crack.'

What I could see about her that night: that she didn't talk about herself at all, using the device of asking people about themselves to deflect curiosity about her; that she was contemptuous of coupley-ness (her lower lip stiffened as a woman opposite sat on her boyfriend's lap during dessert); that she wore designer underwear (as she leant forwards at one point, the waistband of her skirt slid down to reveal her lower back and a label name that ran repeated round the elastic top of her knickers); that she didn't like smoking (she flinched slightly as someone lit up); that she suffered from wrist and shoulder problems and would probably develop lumber pain in later life if she didn't attend to it soon.

When I saw her next she'd cut her hair. It lay in sharp, defined line against her cheekbones. I told her I liked it and she said she was in a constant state of flux with my hair. I grow it, I cut it, I grow it, I cut it. It's a little game I play with myself. It was summertime and we were standing on the balding lawn of another friend. She had sunglasses hooked into the neckline of her T-shirt. A barbecue coughed out charcoal smoke in the corner, and people wandered about with boxes of wine that you had to hold your glass underneath and press a plastic valve to release a thin stream of sticky burgundy liquid. She remembered my name. I saw her four more times that summer. There was another barbecue, and then another dinner party where she and I talked across a table about a film that had just come out. Then a few of us went to the cinema to see the film. She sat next to me, relaxed, her palms resting on her thighs. At one point she leaned across to say something to me and her lip touched my earlobe. I was surprised how hot it was. At the end of the evening, she and I were standing on a pavement when she suddenly stretched up on tiptoe like a ballerina, the material of her dress strained against her body, her arm up in the air. A taxi swerved to a standstill next to us. Bye, she called as she jumped in, bye. I told myself that it was OK, that it wasn't a disaster, not yet, that I would see her in three days' time. A group of us had arranged to go on a trip to the sea.

The two of them walked ahead. She was holding her shoes in one hand; the other dangled next to his. He was loose-limbed, blue-eyed, resonant-voiced. He watched her as she swam, holding her shirt like the husband of a selkie. He and I only exchanged two sentences. There had been no individual introductions. 'Everyone, this is Pierre,' Paul had said as we all got into the cars, and then swept his hand over us, 'Pierre, this is everyone.' She was standing quite close to him at that point and he smiled directly at her, nodding his head. Paul had met him while working a costume drama for Christmas TV in Paris. 'He's an expert on the Revolution,' he told me as we walked behind them along the beach, 'he's great, isn't he?' 'So, you are the man with the bread?' he said to me. His voice was almost accentless: his 'wiz' rather than 'with' gave him away. 'Yes,' I said, and from the paper bag next to me, I pulled two loaves. 'White or brown?' 'White. Please. Thank you.' He took it, and returned to where she was lying, propped up on one elbow, her hair wet to her head. He put his fingers in the loaf's cleft and, parting the two halves, handed one to her. She looked up at him as she took it, and it was then I knew. A few feet away, the sea sucked and sighed. The sky above us was striated with cirrus wisps. Their faces were close together, his hand resting on the corner of her towel. She didn't return his smile; her expression was assessing, unsettled. At the end of the day, when we'd returned to the city, prickly with salt and sunburn, I was walking away, fast, and I still managed to catch, on some late summer movement of air, the sound of him asking her if she would give him her number so they could go for dinner maybe, or perhaps a play or something if she preferred...

It's night and I cannot sleep. I think of her wandering about Amsterdam with one glove, her breath steaming from her mouth, ice floes creaking in the canals.

I was washing my hands ready for my noon appointment when she appeared in the doorway of my consulting room. My hands fumbled under the jet of hot water. Neither of us spoke. She turned and closed the door behind her, walked across the room and sat in the chair next to the desk. I turned off the tap and shook water from my hands. 'I have a patient at twelve,' I heard myself say to the back of her head. She leaned over and placed her bag on the floor. 'That's me. I made an appointment.' I sat down in my chair, but this consultant-patient arrangement felt odd so I stood up again. Walked to the window, leaned my back against it, crossed my arms. 'Are you here ...' I struggled to catch up, understand, 'do you want to see me ... professionally?' She smiled then, but only briefly, then shook her head. 'No. I-' she stopped. 'Sam ...' She laced her fingers into each other, then spread them out on her knees. It had been a week since the day at the beach. From another room somewhere in the practice, there came the high whine of a whale music tape. 'You know, I could fall in love with Pierre Kant.' Her words were clear. She looked at the wall in front of her as she spoke them. Her hands twisted in her lap, then darted to her hair, pushing a strand of it behind her ear. She glanced at me then and her face was pressed and panicked. I saw that she wasn't used to situations like this, that she wasn't a woman to say these things lightly, that this was not something she would say again. 'Do you ...' she began, uncertain, 'does that ... are you at all interested in that?'

I didn't return to my flat for two weeks. When I finally did go back it seemed unfamiliar, altered, like a house I once visited a long time ago and remembered inaccurately. I never asked her about Pierre Kant, about what had happened in that week, about what was said between them, whether they'd slept together, about how she explained me to him, whether he remembered me, the man with the bread; we never mentioned him again.

The next day, I curl my hands around the pipes. The central heating, turned low, rumbles through them. Watch out for burst pipes, she instructed me. The terrapin swims, fins extended like spades from one end of the tank to the other, its gills red, its eyes open. It doesn't see me. Or if it does it doesn't show it. The parcel I have placed on the bookcase in the hall. I remember what clothes she was wearing when she set off to the airport: a black translucent blouse that she wears open to the dip between her breasts, her grey trousers, a red sweater. I water the cacti again, even though they don't need it. On a piece of paper by the phone, a list: 'Call A. Read Levy. Arrange Tanzania meeting.'

My girlfriend sleeps on her front, one arm underneath her. Don't you ever get pins and needles, I asked her once. Only when I'm asleep, she said. My girlfriend always paints her toenails, a dark midnight blue. My girlfriend spends the longest time I have ever known brushing her teeth. My girlfriend never breaks the spine of books. My girlfriend has looped lines on all her fingerprints except one, her left hand middle finger, which is whorled. My girlfriend speaks to her sister on the phone every day. My girlfriend hates rollercoasters and deep-fried food and bars that play music too loudly and Valentine's cards and machines that don't work. My girlfriend can make the exact noise of a fork entering a piece of wood at speed. My girlfriend claims hats give her a headache. My girlfriend kissed a woman once: but I don't really do business that way, she told me. My girlfriend has her CDs ordered a-z. My girlfriend does housework when she's angry.

'I just felt a twang, like something broke or snapped,' the woman in my consulting room says. 'And what position was your arm when this happened?'

I could throw it away. She'd never know. Unless he called up to check she got it. Unless she's expecting it. Unless they're in touch all the time.

They're getting there, she tells me on the phone, it's going better than she expected. People are co-operating. The authorities have agreed to them filming in the streets. It will be a good one, she thinks, she hopes. What have you been doing ? Nothing, I say. Well, the usual. Working. You know. Suddenly I can tell her attention isn't on me anymore – there's a change in the rhythm of her breathing. Hang on a sec, she says. A man's voice rumbles in the background. He's saying her name a lot. Asking her something, trying to persuade her to do something. Two minutes, she says to him, two minutes. Hi. She's back. We're going for a Turkish bath. How are you? You sound a bit ... flat. I'm fine, I say, really I am.

I carry it from the bookshelves in the hall to the kitchen, test its length, breadth and weight between my hands. It's not a book. It's not clothes. But it's oblong, wider at one end, ridged, hard beneath the wrapping. I turn it over. The stamp, his name, his department, his address is still there. I have an urge to wet my finger and rub at it until the ink blurs into illegibility. I could open it, could tear apart the brown paper and tape he assembled with such care, pull out whatever it is he's sent her. It would be so easy. The paper is thin. Then I'd know. But how would I explain it? And what would she say?

I lay out a young woman on the table, on her side, flex her arm in my hands until I feel its weight relax into my grasp. Then I place it, crooked at the elbow, in front of her face. The vertebrae in her neck, I can tell, are cranked together, pulling on all the muscles in her shoulders and upper back. She cannot turn her head to the left. I ease one leg up so the knee is balancing her, supporting her weight. Then I place one hand on her hip and the other on her shoulder. She breathes in and out. I count two. I wait until she has drawn in her lung's capacity of air and then I push down quickly, twisting the two halves of her body in two different directions. There is a loud crunch, the sound of vertebrae moving against each other, the sound of synovial fluid rushing in on a joint. Her eyes widen in alarm, in expectancy of pain. Then her face relaxes first into relief, then into pleasure. She sits up, flexes her neck from side to side, like a bird preparing for flight. 'Wow,' she laughs, 'wow. That's incredible.'

Paris. I went there once with an ex-girlfriend. It was autumn and a bitter wind kept tossing newspapers and rubbish up into our faces. We had to rush between museums and galleries and cafes to stay out of the cold. She told me, on the third day, over an oiled salad, that our expectancies in life weren't compatible. The Seine was grey, its surface twisting, muscled like the backs of serpents.

I've been out to see Paul. His wife is pregnant. During the meal, the foetus-baby got hiccups: the dome of Gina's stomach convulsed every few seconds, then wriggled, affronted, in surprise. When I get back, an answaphone message: It's me. Are you there? No? You must be out gallivanting. OK. I've got two things to tell you: it's warmer here today and I went to a flower market and bought you some bulbs. Not tulips. I got narcissus and ... um. I've forgotten what the others are. They're in my suitcase. I'll see you tomorrow. That's three things. I should be back around seven. That's four. Bye. That's five. Right I'm going now. Bye.

I think of them together over and over: the way they walked ahead of me on that beach; how her wrist swung next to his; the flash of white as her bare soles left the sand; her wet head out to sea and him holding her shirt in his hands; him standing before her on the kerb as he asked for her telephone number. I thought their story had ended there, that he was just a catalyst for me and her, that there were no more of 'them' only 'him' and 'her' in separate lives, in separate cities. I discover that the thought of her body with someone else's gives me actual pain, just below my sternum.

The terrapin is out, standing resolutely on its gravel, exercising its lungs, its gills folded away. Onto the surface of its water, I release dried flakes of its food that smell vaguely of woodchips and sawmills; it stays staring into its dormant UV light. The flat has a feel today of, not neglect, but stasis. The air in the rooms feels heavy somehow, undisturbed. I wait for her, sitting at the table. I can't do anything – read a newspaper, listen to the radio, update my patient notes; my mind, failing to find any purchase, keeps slipping. So I sit, my elbows resting on my knees. I notice several things: her hot tap drips, the pens in a jar beside the phone, the handcream among the cutlery, onions leaning against each other on a shelf. She is late. The parcel lies on the table beside me. Then her key is grinding in the lock, and I had not planned, because you can never say you plan these things, I had envisaged that I would stand up and walk down the hall to greet her. But suddenly I cannot move, I cannot rise to my feet because blood is being propelled urgently from my heart, swelling my veins with heat; so I sit, one hand on the keys on her table, watching as she comes down the hall towards me, bag over her shoulder, saying something to me, pushing her hair away from her face.

Maggie O'Farrell

Hounds Ghyll Viaduct

(air: *She Moved through the Fair*)

1

'Farewell the world,
Farewell to the night',
Farewell my family,
Forgive me this flight

2

As I did my husband's
Though with him was gone
Some of the best times
For me and my son.

3

I served my son bread
Though life served me stones;
Now ground in its mill,
I'm down to my bones.

4

Life gave us rough service,
A stone for its host –
My son you are special,
Different from most

5

And most take against
The different as strange;
With names if not stones
It takes its revenge.

6

We'll turn to air
That no stone can touch;
You made my life son,
I love you so much.

7

'Then she went her way homeward
With one star awake
As the swan in the evening
Moves over the lake.'

8

Wind from the wheatfieds
lows through Bridgehill,
The last light of summer
Falls on Blackhill;

9

It falls still on Consett
And Leadgate and Delves –
This song is over,
Look after yourselves.

Ian Duhig

Ian Duhig writes: 'I wrote this in the formal and ritual style of the Japanese Love Suicide genre (the first two lines quote one by Chikamatsu) partly because it is a tradition more forgiving of this desperate act, but mainly because the events inspiring it were so heartbreaking they overwhelmed my attempts to treat it more directly. Where I was working recently an NHS employee, married to another NHS employee, was trying to raise their autistic child. Despite being at the heart of this vast care organisation the pressures of caring destroyed their marriage, and led eventually to her jumping to her death with her child in her arms, who also died, at a beauty spot already too well-known for such sad leavings. My wife Jane works for the NHS and through her I have met many women staff in danger of, or actually being on, a treadmill of caring at work and at home with their own needs crushed, sometimes with tragic results. This poem is dedicated to them, and to the memory of Helen Rogan.'

from *What a Carve Up!*

I took the beakers of orange juice and carried them back to the cubicle. Fiona drank hers slowly and gratefully: then she drank half of mine. She said that I looked a bit distracted and asked me what had happened.

'This guy's just been brought in. He's unconscious, and he's in a pretty bad way. It just gave me a bit of a shock.'

Fiona said: 'I'm sorry. This is a terrible way to start the New Year.'

I said: 'Don't be silly.'

She was getting weaker, I could see. After her drink she lay back on the trolley and didn't try to speak again until the nurse reappeared.

'Progress report,' she said brightly. 'The sister's trying to find you a bed, and as soon as we've got one, you can go onto the ward and Doctor Bishop will give you your antibiotics. Doctor Gillam, our registrar, is very busy at the moment, so she'll have to come and see you in the morning.'

This didn't sound very much like progress to me.

'But they've been looking for a bed for more than half an hour, now. What's the problem?'

'Things are very tight,' she said. 'There were some surgical wards closed just before Christmas and that has a knock-on effect. It means that a lot of the surgical patients are now on the medical wards. We keep a chart of all the beds available but it has to be updated all the time. We did think we'd found one for you just now, and we sent the sister along to check but she found there was already someone in it. Anyway, it really shouldn't be much longer.'

'Fine,' I said, with a touch of grimness.

'There is one problem, though.'

'Oh?'

There was a pause. I could tell it was something she was embarrassed about.

'Well, the thing is, we need this cubicle. I'm afraid we're going to have to move you.'

'Move us? But I thought you didn't have anywhere to move us to.'

It turned out that they did. They wheeled Fiona's trolley out into the corridor, pulled up a chair for me to sit beside her, and left us there. It took another ninety minutes to find the bed. We didn't get to see any more doctors in that time: both the houseman and the elusive Dr Gillam were fully occupied, so I gathered, dealing with the new arrival – the man I'd half-recognised – who it seemed they had somehow managed to revive. It was almost two o'clock when the nurses came to take Fiona away, and by then she looked helpless and frightened. I clasped her hand tightly and kissed her on the lips. They were very cold. Then I watched as they wheeled her off down the corridor.

•

The staff had insisted that I went home and got some rest, but I was only able to carry out the first half of this instruction. Physically I was exhausted, not least because I walked all the way back from the hospital, reaching the flat some time after four o'clock. But I'd never felt less like sleep, knowing as I did that in a darkened ward three or four miles away Fiona too was lying awake, her gaze fixed blankly on the ceiling. How could it have taken them so long to get her there? After I'd found her kneeling in front of the wardrobe, it had been more than five hours before she was put safely in that bed – hours in which her condition had clearly worsened. And yet nobody had been negligent, as far as I could see: the atmosphere had been one of frantic, resolute efficiency under pressure. So how could it have taken them so long?

I lay fully clothed on my bed, with the curtains open. A bed was a simple thing, or so I'd always thought. As far as I could remember there could hardly have been more than a dozen nights in my whole life when I hadn't slept in a bed somewhere or other. And hospitals were full of beds. That was the whole point about hospitals: they were just rooms full of beds. It was true that my faith in medical science had always been limited. I knew there were many ailments which it was powerless to treat, but it would never have occurred to me that a bunch of highly qualified doctors and nurses could have such difficulty simply transferring a patient from one place to another: from a cubicle to a bed. I wondered who was responsible for this state of affairs (yes, Fiona, I still believed in conspiracies), what vested interest they might have in making these people's lives even harder than they already were.

I'd been told to phone the hospital at about ten o'clock in the morning. Was there anyone else I should contact in the meantime? I got up and went into Fiona's flat to fetch her address book. It was full of names she'd never mentioned to me, and there was a letter folded inside the back cover, dated March 1984. Probably most of the people in this book hadn't heard from her in about six or seven years. One of them, presumably, was her ex-husband, the born-again Christian. As far as I knew they hadn't spoken to each other since the divorce, so there was no point involving him. She always spoke quite fondly of her colleagues at work: perhaps I should give them a call. But of course they wouldn't be in for another day or two.

She was alone: very much alone. We both were.

The table in my sitting room was still laid for our candlelit dinner, so I cleared everything away and then watched the first day of the New Year dawn feebly over Battersea. When it was light I considered taking a shower but settled for two cups of strong coffee instead. The prospect of waiting another three hours appalled me. I thought of my mother, and how she had done her best to fill out the empty days while my father lay in hospital. There were plenty of old newspapers in the flat so I gathered them together and started doing the crossword puzzles. I did half a dozen of the quick crosswords in no time at all and then got stuck into a jumbo-sized cryptic puzzle which required the use of dictionaries and reference books and a thesaurus. It didn't actually take my mind off anything, but it was better than just sitting around. It kept me going until twenty to ten, when I phoned the hospital.

I was put through to a nurse who told me that Fiona was still looking 'pretty poorly', and said that I could come in and see her now if I wanted to. Rudely, I put the receiver down without even thanking her, and almost broke a leg running down the staircase.

•

The ward was full but quiet: most of the patients looked bored rather than seriously ill. Fiona was in a bed near the nurses' room. I didn't recognise her at first, because she had an oxygen mask over her nose and mouth. There was a drip attached to her arm. I had to tap her on the shoulder before she realised I was there.

'Hello,' I said. 'I didn't know what to get you, so I brought some grapes. Not very original.'

She took the mask off and smiled. Her lips were turning slightly blue.

'They're seedless,' I added.

'I'll have some later.'

I held her hand, which was icy, and waited while she took some more breaths from the mask.

Fiona said: 'They're going to move me. To another ward.'

I said: 'How come?'

She said: 'Intensive care.'

I tried not to let the panic show in my face.

She said: 'They did all these things to me this morning. It took about an hour. It was awful.'

I said: 'What sort of things?'

She said: 'First of all, I saw Dr Gillam. The registrar. She was very nice, but she seemed a bit angry about something. She made them do an X-ray here. Right away. I had to sit up in bed and they put this plate behind my back. Then I had to keep breathing in. That was quite bad. Then they wanted to do a blood gases test, so they got this needle and had to find an artery. Here.' She showed me her wrist, which had several puncture marks. 'I think it must be difficult to get it right first time.'

I said: 'When are they moving you?'

She said: 'Soon, I think. I don't know what the delay is.'

I said: 'Have they told you what's wrong?'

She shook her head.

Dr Gillam took me aside into a private room. First of all she asked me if I was next of kin, and I said no, I was just a friend. She asked me how long I'd known Fiona and I said about four months, and she asked me if Fiona had any family and I said no, not unless there were uncles or cousins or things that I didn't know about. Then I asked her why Fiona was suddenly so ill and she told me everything, starting with the pneumonia. She'd picked up a severe pneumonia from somewhere and her body wasn't fighting it properly. The explanation for that lay in the X-rays (and, of course, in the consultant's notes, locked up somewhere in a filing cabinet), which revealed large growths in the centre of her chest: a lymphoma, in fact. The word meant nothing to me so Dr Gillam explained that it was a form of cancer, and seemed, in this case, to be quite advanced.

'How advanced?' I said. 'I mean, it's not too late to do anything about this, is it?'

Dr Gillam was a tall woman whose jet-black hair was cut in a bob and whose small, gold-rimmed glasses framed a pair of striking and combative brown eyes. She thought carefully before answering.

'If we could have got at this a bit earlier, we may have had a better chance.' She gave the impression of holding something back, at this point. Like Fiona, I could sense a closely guarded anger. 'As it is,' she continued, 'her blood oxygen level's been allowed to get very low. The only thing we can do is move her to intensive care and keep a close eye on her.'

'So what are you waiting for?'

'Well, it's not quite that simple. You see, first of all - '

I knew what was coming.

' – we've got to find her a bed.'

•

I stayed at the hospital until the bed was found. This time it only took about another half hour. It involved several telephone calls and appeared to depend, finally, on finding a patient two or three beds down the chain, throwing him off his ward and making him wait in the day room until he could be officially discharged. Then Fiona was taken away from me again and there was nothing I could do. I went home.

I didn't have any medical books but the dictionaries I'd used for the crossword were still lying on the table, so I looked up 'lymphoma'. All it said was, 'A tumour having the structure of a lymphatic gland'. Put like that it didn't sound very frightening but apparently this was the cause of all those months of sore throats and fevers, and this was the reason her immune system had all but closed down and surrendered to the first infection that came its way. I stared at the word again, stared at it for so long that it stopped making any kind of sense and began to look like nothing but a meaningless jumble of letters. How could anything so small, so random as this silly little word possibly do so much damage? How could it (but this wasn't going to happen) destroy a person?

It wasn't going to happen.

Suddenly revolted by the sight of the half-finished crossword, which seemed trivial and offensive, I screwed the newspaper up into a ball and in the process knocked over the cold remains of my second cup of coffee. Then, after fetching a cloth and wiping away the stain, I fell into a frenzy of cleaning. I polished the table, dusted the shelves and attacked the skirting board. I marshalled scourers and J-cloths, Pledge, Jif and Windolene. I went at it so ferociously that I started to take the paint off the window frames and the veneer off the coffee table. But even this wasn't enough. I piled all the furniture from my sitting room into the hallway and vacuumed the carpet. I took a mop to the bathroom floor and polished the taps and the shower fittings and the mirrors. I cleaned out the lavatory bowl. Then I went round the flat with two big black dustbin liners, throwing in every out-of-date magazine, every wad of yellowing newsprint, every discarded note and scrap of paper. I didn't stop, in fact, until I came upon an unopened Jiffy bag, containing my parcel of books from the Peacock Press. Seized by an absurd, almost hysterical curiosity, I tore it open and looked at the three volumes. I wanted to see something that would make me laugh.

There was a slender pamphlet entitled Architectural Beauties Of Croydon, which boasted, according to the flyleaf, 'three black and white illustations'. Plinths! Plinths! Plinths!, by the Reverend J. W. Pottage, promised to be 'the most accessible and humorous offering yet to fall from the pen of an author now internationally recognised as an authority in his field'. And the third book seemed to be yet another volume of war memoirs, bearing the somewhat enigmatic title, I Was "Celery".

Before I'd had time to attach any significance to this, the telephone rang. I threw the book down at once and went to answer it. It was the hospital. They were putting Fiona onto a ventilator and if I wanted to talk to her I should come right away.

●

'There's been a circulatory collapse,' Dr Gillam explained. 'We've been treating her with high concentrations of oxygen, but the level in her blood's still very low. So we'll have to try the ventilator. Once she's on it, though, she won't be able to talk. I thought you'd better see her first.'

She could barely talk even now.

She said: 'I can't understand it.'

And: 'Thanks for being here.'

And: 'You look tired.'

And: 'What happened to the lasagne?'

I said: 'You'll be all right.'

And: 'Are you comfortable?'

And: 'The doctors here are very good.'

And: 'You'll be all right.'

It was nothing special, as conversations go. I suppose none of our conversations had ever been all that special. Especially special, I nearly wrote. I think I must be going to pieces.

●

They said it would take about ninety minutes to set the ventilator up and fit all the necessary drips, and after that I could go back to see her. I lingered for a few minutes in the Relatives' Room, a functional-enough waiting area with a few unyielding black vinyl chairs and a selection of newspapers and magazines which seemed slightly more upmarket than usual. Then I went to get a cup of coffee, and managed to find a canteen which I think was intended for the use of staff rather than visitors, although nobody seemed to object when I took my seat. I'd been there for a while, drinking black coffee and getting through two and a half bars of Fruit and Nut, when someone stopped by my table and said hello.

I glanced up. It was the nurse who had been looking after Fiona that morning.

'How is she now?' she asked.

'Well, they're putting her on a ventilator at the moment,' I said. 'I assume that means things are fairly serious.'

Her response was non-commital. 'She'll be very well looked after.'

I nodded glumly, and she sat down in the chair opposite me.

'How are you feeling, though?'

I hadn't really thought about this. After a second or two I said, rather to my own surprise: 'I'm not sure. Angry, if anything.'

'Not with Dr Bishop, I hope.'

'No, not with anyone specific. I'd say it was with fate, except that I don't actually believe in fate. With the particular chain of circumstances, I suppose, which has

240

brought – ' Suddenly it struck me that I hadn't understood her remark. 'Why should I be angry with Dr Bishop?'

'Well, it probably would have been better if she'd been given the antibiotics last night,' she said doubtfully. 'She might at least have been more comfortable that way. Not that it ought to make that much difference, in the long run ...'

'Hang on,' I said: 'I thought she did have them last night. I mean, that's what they told me was going to happen.'

I could see it dawning on her that she shouldn't have told me. She must have assumed that I already knew.

'Look,' she said, 'I ought to be getting back to the ward ...'

I followed her into the corridor but she wouldn't answer any more of my questions, and I gave up when I caught sight of Dr Gillam out in the car park, wrapped up against the winter cold in her gloves and trench coat. I hurried to the main entrance and ran after her, catching up just as she was fumbling in her pocket for the car keys.

'Can I have a word with you?' I said.

'Of course.'

'I don't want to keep you, if you've finished for the day ...'

'Never mind that. Was there something you wanted to know?'

'Yes, there was.' I hesitated. There seemed to be no tactful way of approaching this. 'Is it true that Dr Bishop forgot to give Fiona her antibiotics last night?'

She said: 'Where did you hear that?'

I said: 'Is that what you were so angry about this morning?'

She said: 'It might be a good idea if we went for a drink.'

As it was a Bank Holiday and the middle of the afternoon, all the pubs were shut. We were in a gloomy backwater of South West London. The best we could manage, in the end, was a bleak and characterless little café, rendered all the more tacky by the fact that it had obviously been designed to fool unwary customers into thinking that it was part of a well-known fast food chain. It called itself 'Nantucket Fried Chicken'.

'I think I've got the coffee,' said Dr Gillam, after sipping from her paper cup. We swapped drinks.

'No, this could be the tea,' I said, testing it doubtfully. But we didn't swap again. There didn't seem much point.

'You went through quite an ordeal last night,' she began, after a few moments' thought. 'In fact, what you went through was unacceptable. But I'm afraid I can't apologise, because it happens all the time, and it would have happened anywhere else.'

'It wasn't quite what I ... would have expected,' I said, not sure where any of this was leading.

'This is my last month as a doctor,' she now announced, abruptly.

I nodded, more confused than ever.

'I'm going to have a baby.'

'Congratulations.'

'I don't mean that I'm pregnant. I mean that I might as well have a baby now, while I'm trying to decide what to do next. The fact is that I can't really put up with this job any more. It depresses me too much.'

241

'Why become a doctor in the first place,' I asked, 'if illness depresses you?'

'Illness is only one of the things we're fighting against.'

'What are the others?'

She considered. '"Interference" would be the best word, I suppose.' She brushed this line of argument aside angrily. 'I'm sorry, I don't want this to turn into a political lecture. We should be talking about Fiona.'

'Or Dr Bishop,' I said. Then asked: 'Is it true?'

'The point is,' she said, leaning forward, 'that it's no use trying to find scapegoats. He'd been on call for twenty-six hours. And they found the bed as quickly as they could. I was horrified when I heard about it this morning, but I don't know why. As I said, it happens all the time.'

I tried to take this in. 'So ...I mean, what kind of effect are we talking about here?'

'It's hard to say. I don't think the pneumonia would necessarily have taken hold the way it did. Not if she'd been put onto a ward straight away, and given her antibiotics last night.'

'Look, if you're telling me that her life – ' I didn't want to say this; just by saying it, there was a danger of making it real: ' – that her life has been put in danger through somebody's negligence – '

'I'm not talking about negligence. I'm talking about people trying to work under conditions which are becoming impossible.'

'Somebody must create those conditions!'

'The decision to close wards is taken by managers.'

'Yes, but on what basis?'

She sighed. 'These are not people who feel a personal involvement with the hospital. They're brought in from outside on short-term contracts to balance the books. If they balance the books by the end of the financial year then they get their bonus. Simple.'

'And whose bright idea was that?'

'Who knows? Some cabinet minister, some civil servant, some academic guru sitting on a policy-making committee.'

A name immediately flashed through my mind: Henry.

I said: 'But that's the only consideration, is it – finance?'

'Not always.' Doctor Gillam smiled bitterly. 'Another ward was closed a few days ago. Do you know why?'

'Go on, I'll buy it.'

'War casualties.'

'But we're not at war,' I said, not even certain that I'd heard her properly.

'Well, somebody obviously thinks we will be soon, unless Saddam pulls his finger out. And this is one of the hospitals which has been told to clear some room for our gallant lads out at the front.'

There was no option but to believe her, however incredible it might seem. But I hated the way we were now expected to take this war for granted: where had it come from, this breezy assumption of inevitability? In any case, it was supposed to be nothing to do with me – something that was happening thousands of miles away, on the other side of the world: on the other side (which was further still) of a television screen. So how could I suddenly accept that it was now one of the forces conspiring against Fiona: that it had already crept into her blameless life? It was as if cracks had started to appear in the screen and this awful reality was leaking out: or as if the glass barrier itself had magically turned to liquid and without knowing it I had slipped across the divide, like a dreaming Orpheus.

All my life I'd been trying to find my way to the other side of the screen: ever since my visit to the cinema in Weston-Super-Mare. Did this mean that I'd made it at last?

Jonathan Coe

the underfunders' utopia

the state hospital
with one bed

always full
always efficient

Tom Leonard

High Altitude Lavender

When snow fell for six hours
in an unforeseen direction,
the winter of fruit skins
recovered the footlight glow
of the sun as solid silver.

A gothic bouquet
of bronze-coloured roses,
standing up in a military elegance
shackled to a trance,
flexed gleaming silken arches.

A stem of body-bound
orchids on a breathless postcard
changed their florid despair
to a midnight-blue glance,
and accepted to speak about next year.

A sheaf of country dahlias
in a communal ward
turned their humbled palms out
with morbid homage to embrace
the rustle of live wings.

I kept colliding with the absence
of my own heavy family,
fiery as this year's grapes
that the dew considered heartless,
as though they had grown deafer;

and addresses a conversation
to no one among us,
to the gardens framed by your windows,
that can imitate the shape of flowers
with their mere mouth and their empty fingers.

Bleu de Paris

After two weeks, you cannot find a scar
To dye the heavens with purple, only
A remembered colour, or a scent
Associated with new mown hay.

Everywhere the eye is struck
With a little creeping pain,
Bright red needles
In the composition of the air.

We forget that we enjoyed
The more subdued and pensive
Harmonies, our common vision
Of God, on a day of many blooms,

Most of them mauve,
When the imprisoned spirits of the rain
Bow had a sweet taste
For her human eye,

Preparing the fastest blue
And fastening against water and light
Her tar-distilled crimson,
Her coal-derived blues.

Medbh McGuckian

Medbh McGuckian writes:

High Altitude Lavender
'There is a lot of imagery about "feet" and "arches" in this, since it was written last autumn/winter when my mother, aged 82, was recovering from an operation to amputate her right lower leg after an incurable breakage to the bone. Due to her own remarkable courage and high-spirit, but also most categorically to the care and judgement of her nurses, doctors and consultants, six of whom performed this difficult operation on her without a general anaesthetic, she has been restored to health. I was also thinking in the poem about the magnificent efforts of people who helped her in the long rehabilitation period which could have been very depressing for all of us. All along she was given special attention and private rooms. Thanks to a very generous "care package", with home visits and free wheel-chairs and beds, she is still able to live with my sister in her own house. The other day her normal hospital bed was exchanged for one safer, with sides, more comfortable, thanks to someone's consideration. Her quality of life we owe in large part to the kindness, the work and humanity of the NHS.'

Bleu de Paris
'The story of this poem is of this past autumn. My only daughter aged 12, was badly injured in some of the violence we have had in the city here recently. I have to thank from the bottom of my heart the many, many workers of the Royal Belfast Hospital for Sick Children who looked after her in the worst hours of intensive care. There was not a moment when she was left alone, in fact there were usually three or four people monitoring or checking her constantly. The facilities for parents to stay with their children were excellent and I was most grateful to be able to stay with her overnight.

246

Her distress at being ill was much alleviated by the provision of her our bedside "phone and television set". I had the use of a kitchen to bring her toast and tea whenever she felt like it. It sounds trivial but it was very important during those days to spoil her more than usual. The eye-doctor who examined her for any damage to the precious eye spent a whole morning on complex tests which relieved all my anxieties for her, which were many. The atmosphere of warmth, interest, co-operation, even enthusiasm, in a place where much of the suffering is so unnecessary, made me compare our situation here with that of Afghanistan, where few medical helpers if any are available for those, especially children, wounded in the battles. The list of my debts to the NHS, on a personal level, is too long, and I offer these two poems in very partial appreciation for a lifetime's experience, of both births and deaths.'

How Things Were

My mother was a nurse in the old Royal Free Hospital when it was in the East End of London, long before it moved to the heights of Hampstead. It was one of the first charity hospitals, financed by Royalty and the rich. Hospitals then had long wards with high ceilings and tall windows and acres of polished floors. No curtains, hygiene forbade them. The ghost of Florence Nightingale still ruled.

The nursing staff was as structured as the army. The lowest were the probationers, then the first, second, third year and staff nurses, then the ward sisters and over all Matron, whose martinet eye did not miss a grain of dust or a bed whose corners were half an inch out.

My mother fought with her father to be a nurse: he could not agree; middleclass girls did not become nurses. Defying him she left home and without any support from him worked her way up that jealous hierarchy. Pay was bad, and the food poor. Most nurses had help from their families. It was hard for her, but she did it, and became Sister in time for the First World War. For the four years of that war she nursed the wounded soldiers sent back to the hospital in Britain from the casualty stations and makeshift hospitals in France and Belgium. The Royal Free was overfull with soldiers, one of them my father who always considered himself lucky to have got shrapnel in his leg in time to get him sent home before the battle of Passchendaele where every man in his company was killed. When the war ended she was offered the job of matron in the old St George's Hospital on Hyde Park Corner, now a prestigious hotel, nothing left of the tall hall-like wards, the tall austere windows. She was thirty-two, and young for that coveted position. It must have been hard to turn down something so suited to her talents and her temperament, but she did, and in due course found herself on a farm in the old Rhodesia, in a house that was an elongated mud hut, rooms one, two, three, four under thatch. In a trunk was her Sister McVeagh's uniform, and the nursing manual from her student days, which I devoured, aged eight, nine, ten, with incredulity.

There, on that hill, around and through the house dust blew in the dry season, or bits of burned grass from the bush fires; straws, loosened by borers, fell from the thatch where mice, and more than once, little monkeys scurried and played. Over whitewashed walls white ants made ingenious tunnels of red earth which had to be brushed off when they dried, leaving faint pink stains. I liked to keep the door open, though frogs did hop in and out of the room, mosquitoes hunted for their blood feasts, and mosquito nets bundled over the beds could easily have dust in them or a blown leaf.

Thus surrounded, I read about the day and night vigilance to preserve hygiene, in the old Royal Free Hospital.

Every bed frame, locker, bed table, light bracket, chair, had to be wiped with disinfectant every day. The walls and ceilings were wiped over with disinfectant once a week. Floors were scoured daily. Bedding was changed every day. Patients were washed or washed themselves, face and hands, twice a day and all over once a day. Every time a patient was moved from one room to another, or left, and a new one brought in, each surface had to be scrubbed with disinfectant, floors, walls, ceilings, bed, locker, table, chair.

Bedpans had a room to themselves and were continually being sluiced with boiling water and disinfectant. Nowhere more than here lingered memories of the typhoid and cholera of past wars where more soldiers died from them than they ever did from bullets.

Each ward had a kitchenette where tea, beef tea, hot drinks, jellies, and special delicacies like arrowroot jelly and calfsfoot jelly could be prepared, to tempt sick appetites.

On a wall in the staffroom a notice exhorted: 'Never forget! The cleanliness of the nurses is of equal importance to that of the patients!'

Nurses' hands, forearms, nails, and hair were examined by the sisters, and everyone was monitored by Matron.

Doctors were on a parallel ladder of achievement, and had nothing to do with this ferocious structure of cleanliness and discipline. Matron, I think, would not dare to examine their nails and hands and hair for dirt, though it is hard to imagine a doctor, no matter how senior, withstanding Matron's cold stare at finger nails or hands.

All this I read about, lying in bed, in the middle of southern Africa, while the many winds of heaven wafted what they willed into and around the house, and in the dry season my bathwater might be red with the day's dust. My mother, Sister McVeagh, countered my incredulity with, 'You see, if you are nursing people, there are all those germs about, so *of course* it is important to have *absolute* hygiene.'

Last year I sat by a bed in the new Royal Free, in Intensive Care. What expertise, skill, dedication, devotion; how moving it was to see. What wonderful care my sick relative was getting. But the hours passed, and then a day, and another, and I entertained myself with imagining that Sister McVeagh walked in, a tall and commanding figure, with her full crisp white veil, her little cape, not a hair out of its place. There is a photograph of her in this outfit.

She is bewildered.

'Who are all these people?' she demands.

'They are the doctors and nurses.'

'Why are they wearing pyjamas?'

'Don't you see? These cotton tops and pants, they are also so practical, they don't get in the way when they work, and then into the washing machine they go... .'

She sighs. 'Washing machines ... now, if we'd had those ... keeping those mountains of sheets and pillowcases clean, it was a nightmare. The laundry, it was the most important place in the hospital. But when you went in – you had to sometimes – you'd think it was an inferno, it was so hot, and the clouds of steam ... the washing women always had coughs, it was not a place anyone would work in unless they had to.'

Now she is looking at the beds, and at the patients in them, each one with two or three or sometimes up to five lines attached to them, and the equipment: she is listening to the clicks and calls and chattering of the machines.

Eighty years or so of evolving hospital techniques means that Sister McVeagh, who in her time was as skilled as anyone in her profession, doesn't know what she is looking at, and would hardly dare to try and read a dial or adjust a tube.

A nurse – a little girl – so it would seem – goes to a patient with a thermometer, and lifts the wrist to check the pulse. This at least is the same.

'She is so small' my mother whispers, but she is overheard, and the nurse – she is from Taiwan – says smartly, 'But I'm strong.' She is eyeing Sister McVeagh, wondering part of the hospital she can be from. She has never seen anything like the full veil, the starched cuffs, and cufflinks, the gleaming starched collar.

'Will you explain these machines to me?' My mother realises she sounds commanding, and though this is hardly correct, from a sister to a mere nurse, adds, humbly, 'Please.'

The nurse is busy, and she is tired, being in the eleventh hour of a twelve hour shift: this at least she shares with Sister McVeagh – being overworked – but she says politely, 'This one here, it monitors the heart beat: it calls us if the heart gets out of phase. This tube – it's for rehydration: this patient is badly dehydrated. This is blood. This dial monitors blood pressure. This is for intravenal feeding. This is oxygen. This is for antibiotics... .'

'Well, we did have oxygen' my mother says and I can tell she is ready to cry. 'If we had these things, if we had had them, then those poor boys wouldn't have died so often, my poor boys wouldn't have died, and they were so young, some of them, it was dreadful, sometimes it didn't matter what we did, we couldn't save them. Those poor tommies, if we had these things then... .'

The nurse is being called from a near bed, where colleagues have arrived to deal with a crisis. She wants to leave, but Sister McVeagh is going on, she has to, she needs so badly that this young woman should understand her, acknowledge her.

'After big battles like the Somme, like Passchendaele, the stretcher bearers were bringing in the wounded off the lorries and the carts for hours. The men lay on their stretchers all along the corridors, calling and crying for help. Dreadfully wounded men. Sometimes they died before we could get to them. All the hospitals in London were the same. And we got them into the beds, those poor tommies... if we had then what you have now...antibiotics, you say...is that disinfectant?'

The nurse has to go. She gives a last puzzled look at this extraordinary figure and she is thinking, Did they call patients tommies then? Her boys, she says...which war was that? – But it is all too difficult and she is already with the other nurses and doctors by the crisis bed.

Sister McVeagh stands watching. The concentration, the dedication, is familiar, yes, once she herself... but she understands nothing of what they are doing with this patient.

I hear her sigh. I hear her murmur: 'If we had had these things, don't you see? – they needn't have died, at least not so much, the poor boys... .'

I watch her walk away out of Intensive Care and back into the past.

Doris Lessing

Case Notes

Dannie Abse is both Jewish and Welsh, both medical physician and poet. He has drawn upon seemingly disparate elements of his life in an extensive body of work that includes ten volumes of poetry (the first published while he was still a medical student), three novels, plays, and autobiographical works.

Lynne Alexander was born in Brooklyn, New York, and has lived in the U.K. since 1970. Her first novel, *Safe Houses*, was published in Britain in 1984 and has been translated into 8 languages. Since then she has published four more novels: *Resonating Bodies*, *Taking Heart*, *Adolf's Revenge* and *Intimate Cartographies*.

Moniza Alvi was born in Pakistan and grew up in Hertfordshire. She taught in London comprehensive schools for many years, and has written four books of poetry. Her compendium collection *Carrying My Wife* (2000) was published by Bloodaxe. Her latest collection is *Souls* (Bloodaxe, 2002).

Susan Bassnett has published books on comparative literature, translation, women's writing, theatre history, Shakespeare, and the feminist movement in various cultures. Her most recent book, co-edited with Ulrich Broich, is *Britain at the Turn of the Twenty-first Century*. A book of poems, *Exchanging Lives*, was published in 2002.

Gerard Benson writes for both children and adults, and is co-founder and –organiser of *Poems on the Underground*. He worked for ten years with psychiatric patients at the North Middlesex Hospital. He was recently poet-in-practice in a GP's surgery in inner-city Bradford.

Christopher Bigsby is the author of three novels: *Hester*, *Pearl* and *Still Lives*. He is Professor of American Literature at the University of East Anglia and a regular presenter of arts programmes for the BBC.

Peter Blegvad is an American writer, illustrator, musician, songwriter and pamphleteer. His weekly cartoon strip, 'Leviathan', ran in the *Independent on Sunday* from 1991-98. *The Book of Leviathan* was published by Sort of Books in London in 2000 and by the Overlook Press, New York City, in 2001. In 1994, a slim volume of his writings and drawings *Headcheese* was published by Atlas Press.

Zoe Brigley is a new Welsh writer. Her work has appeared in various journals and anthologies, and she has led writing workshops in schools and colleges.

Andy Brown is Lecturer in Creative Writing at Exeter University, and has been Centre Director for the Arvon Foundation for over five years. His third poetry collection, *From A Cliff* was published by Arc in 2002. New poems also appeared in *Of Science* (The Worple Press). He has recently finished his first novel.

John Burnside lives and works in East Fife. His latest collection of poetry, *The Light Trap*, was published by Jonathan Cape in 2002. He is currently working on a novel.

Peter Carpenter is a poet whose collections include: *Choosing an England, No Age* and *The Blackout Book*. He co-directs The Worple Press.

Candida Clark has published two novels, *The Last Look* and *The Constant Eye*, available in Vintage paperback. Her third, *The Mariner's Star*, was published by

Headline Review in 2002. She is currently at work on a fourth. She has also published short stories, poetry and criticism.

Jonathan Coe is the author of five previous novels: *The Accidental Woman*, *A Touch of Love*, *The Dwarves of Death*, *What a Carve Up!*, which won the 1995 John Llewellyn Rhys Prize and the French Prix du Meilleur Livre Etranger and *The House of Sleep*, which won the Writer's Guild Best Fiction Award in 1997. His latest book is *The Rotters' Club*.

David Constantine has published half a dozen volumes of poetry with Bloodaxe Books, most recently *Something for the Ghosts* in which the poems in this anthology are published. In addition, he is the author of a novel and a collection of short stories. Until 2000 he was Fellow in German at the Queen's College, Oxford, and works full-time now as a writer and translator.

Robert Crawford is Professor of English at the University of St Andrews. In addition to academic work and the editing of literary anthologies, he has published a number of volumes of poetry including *Spirit Machines*, *Talkies*, *Masculinity* and *A Scottish Assembly*.

Susan Crawford was born in Birmingham and works as a specialist nurse in Haemoglobinopathies. This poem was inspired by her son, Jamie, to give insight.

David Dabydeen is a poet and novelist. His works include *Slave Song* (winner of Commonwealth Poetry Prize, 1984), *Coolie Odyssey*, *Turner*, *The Counting House*, and *A Harlot's Progress*. David Dabydeen is also Guyana's ambassador-at-large and a member of UNESCO's Executive Board.

Julia Darling is a playwright, poet and fiction writer. She has worked as a performance poet with the Poetry Virgins, and published poems in their anthology *Sauce*, and *Modern Goddess*. *Eating the Elephant*, her last full length work, toured the country several times and was also produced in the States. Her first novel *Crocodile Soup* was published in 1998 by Transworld.

Stevie Davies is a novelist, literary critic, biographer and historian. She was born in Wales and is a Fellow of the Royal Society of Literature, a Member of the Academi Gymreig and is the Royal Literary Fund Fellow at the University of Wales, Swansea.

Michael Donaghy was born in the Bronx, New York. His most recent collection, *Conjure*, was a PBS Choice and won the Forward Prize. His previous collections have won the Whitbread and Geoffrey Faber Memorial Prizes. He teaches at City University and Birkbeck College and he is a Fellow of The Royal Society of Literature.

Maura Dooley is a poet who also works in film and theatre. In film, she has recently worked as part of a creative team developing educational films for Jim Henson Productions. In theatre, she has coordinated experimental workshops for Performing Arts Labs, creating new plays for younger audiences. Her volumes of poetry include *Ivy Leaves and Arrows*, *Explaining Magnetism*, *Kissing a Bone*, all with Bloodaxe Books.

Carol Ann Duffy has published several collections of poetry for both children and adults. Her latest collection *Feminine Gospels* will appear in 2002 from Picador and she has several new children's titles appearing in 2002 and 2003. She is currently the recipient of a NESTA Fellowship for new work and is completing a third collection of new poems for young readers.

Ian Duhig worked with homeless people for 15 years before becoming a freelance teacher and writer. He has received Arts Council and Cholmondeley Awards, won the National Poetry Competition twice and the Forward Tolman Cunard Prize. His most recent book is *Nominies* (Bloodaxe 1998). His next is forthcoming from Picador.

Douglas Dunn has published ten collections of poems, the most recent being *The Donkey's Ears* and *The Year's Afternoon*. His *New Selected Poems 1964 - 2000* will appear in 2002. He is Director of the Scottish Studies Institute and Professor of English at the University of St Andrews.

U.A. Fanthorpe became an assistant English teacher, and then later head of English at the independent girls' school, Cheltenham Ladies' College. She found the teaching post demanding and left in 1972 to take a job as an admissions clerk in a Bristol Hospital which she did until 1983. She found time to start writing poetry, and when she was nearly 50 she compiled her first collection as *Side Effects* in 1978. Her subsequent books include *A Watching Brief, Neck-Verse, Safe as Houses*, and *Consequences*.

Michael Foxton went to Oxford and St Mary's medical schools, and is now a junior doctor in the north of England. He also writes *Bedside Stories, The Life of a Junior Doctor*, for the *Guardian* Health pages.

Maureen Freely was born in Neptune, New Jersey, and grew up in Istanbul, Turkey. Since graduating from Harvard in 1974, she has lived mostly in England. She is the author of five novels – *Mother's Helper, The Life of the Party, The Stork Club, Under the Vulcania*, and *The Other Rebecca* – and three works of non-fiction – *Pandora's Clock, What About Us?* and *The Parent Trap*. She is a regular contributor to *The Guardian, Observer, Sunday Times, Daily Mail*, and *The Independent*.

Katherine Gallagher is a widely-published poet and her books include *Fish-Rings on Water* (Forest Books, l989), *Finding the Prince* (Hearing Eye Pamphlet Series, 1993), a translation of Jean-Jacques Celly's poems, *The Sleepwalker with Eyes of Clay* (Forest Books, 1994) and *Tigers on the Silk Road* (Arc Publications, 2000).

Peter Goldsworthy is an MD. His most recent book is *This Goes With That: Selected Poems* (Leviathan, UK, 2001). His novels *Maestro, Honk If You Are Jesus* and *Wish* are best-sellers in Australia, have also been translated into many European and Asian languages. He lives in Adelaide, where he divides his time between writing and medicine.

Sophie Hannah lives in Bingley.Her latest novel, *The Superpower of Love* has just been published by Arrow, and her three poetry collections are published by Carcanet. She teaches at the Writing School at Manchester Metropolitan University.

David Hart has been university chaplain, theatre critic and arts administrator, and is the author of the poetry collection *Setting the poem to words*. He was Poet in Residence for Worcester Cathedral, South Birmingham Mental Health NHS Trust and the Aldeburgh Poetry Festival, and runs a literature course for post-graduate doctors at Heartlands Hospital, Birmingham.

John Hegley is widely known in Britain as a populariser of poetry. He is also known for his spectacles and a penchant for dogs and potatoes. He adds dance, mandolin playing, and drawing to his performances, which create a warm family atmosphere, with something of a medicinal quality.

W.N. Herbert is a highly versatile poet who writes both in English and Scots. He established his reputation with two collections from Bloodaxe, *Forked Tongue* and *Cabaret McGonagall*. His other books include a critical study, *To Circumjack MacDiarmid* and *The Testament of the Reverend Thomas Dick*. He is co-editor with Matthew Hollis of *Strong Words: modern poets on modern poetry* (Bloodaxe).

Selima Hill lives in Lyme Regis, Dorset and is the only poet to have been shortlisted for the Whitbread, Forward and T S Eliot Prizes with her seventh collection *Violet*. Her eighth collection *Bunny* was the Poetry Book Society Choice in 2001 and won the Whitbread Poetry Prize in 2002. She is currently working as a tutor at the South Bank Centre and at the Poetry School, in London.

Douglas Houston was born in Cardiff, and grew up in Scotland, and later became a Hull poet – his work was featured in Douglas Dunn's seminal anthology *A Rumoured City*. He has published several collections of poetry including *With the Offal Eaters* and *The Hunters in the Snow* both from Bloodaxe.

Kim Hudson has been in nursing for over 20 years in both Primary and Secondary care in Birmingham. She has officially spent half her life in the NHS.

Glyn Hughes was awarded the Guardian Fiction Prize as well as the David Higham Prize for his first novel, *Where I Used To Play On The Green*. He was short-listed for The Whitbread Novel of the Year for *The Antique Collector* and has won national prizes and awards for his poetry collections. His latest novel was *Bronte,* a life of the Bronte family.

Siân Hughes's publications include *Saltpetre*, a Smith/Doorstop poetry pamphlet in 1998. In 2000 she was awarded a Southern Arts writers award and her poetry appeared in *Anvil New Poets 3*, 2001. She works as a freelance writer and education consultant, and lives in Oxfordshire.

Michael Hulse's selected poems were published in 2002 by Salt under the title *Empires and Holy Lands*. The acclaimed translator of more than fifty books from the German, he is also a prolific critic, co-edited the best-selling anthology *The New Poetry*, and recently established the poetry press Leviathan.

Kathleen Jamie has published four collections of poetry and a travel book: *Black Spiders*, *The Way We Live*, *The Golden Peak: travels in Northern Pakistan*, *The Queen of Sheba* and *Jizzen*. Kathleen Jamie lives in north Fife, Scotland with her young family, and teaches at the University of St Andrews.

Russell Celyn Jones is an award-winning novelist, and short story writer. His books include novels, *Soldiers and Innocents*, *Small Times*, *An Interference of Light*, *The Eros Hunter*, and anthologies *The Time Out Book of New York Short Stories* and *The Ex-Files*. He also reviews for *The Sunday Times* and *The London Review of Books* and writes screenplays.

Jackie Kay is an award-winning poet and novelist. Her novel *Trumpet* won the Guardian Fiction award. She was born and brought up in Scotland. Her latest collection of short stories, *Why Don't You Stop Talking* is published by Picador.

A.L. Kennedy is the author of two award-winning collections of short stories, three award-winning novels and the award-winning *Original Bliss*: short stories and a novella. She has also written two non-fiction books and a variety of journalism. She was listed among Granta's Best of Young British novelists, and is a Fellow of the Royal Society of Literature and has sold brushes door-to-door.

John Kinsella has published *The Silo* (Arc), *Poems1980-1994* (Bloodaxe), and *The Hierarchy of Sheep* (Bloodaxe). He also writes novels, short fiction, plays, essays, and is poetry critic with the *Observer* newspaper. He is a commissioning editor for Arc and Salt publications, and international editor for *The Kenyon Review*.

Bill Kirton has published two crime novels, *Material Evidence* and *Rough Justice* both with Piatkus, and his short story 'Missing' was included in the Crime Writers Associations 1999 *Anthology*. In the same year, his verse translation of Molière's *Sganarelle* won a BCLA translation prize.

Hanif Kureishi was born in Bromley. His most well-known novels are arguably *The Buddha of Suburbia* and *The Black Album*. He wrote the screen-play for *My Beautiful Laundrette* and *Sammy and Rosie Get Laid. My Beautiful Laundrette* was awarded Best Screenplay award from the New York Film Critics Circle. *The Buddha of Suburbia* won Whitbread Book of the Year Award. He has written two collections of short stories, *Love in a Blue Time*, and *Midnight All Day*, and his last novel was *Intimacy*. His most recently published novel is *Gabriel's Gift*.

Joel Lane lives in Birmingham and is the author of *From Blue to Black* and *The Earth Wire and Other Stories.* He is also the notable poet of *The Edge of the Screen.*

Anna Lea has been writing poetry for three years, dividing her time between England and Spain. She is currently completing her BA in Writing and is working on her first collection of poetry.

Tom Leonard is a poet who was born in Glasgow in 1944. He has published collections of poetry, biography and political satire. He is currently on Duovent inhaler and has moved from Becloforte to the new Symbicort turbohaler.

Doris Lessing was born in 1919 in Khermanshah, Persia. In 1927, the family moved to Southern Rhodesia (Zimbabwe). In 1949, Lessing travelled to England with her son and a manuscript of *The Grass is Singing*. This was published in 1950 to immediate acclaim. It was followed by *This was the old Chief's Country* (1951), a volume of short stories that was also well received by the critics. *The Golden Notebook* (1962) won praise as a feminist text, although it was not conceived as such. She has been awarded numerous prizes including the Somerset Maugham Award in 1956 and the W.H.Smith Award in 1986.

Rupert Loydell is the Managing Editor of Stride Publications, and Visiting Fellow of Poetry at Warwick University. His poetry publications include *Home All Along, The Museum of Improvisation* and the collaborative *A Hawk Into Everywhere. The Museum of Light* was published by Arc in 2002.

Medbh McGuckian was born in Belfast. Her collections of poetry include *The Flower Master, Venus and the Rain, On Ballycastle Beach, Marconi's Cottage, Captain Lavender, Selected Poems*, and *Drawing Ballerinas*. Her awards include

The Cheltenham Award, The Alice Hunt Bartlett Prize, and the Bass Ireland Award for Literature in 1991. *Marconi's Cottage* was shortlisted for the Irish Times/Aer Lingus Irish Literature Prize for Poetry.

Katharine McMahon is the author of four novels. The latest *After Mary* (Flamingo) explores the extraordinary lives of a revolutionary group of seventeenth century English women. Katharine has also written lyrics and the book for a musical, and is a teacher of English and drama.

Edwin Morgan was born in 1920 in Glasgow's West End. His volume of *Collected Poems* (Carcanet Press, 1990) is the largest, a very wide ranging collection. He was announced Glasgow's first Poet Laureate in autumn 1999, and was awarded the Queen's Gold Medal for Poetry in 2000. He recently received the prestigious Weidenfeld Prize for Translation, the winning book being *Phaedra* (Carcanet).

Esther Morgan completed an MA in Creative Writing at the University of East Anglia and edits an annual anthology of new poetry *Reactions* for the university's small press, Pen&inc. Her first collection *Beyond Calling Distance* was published by Bloodaxe in 2001 and won the Aldeburgh Poetry Festival's first collection prize.

David Morley was a research biologist for many years. He is Director of the Writing Programme at Warwick University, where he develops new teaching and research for scientific, medical and creative writing. He co-edited *The New Poetry* for Bloodaxe. Recent poems are collected in *Ludus Coventriae* and *Scientific Papers* (Carcanet).

Blake Morrison's books include two collections of poems, *Dark Glasses* and *The Ballad of the Yorkshire Ripper*; a bestselling memoir, *And When Did You Last See Your Father?*; an account of the James Bulger murder case, *As If*; a children's book, *The Yellow House*; a collection of stories and journalism *Too True*; and, most recently, a novel, *The Justification of Johann Gutenberg*. His next book is a work of non-fiction, *Things My Mother Never Told Me*.

Andrew Motion is the Poet Laureate and Professor of Creative Writing at the University of East Anglia. He is as well-known for his biographies as he is for his poems, and is the author of *The Lamberts* (1987), *Philip Larkin: A Writer's Life* (1993), and *Keats* (1997). His most recent collections of poetry are *Salt Water*(1997)and *Selected Poems*(1998). He has also edited editions of *William Barnes* and *Thomas Hardy*. His work has been awarded the John Llewelyn Rhys Prize, the Somerset Maugham Prize, and the Whitbread Prize for biography.

Najam Mughal works for the NHS in Birmingham.

Paul Muldoon is one of the most innovative poets of his generation. His poetry – from his debut *New Weather* (1973) to *Hay* (1998), via a *New Selected Poems* – represents an influential body of work. He has received many accolades, including the T.S. Eliot Prize for *The Annals of Chile* in 1995. He is Oxford Professor of Poetry, President of The Poetry Society, and he directs the Princeton Writing Programme in the United States.

Elizabeth Mulrey works for the NHS in Birmingham.

Les Murray is Australia's leading poet and one of the finest contemporary poets writing in English. He has won many literary awards, including the Grace Leven

Prize (1980 and 1990), the Petrarch Prize (1995), and the prestigious TS Eliot Award (1996). In 2000 he was awarded the Queens Gold Medal for Poetry on the recommendation of Ted Hughes. He is published in Britain by Carcanet Press.

Matt Nunn is a West Midlands Arts Creative Writing Fellow at Warwick University and poet-in-residence at Birmingham City Football club. His first collection of poems *Apocalyptic Bubblegum* was published in 2002.

Sean O'Brien is an award-winning poet, critic, playwright, broadcaster, anthologist and editor. He has published five collections of poetry, most recently *Downriver* (Picador) in which 'Poem for a Psychiatric Conference' appears. This poem was originally commissioned by the Neuropsychiatric Department of Newcastle Royal Victorian Hospital.

Bernard O'Donoghue is an Irish poet. He lectures in Oxford at Wadham College. Whitbread Prize winner, O'Donoghue is the author of important critical studies on Shakespeare and has published a monograph study on the poetry of Seamus Heaney, entitled *Seamus Heaney and the Language of Poetry* (1995). In 1995, his collection of poems *Gunpowder* (Chatto & Windus) was nominated the Book of the Year.

Maggie O'Farrell was born in Northern Ireland, and grew up in Wales and Scotland. She worked as a waitress, chambermaid, cycle courier, teacher, arts administrator and journalist before writing her first novel, *After You'd Gone*. Her second novel, *My Lover's Lover*, was published in 2002.

Miriam Obrey is a part time counsellor for Relate. She has led writing workshops through the Poetry Society's Poetry Placements scheme. Her poems have appeared in the national press and literary magazines. Her pamphlet *A Case For More Heads* was published by Flarestack in 1996.

Cheryl Palmer is a Speech and Language Therapist and has worked for the National Health Service for eleven years.

William Parry, FRS, is Professor of Mathematics at Warwick University.

Don Paterson was born in Dundee. After many years working in South East England, he now lives in Kirriemuir, Angus. He works as a writer, musician and editor; his most recent collection is *The Eyes* (Faber). He has won the Forward Prize, the Geoffrey Faber Award, the T.S. Eliot Prize and the Arvon Poetry Competition.

Tom Paulin was born in Leeds, and grew up in Belfast. He was educated at the universities of Hull and Oxford, and is now Lecturer in English at Hertford College, Oxford. His most famous poetry collections are *The Strange Museum* (1980), *Liberty Tree* (1983), Fivemiletown (1987), *Selected Poems,* Faber & Faber,(1990). He has also published *The Faber Book of Political Verse*. He is a regular critic on BBC2's *Late Review*. His most recent volumes of poems are *The Wind Dog* and *The Invasion Handbook*.

Pascal Petit was born in Paris, has travelled extensively in the Venezuelan Amazon, and lives in London, where she is poetry editor of *Poetry London* and a tutor for The Poetry School. Her first poetry collection was *Heart of a Deer* (Enitharmon, 1998); her second, *The Zoo Father*, is due from Seren Press. She was short-listed for a Forward Prize for best single poem in 2000.

Mario Petrucci is a poet and scientist whose collections include *Shrapnel and Sheets* and *Bosco*. He works widely in universities and schools both in a freelance capacity and as a member of the Poetry Society's Poetryclass project. He is Royal Literary Fund Fellow at Oxford Brookes University.

Milner Place was born in Yorkshire. He has spent most of his life as the skipper of trading vessels and yachts. He has published poems in Spanish and English, and lives in Huddersfield. Chatto and Windus publish his major collection *In a Rare Time of Rain*.

Ian Pople's *The Glass Enclosure* (Arc) was shortlisted for the Forward Prize for First Collection (1997). His son, Ben, was in Booth Hall Children's Hospital, Manchester, with pyloric stenosis at the age of five weeks.

Peter Porter was born in Brisbane, Australia and came to England in 1951. His many poetry collections include *Once Bitten Twice Bitten, Poems Ancient and Modern* and *Words Without Music*. His *Collected Poems* were recently published. Among the awards and honours bestowed on Porter have been Cholmondeley Award, The Duff Cooper Prize and The Whitbread Prize.

Simon Rae is a poet, playwright, biographer and broadcaster. He presented Radio 4's *Poetry Please!* for five years; wrote a regular topical poem for the *Guardian* for ten years and won the National Poetry Competition in 1999. He wrote *W.G.Grace: A Life* (Faber 1998) and *It's Not Cricket* (Faber 2001), and his first stage play, *A Quiet Night In*, was performed in Bristol and London in 1999.

Ravi Randhawa is a story writer and Royal Literary Fund Fellow at Toynbee Hall, London.

Tim Reeves was awarded a Student Fellowship at the Centre for Literary Translation in Spain, and an Arvon Foundation/Jerwood Fellowship for new writers. He is completing his first novel *Walking with Water*.

Michael Symmons Roberts was born in Lancashire. His most recent collection of poems *Burning Babylon* (Cape) was shortlisted for the TS Eliot Prize. He is a regular collaborator with the composer James MacMillan, and an award-winning writer for radio.

Jane Rogers has written six novels, *Separate Tracks*, *Her Living Image* (winner of a Somerset Maugham award), *The Ice is Singing, Mr Wroe's Virgins, Promised Lands* (Writers Guild Best Fiction Award 1996) and *Island* (Little, Brown; 1999). Her novels are published in U.S.A. by Overlook Press. She has written original drama for television, including *Dawn and the Candidate* (C4, Samuel Beckett Award) and adapted *Mr Wroe's Virgins* as an award-winning BBC drama serial. She is a Fellow of the Royal Society of Literature.

Anne Rouse has worked as a general and psychiatric nurse and for a mental health charity. Her poetry has appeared in many periodicals, such as the *Independent, Observer, Atlantic Monthly*, and the *Times Literary Supplement*. Both of her collections, *Sunset Grill* and *Timing*, were Poetry Book Society Recommendations.

W.G. Sebald was born in Wertach im Allgäu,Germany, in 1944. He studied German language and literature in Freiburg, Switzerland and Manchester. In 1966 he took up a position as an assistant lecturer at the University of Manchester, and settled in England for good in 1970. He taught at the University of East Anglia, becoming Professor of European Literature in 1987, and from 1989 to 1994 he was the first Director of the British Centre for Literary Translation at UEA. His novels include *The Emigrants, The Rings of Saturn, Vertigo* and *Austerlitz*. He was killed in a car accident in December 2001.

Jo Shapcott has been a Writers Fellow at The British Library, won the Forward Prize in 1999 and has twice won the National Poetry Competition. She has published several volumes of poetry: *Electroplating the Baby*, *Phrase Book*, *My Life Asleep* and *Tender Taxes*.

Henry Shukman has won several national poetry prizes, as well as awards from the Arts Council of England and Southern Arts. He has worked as a trombonist and travel-writer, and reviews for the *New York Times Book Review*. His first poetry collection was published by Cape in August 2002.

Michael Smith is Principal Immunologist in the Biochemistry Department on Good Hope Hospital, Birmingham.

Jane Stevenson is a novelist and academic. Her books include a sequence of novellas *Several Deceptions* (Cape), and the novels *London Bridges* and *Astraea*. She teaches at the University of Aberdeen.

Lucretia Stewart is the author of *Tiger Balm: Travels in Laos, Vietnam & Cambodia*; *The Weather Prophet: A Caribbean Journey*, and *Making Love: A Romance*. She is also the editor of *Erogenous Zones: An Anthology of Sex Abroad*.

Mall Surjit works for the NHS in Birmingham.

Matthew Sweeney has had numerous occasions to thank the NHS. His books include *The Bridal Suite, A Smell of Fish, Selected Poems* all from Cape. He has also published *Up on the Roof, New and Selected poems for children* (Faber); edited *The New Faber Book of Children's Verse*; and co-edited, with Jo Shapcott, *Emergency Kit: Poems for Strange Times* (Faber). A children's novel, *Fox*, is published by Bloomsbury.

George Szirtes has published many volumes of poetry, including *Portrait of my Father in an English Landscape* (OUP), which was both a PBS recommendation and a Book of the Year, and *The Budapest File* (Bloodaxe). He has won or been short-listed for many major awards including The Faber Memorial Prize, the Whitbread Poetry Prize, the Wiedenfeld Prize and the Forward Prize for Poetry.

Valerie Thornton writes poetry and short stories and, when she's not Royal Literary Fund Fellow at Glasgow University, leads creative writing workshops (in hospitals and elsewhere). *Working Words* (Hodder & Stoughton), is her award-winning creative-writing textbook for schools. *Catacoustics*, her first collection of poems, is published by Mariscat Press.

Charles Tomlinson is recognised as one of the greatest living British poets. He was born in Stoke-on-Trent in 1927. He studied at Cambridge with Donald Davie and taught at the University of Bristol from 1957 until his retirement. He has published many collections, including a *Collected Poems* and *The Vineyard Above the Sea*, available from Carcanet, and volumes of criticism and translation. He also edited the *Oxford Book of Verse in English Translation* (1980).

Michelene Wandor is a playwright, poet and short story writer. She also broadcasts regularly on review programmes on Radios 3 and 4, for which she has written a large number of plays, dramatisations and features. She is Senior Lecturer in Creative Writing at the University of London, and performs 16th and 17th century music with her group, SIENA ENSEMBLE.

Fay Weldon is well-known as a novelist, screenwriter and cultural journalist. Her novels include *The Life and Loves of a She-Devil, Puffball, The Cloning of Joanna May, Affliction* and *Worst Fears*. She scripted Channel 4's recent television series *Big Women*, and has several collections of short stories to her name, in particular *A Hard Time to be a Father*, the title story of which Fay Weldon has given to this anthology.

John Hartley Williams won the Arvon International Poetry Competition. *Bright River Yonder* was published by Bloodaxe, followed by *Cornerless People, Double* and *Canada*. Recent collections include *Spending Time with Walter* and *Mystery in Spiderville* from Jonathan Cape.

Rogan Wolf runs the charity 'Hyphen-21.' Projects include "Poems for the Waiting Room," which offers poems for display in healthcare sites. NHS Estates is helping to distribute the poems. The charity also promotes a strategy for improving staff morale (see www.charts.force9.co.uk.)

Tom Yates has won The Poetry Society's Simon Elvin Award for young poets. His work has appeared in the *Times Educational Supplement*. He is currently completing a degree in writing at Warwick University.

Acknowledgements

Penguin Books for Russell Celyn Jones' *Synapses* from *Surface Tension* (2001); and for the excerpt from Jonathan Coe's *What a Carve Up!* (1995)

Picador (Macmillan) for Sean O'Brien's 'Poem for a Psychiatric Conference' from *Downriver* (2001) and Jackie Kay's 'Out of Hand' from *Why Don't You Stop Talking* (2002).

Bloodaxe Books for poems by David Constantine from *Something for the Ghosts* (2002) and Maura Dooley from *Explaining Magnetism* (1991).

Douglas Dunn and Faber and Faber for Douglas Dunn's 'Reading Pascal in the Lowlands' from *Selected Poems* (1986).

Fay Weldon and Flamingo (Harper Collins) for 'A Hard Time to be a Father' from *A Hard Time to be a Father* (1998).

W.G. Sebald, Jack Murphy and Harvill Press for Chapter 1 of *The Rings of Saturn* by W.G. Sebald from *The Rings of Saturn* translated by Michael Hulse (1998).

Chatto and Windus for 'Lullaby for the Cat' by Elizabeth Bishop from *The Complete Poems* (1983).

Michael Foxton and *The Guardian* for *Two Bedside Stories* from *Bedside Stories* (October 2000-February 2001).

Michael Symmons Roberts and Fiona McLean (BBC Radio 3) for 'Post-Mortem', a Radio 3 commission for the 2001 Poetry Proms.

Rogan Wolf for various work originally used in the Poems in the Waiting Room Project.